AF539604

POP Trash

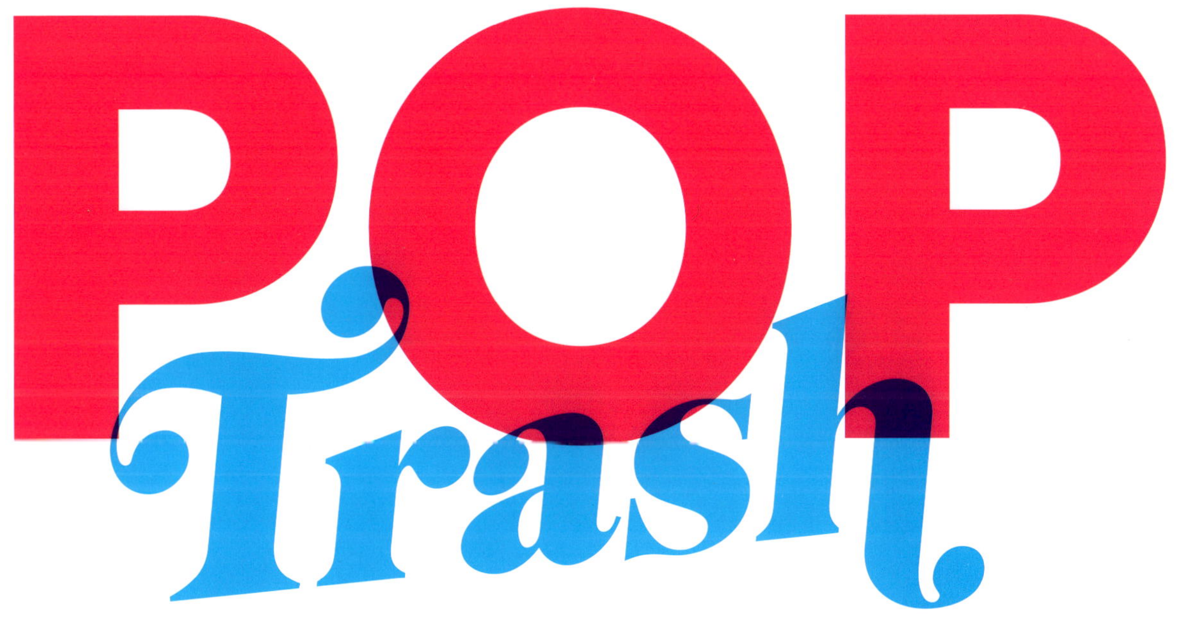

THE AMAZING ART OF JASON MECIER

CHRONICLE BOOKS
SAN FRANCISCO

Library of Congress Cataloging-in-Publication Data

Names: Mecier, Jason, artist.
Title: Pop trash / Jason Mecier.
Description: San Francisco : Chronicle Books, 2018.
Identifiers: LCCN 2018006962 | ISBN 9781452170121 (hardback)
Subjects: LCSH: Mecier, Jason--Themes, motives. | Celebrities--Portraits. |
Assemblage (Art)--United States. | Pop art--United States. | BISAC: ART /
Popular Culture. | ART / Subjects & Themes / Portraits.
Classification: LCC N6537.M3987 A4 2018 | DDC 709.04/071--dc23
LC record available at https://lccn.loc.gov/2018006962

Manufactured in China

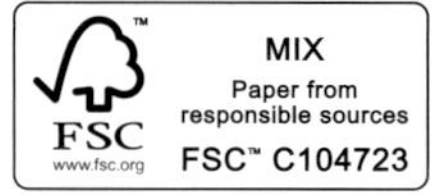

Designed by Michael Morris

10 9 8 7 6 5 4 3 2 1

Chronicle Books LLC
680 Second Street
San Francisco, CA 94107
www.chroniclebooks.com

Chronicle Books publishes distinctive books and gifts. From award-winning children's titles, bestselling cookbooks, and eclectic pop culture to acclaimed works of art and design, stationery, and journals, we craft publishing that's instantly recognizable for its spirit and creativity. Enjoy our publishing and become part of our community at www.chroniclebooks.com.

Contents

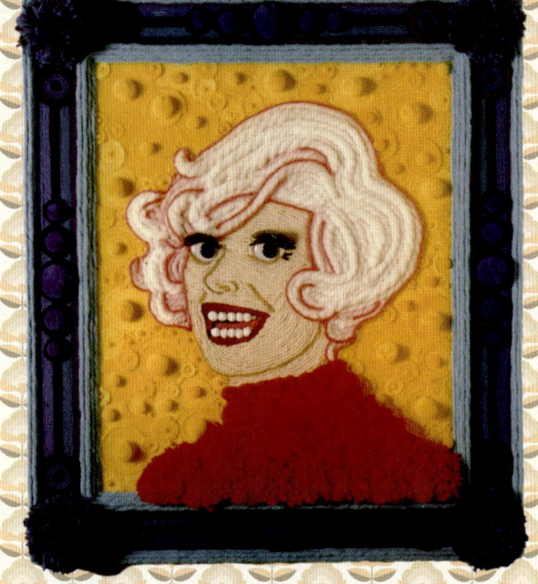

CAROL CHANNING • Yarn, felt, pom-poms, googly eyes, 1997 • **My first yarn portrait.**

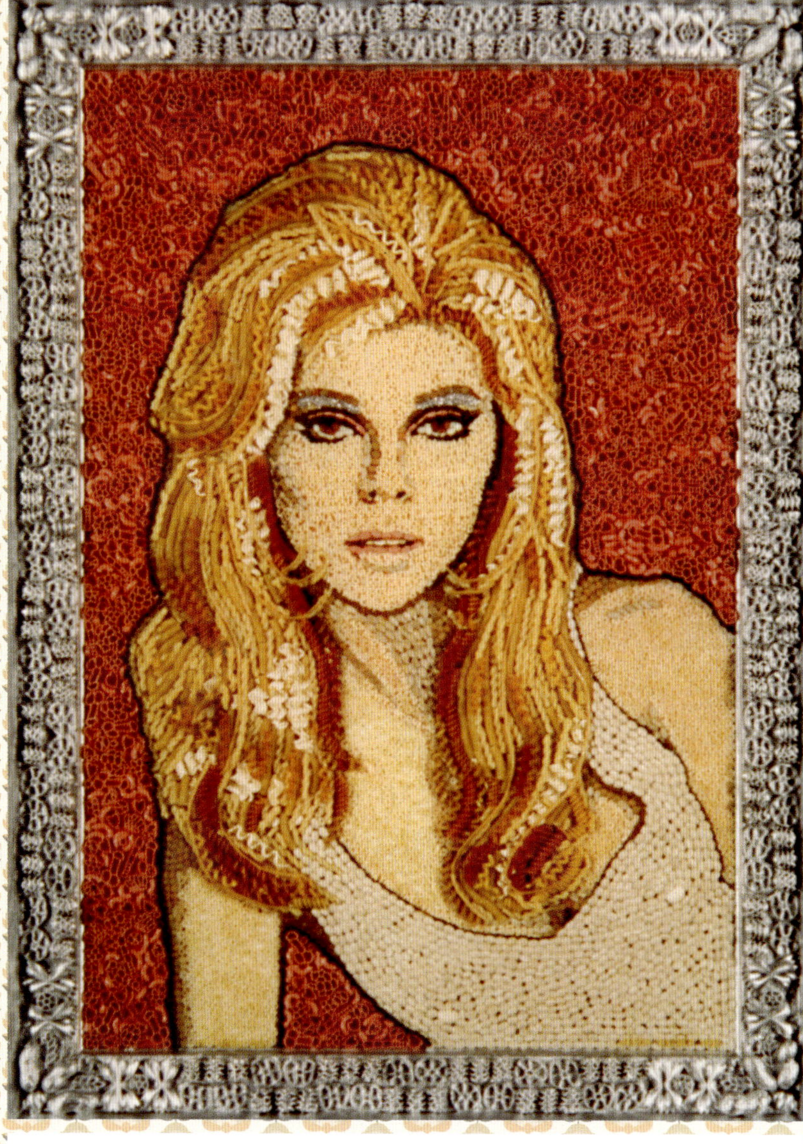

NANCY SINATRA • Beans and noodles, 1995
This was the very first tour poster I did for The Fillmore in San Francisco. Later I would do poster work for Willie Nelson, P!nk, Margaret Cho, Chelsea Handler, Cheech and Chong, and many more.

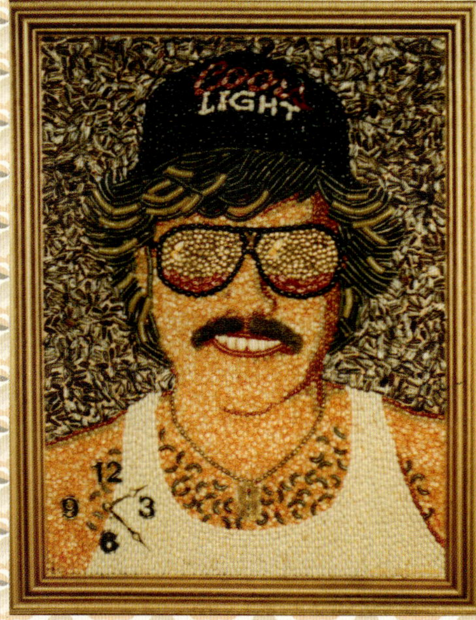

SELF PORTRAIT • Beans, noodles, clock, 1993

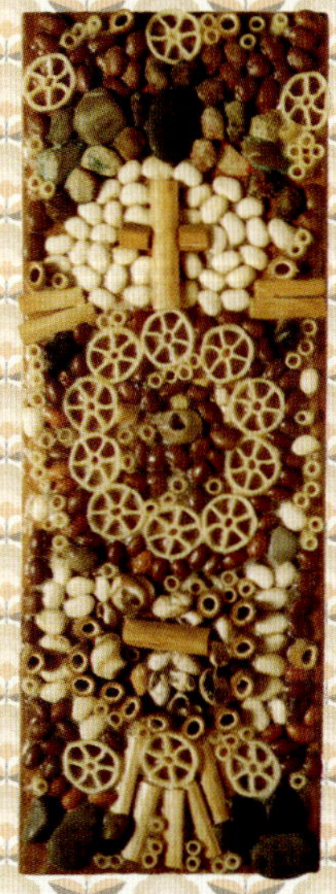

My first mosaic, 1973 (age 5).

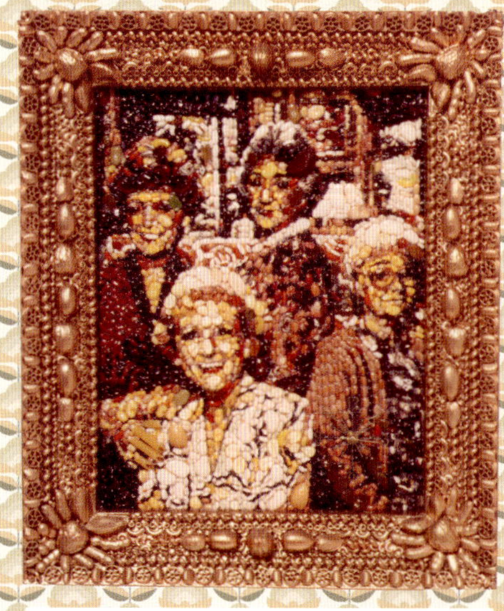

GOLDEN GIRLS • Beans, noodles, clock, 2003

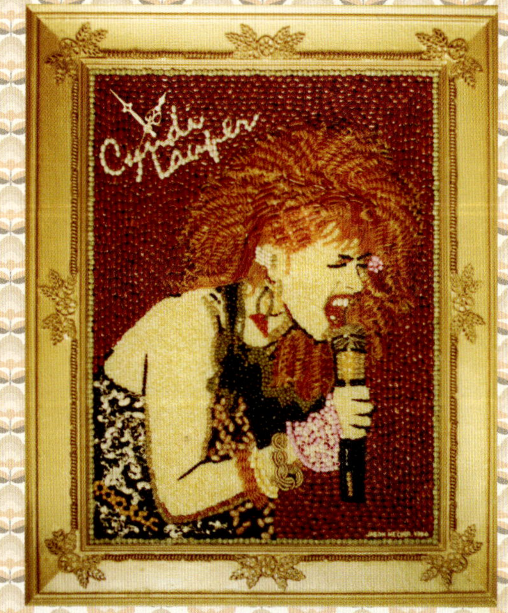

CYNDI LAUPER • Beans, noodles, clock, 1995

Introduction

AS A CHILD, I ALWAYS LOVED VISITING MY GRANDPARENTS' HOUSE.

I was inspired by my grandmother's passion to create, and mesmerized by her paintings, weavings, mosaics, sculptures, collages, and stained-glass work that filled their house and yard. I was also inspired by her resourcefulness—she would rather paint on the back of her cigarette cartons than buy a canvas.

If she was working on an art project, she would set me up at a nearby table with a project of my own to work on. One of my earliest pieces was a mosaic made from beans, noodles, rocks, and cut bamboo sticks glued on a piece of wood, all stuff scavenged from my grandparents' kitchen cupboards and backyard. She would also take me to visit Grandma Prisbey's Bottle Village in Simi Valley, a truly amazing assemblage of shrines and structures built by self-taught artist Tressa Prisbey, where we marveled at the endless bottles, recycled-trash mosaics, and a room covered with pencils. My grandmother encouraged me to create masterpieces using materials readily available to me. I learned from her that I can make art out of anything I want to, and that there are no rules.

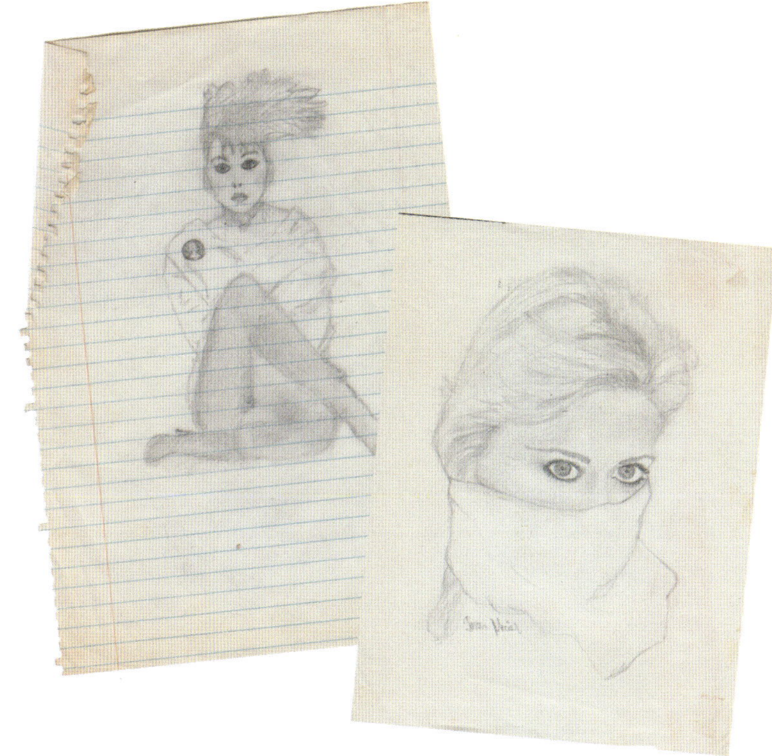

Pencil drawings I did of Pat Benatar and Olivia Newton-John from their album covers in the 1980s.

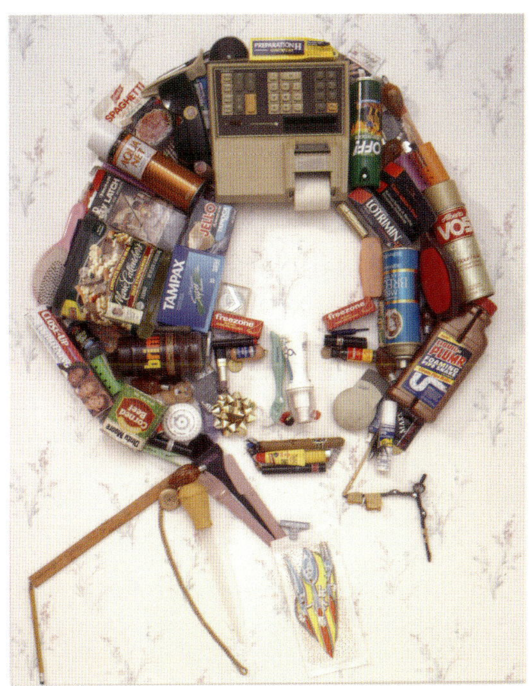

HELEN GURLEY BROWN • Mixed media on panel, 2003
This piece was up at one of my first junk shows at the GlamaRama! salon in San Francisco when I received a phone call. "Hi Jason, um . . . there's something brown leaking from Helen Gurley Brown." It was vintage pudding. Since then I try to be sure to empty all the old packages.

As a kid I remember obsessively clipping and scrapbooking pictures of my favorite shows from the *TV Guide*. In high school I did pencil drawings of my favorite record covers from artists like the Rolling Stones, Olivia Newton-John, and Pat Benatar. Later I did a series of psychedelic collages using *Charlie's Angels* trading cards and pictures of Florence Henderson from the Wesson Oil coupons and ads.

I first started making bean and noodle portraits of my favorite celebrities around 1990, and they were my primary medium for a while. They don't call me the Macaroni Monet for nothing! But at some point I started to feel limited by the earth-toned color palette and moved to yarn, candy, pills, trash . . . finally EVERYTHING was up for consideration as art supplies. One Thanksgiving my partner Adam Ansell was frantically looking for the turkey baster, and I had to fess up that I had glued it onto my Helen Gurley Brown portrait. I'm

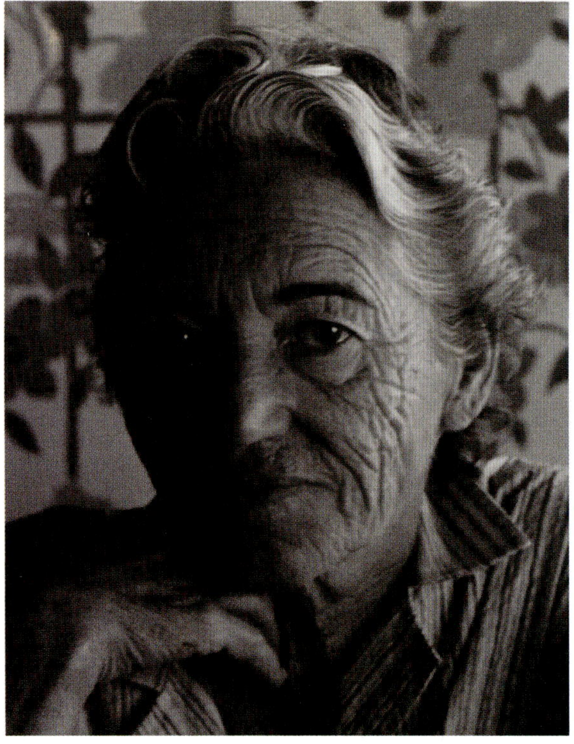

One of my favorite pictures of my grandma. I took this while enrolled in a photography class at Sacramento City College in the 1980s. I later did an abstract food portrait of it.

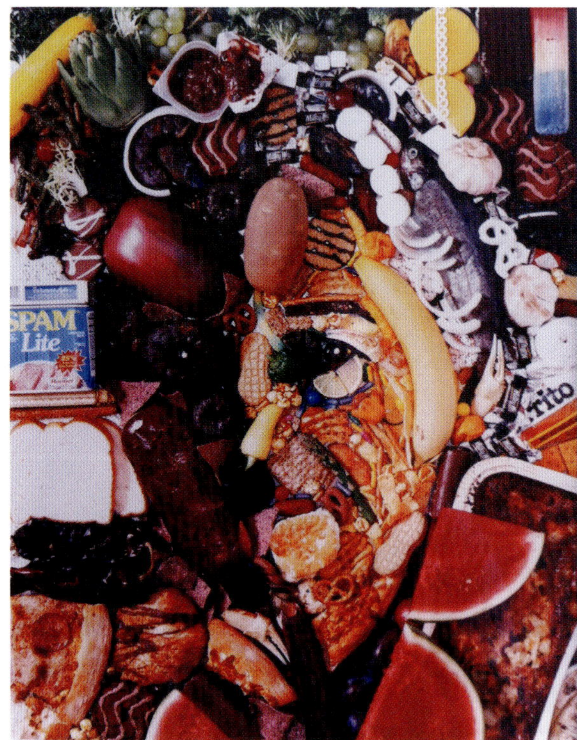

ANITA TOLLEFSON • Pizza crust, fruit, vegetables, junk food, 1998

always getting busted like that. Nothing is safe in my house. Adam and I are both artists, and our home is generally pretty put together except for the art studio, which I hog ninety percent of, and which can look like a room out of an episode of *Hoarders*, although I do try to keep all the materials organized in bins by shape, color, and theme.

In terms of portrait subjects, I generally gravitate towards people who are really recognizable or iconic, who have a built-in theme or are big or outrageous, but my inspiration can also be all over the map. The portraits can take a long time to finish, up to 50 hours or more—the Lady Gaga and giant Farrah Fawcett pieces took me six months!—so there has to be something about the personality of the subject that fascinates me and makes me want to spend that much time interpreting their image. I tend to think and work in series, including Candylebrities (Miley Cyrus, Zach Galifianakis), Man Candy (Tom Hardy, Burt Reynolds), The Real Housewives of Macaroni, and Celebrity Junk Drawer, and while I've had exhibitions for each of these, the series are never really finished and I'll add to them when the inspiration strikes.

Many of the junk portraits are made from the celebrities' own trash (I've indicated which ones in the captions). When I started making the portraits, I would pretend that, say, this was Farrah Fawcett's slipper, makeup container, and Filet-o-Fish wrapper, but then I thought why not ask celebrities for their real trash and see what happens?

Phyllis Diller was the first. I saw online that she was a painter and asked if she'd like to trade art. Within two weeks, she sent me a box of trash full of old prescription bottles, stopwatches, eyeglasses, pinecones, etc. Over the years she has sent close to forty boxes of junk, and I've made three portraits from them so far, which I'm very proud of.

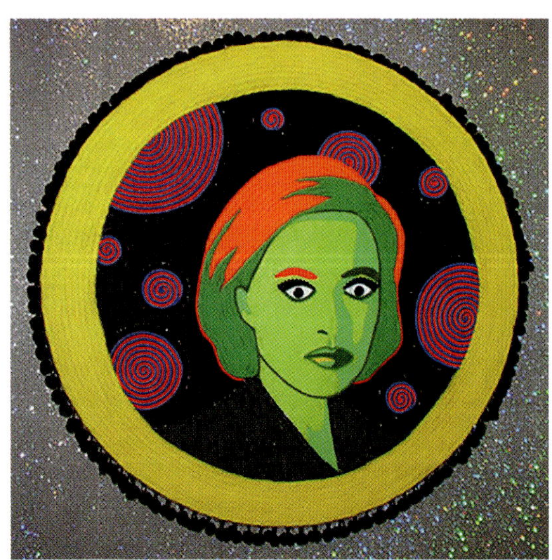

DANA SCULLY • Yarn, felt, pom-poms, googly eyes, 1999

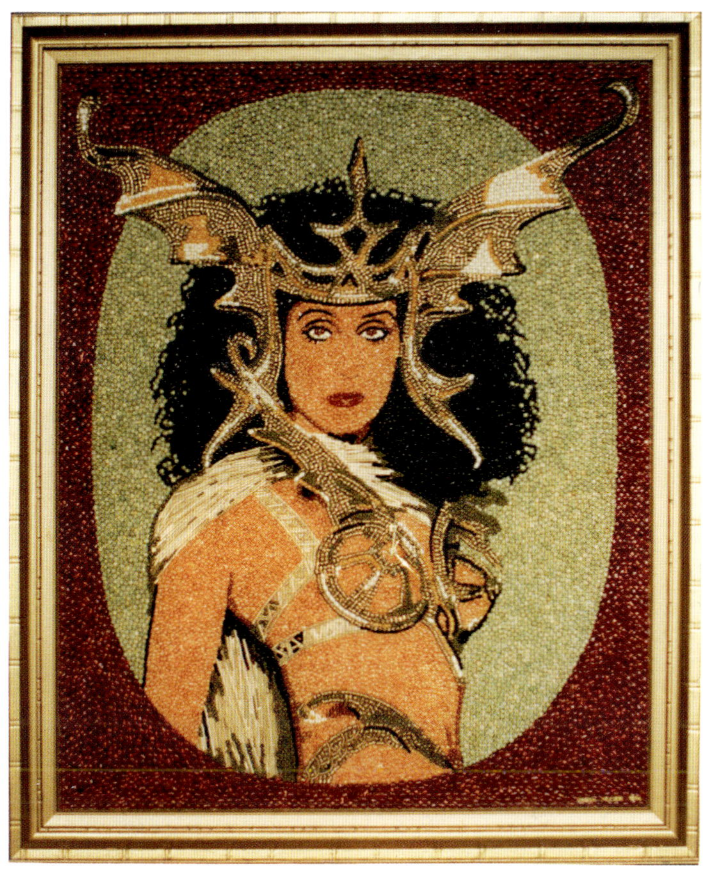

CHER • Beans, noodles, clock, 1992

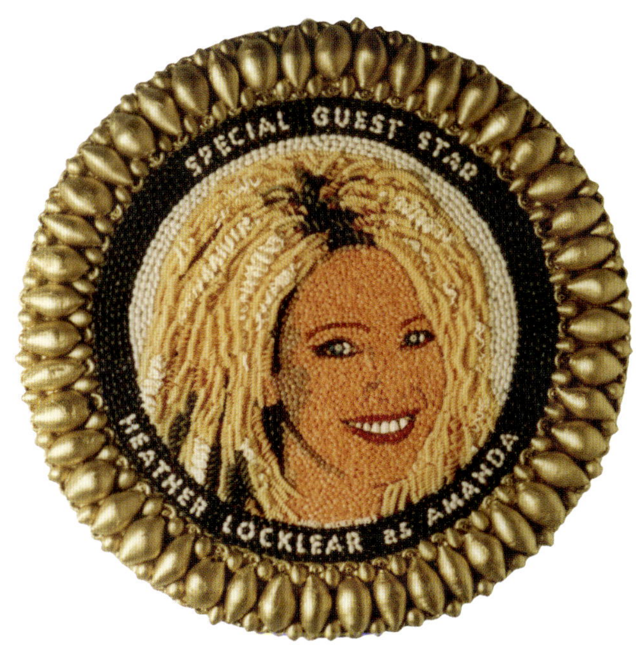

HEATHER LOCKLEAR • Beans and noodles, 1995

Barbie Benton sent me an entire U-Haul truck full of personal keepsakes, such as prom queen crowns, platform shoes, *Hee-Haw* overalls, sunglasses, jewelry, and even the retainer she wore in high school.

I've been given a "key to the city" and silver pumps by Florence Henderson, a leaky black Clairol hair-dye applicator by Jane Wiedlin, and a night guard by Parker Posey (she also gave me a bong that she made in ceramics class).

Once I realized that celebrities would actually send me their junk, my art style took on a life of its own. There's something about the process, and having a connection with or brief relationship with the subject, that thrills me. I think my most successful pieces are the ones that capture the essence of the subject's public personality. My aim is to blur the line between high and low in both art and pop culture, and I like applying a down-to-earth, arts and crafts approach to representing flashy subjects. The addition of using their personal belongings as art supplies makes the art piece more personal and one of a kind, and I know it's fun for people to look at celebrities' actual trash. And really that's kind of the point of all this: to have fun.

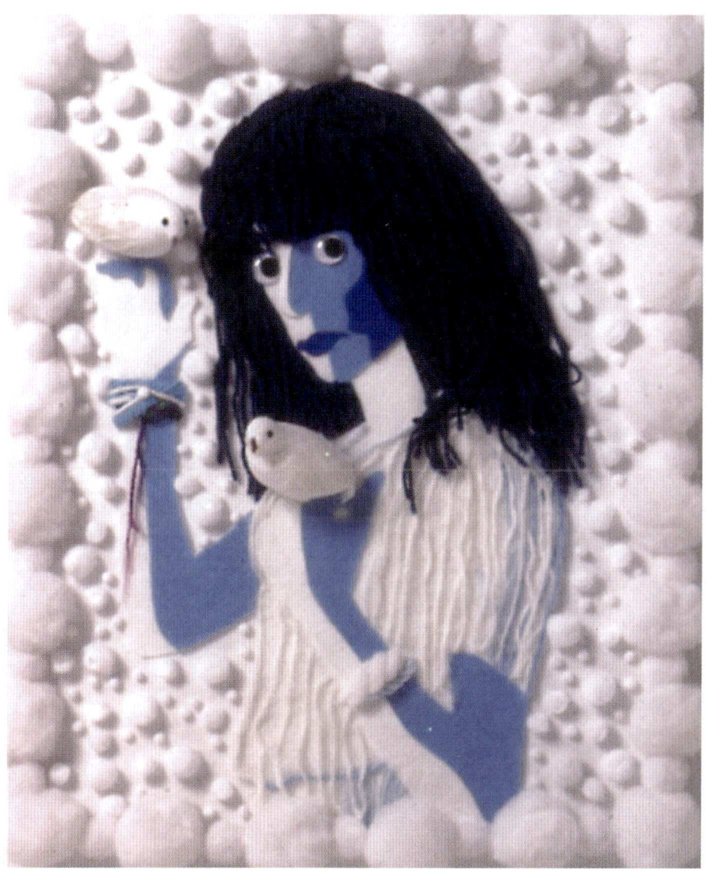

PATTI SMITH • Yarn, felt, pom-poms, googly eyes, 1998

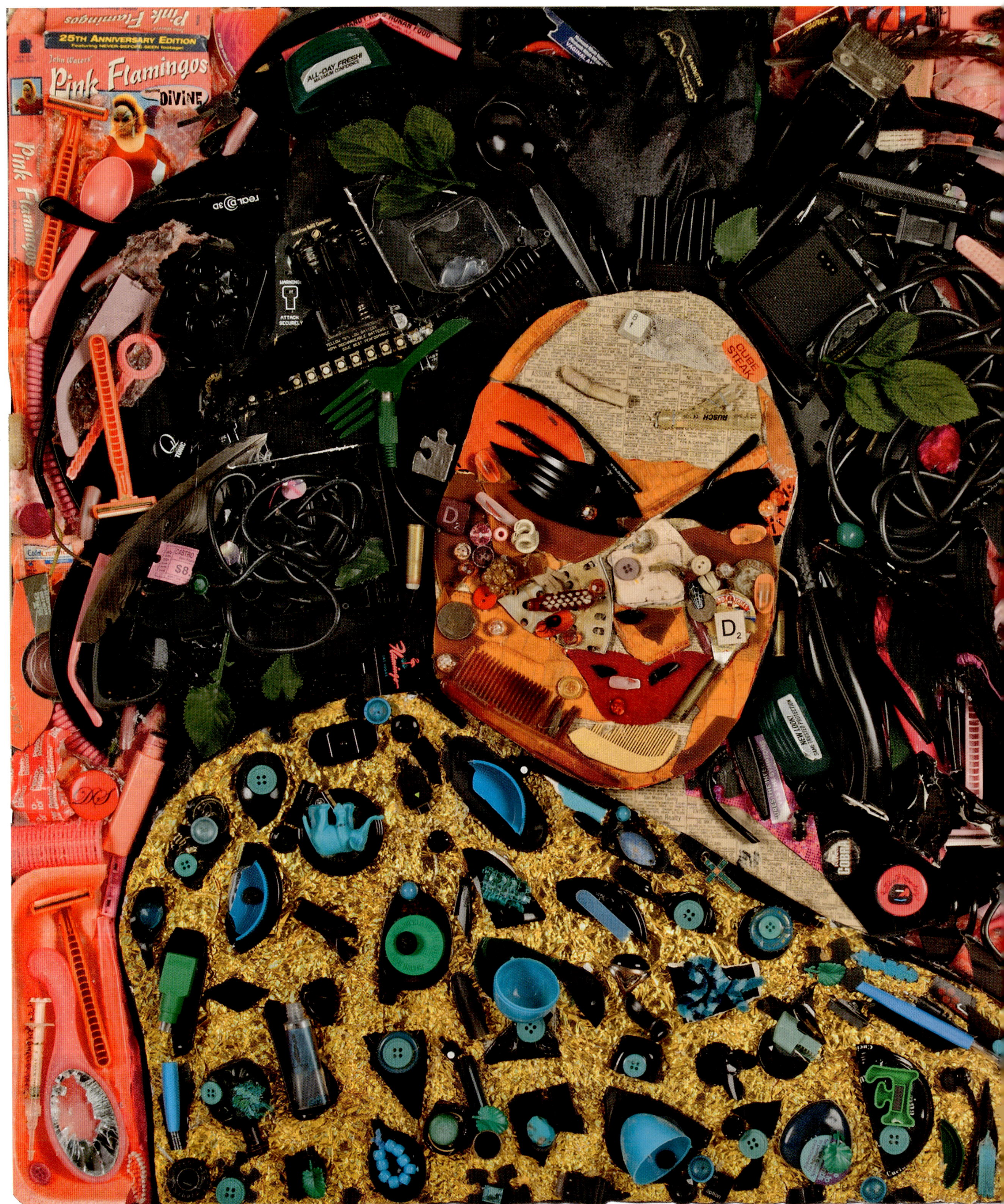
25TH ANNIVERSARY EDITION
John Waters'
Pink Flamingos
DIVINE
ALL-DAY FRESH!
CUBE STEAK
RUSCH
ATTACH SECURELY
COBRA
NEW LOOK!

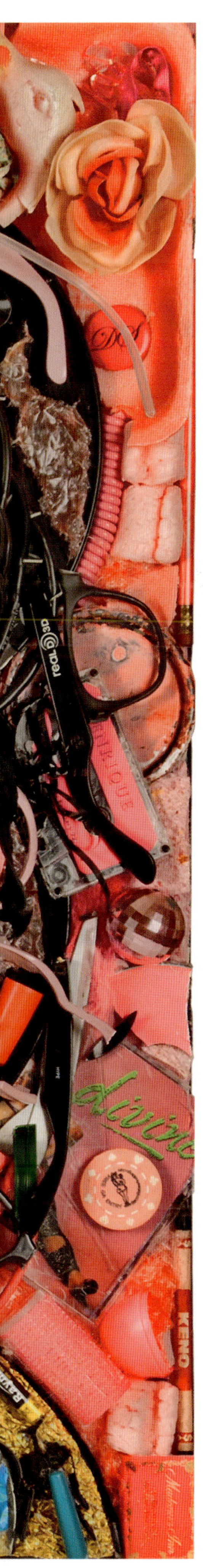

Trash

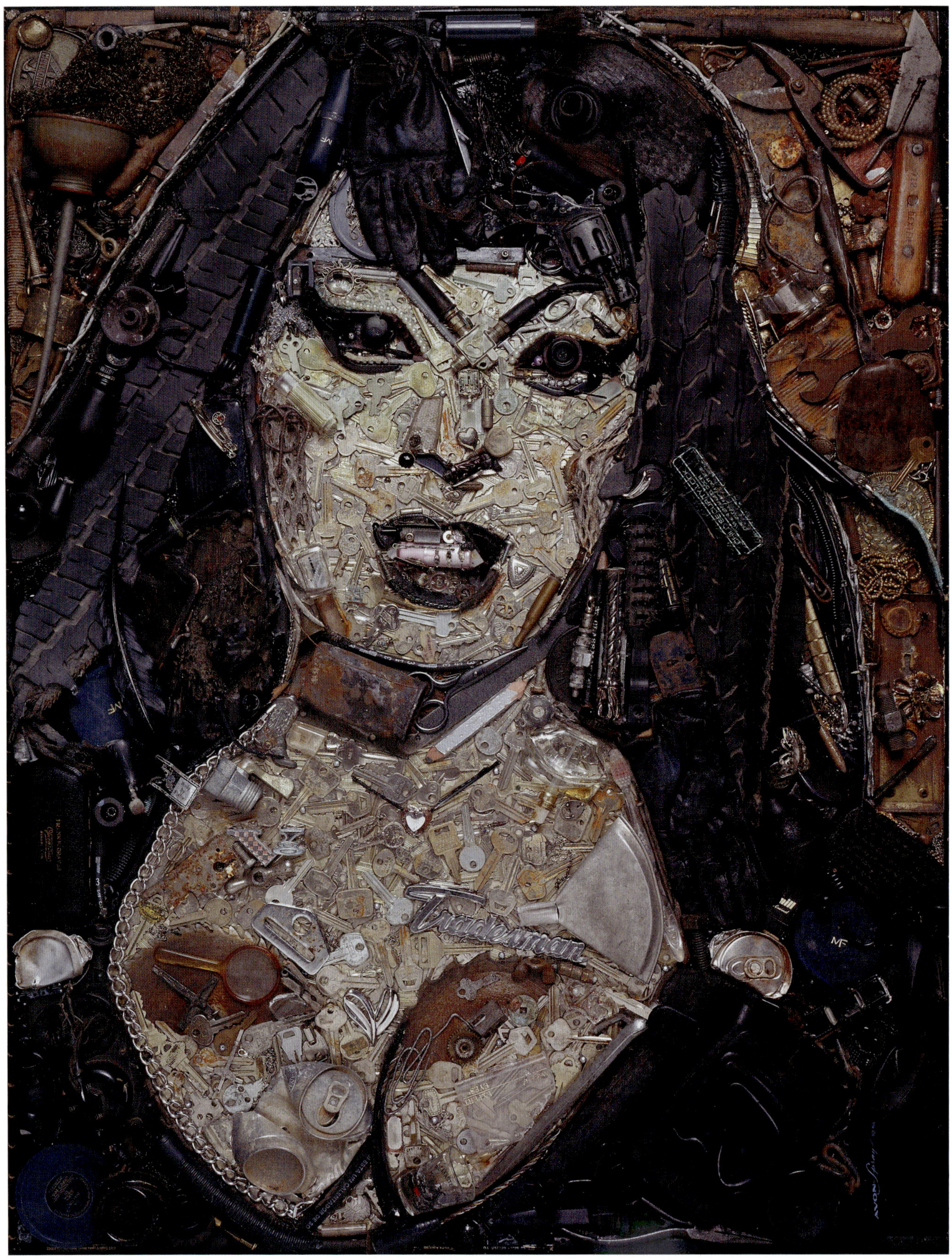

PREVIOUS SPREAD: DIVINE • Plastic razors, broken mirror, videotape packaging, cosmetic items, wire, buttons, gold fabric, 2015

TURA SATANA • Leather gloves, rubber, makeup, jewelry, keys,tools (Satana's own junk), 2007
I got a flat tire while working on the piece and used some of the shredded rubber for her hair.
The black leather gloves are the actual pair she wore in *Faster, Pussycat! Kill! Kill!*

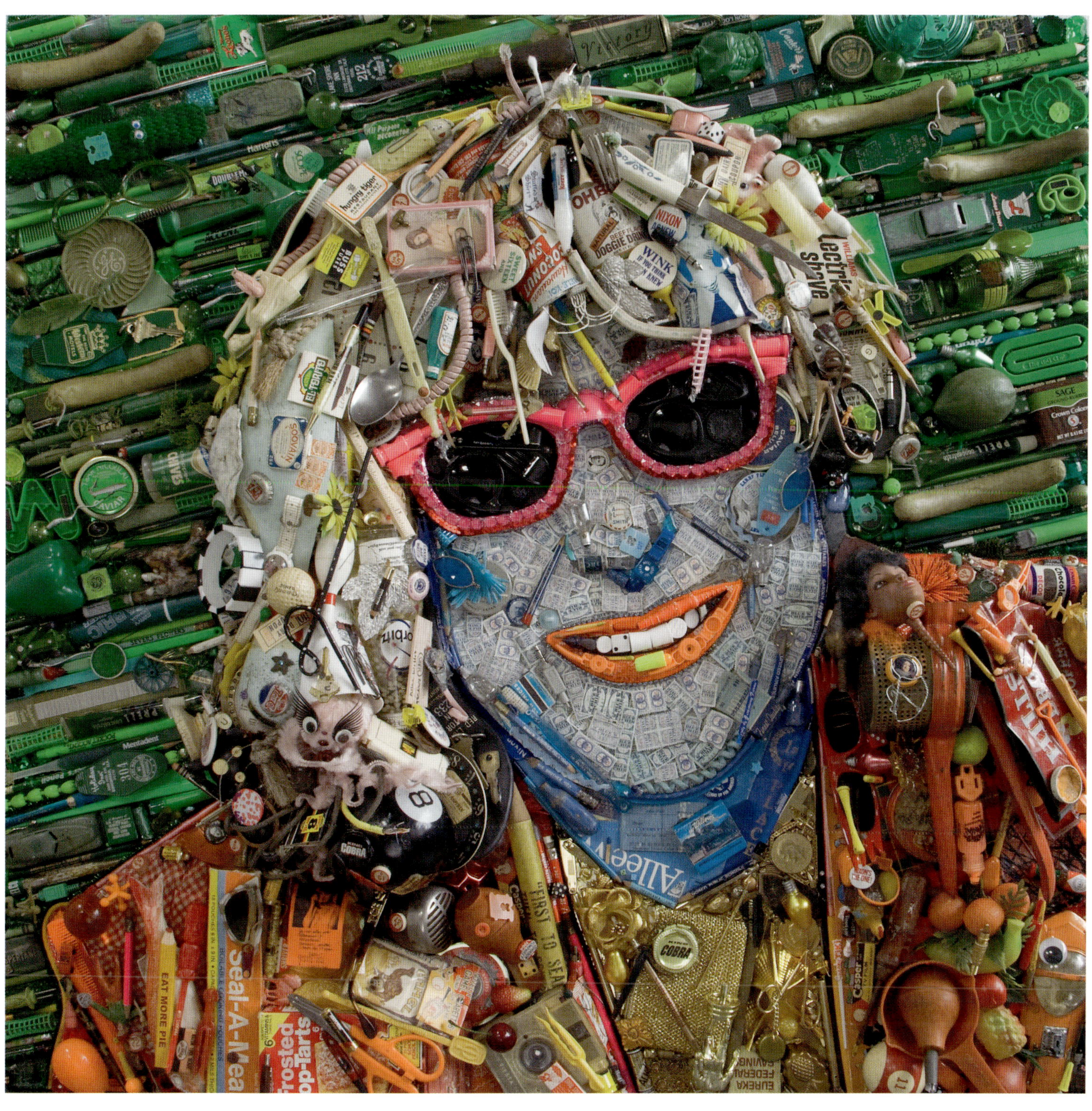

ALLEE WILLIS • Food stamps, plastic toys, hotel room keys, rubber hot dogs, political buttons, 2009
Collection of Allee Willis.

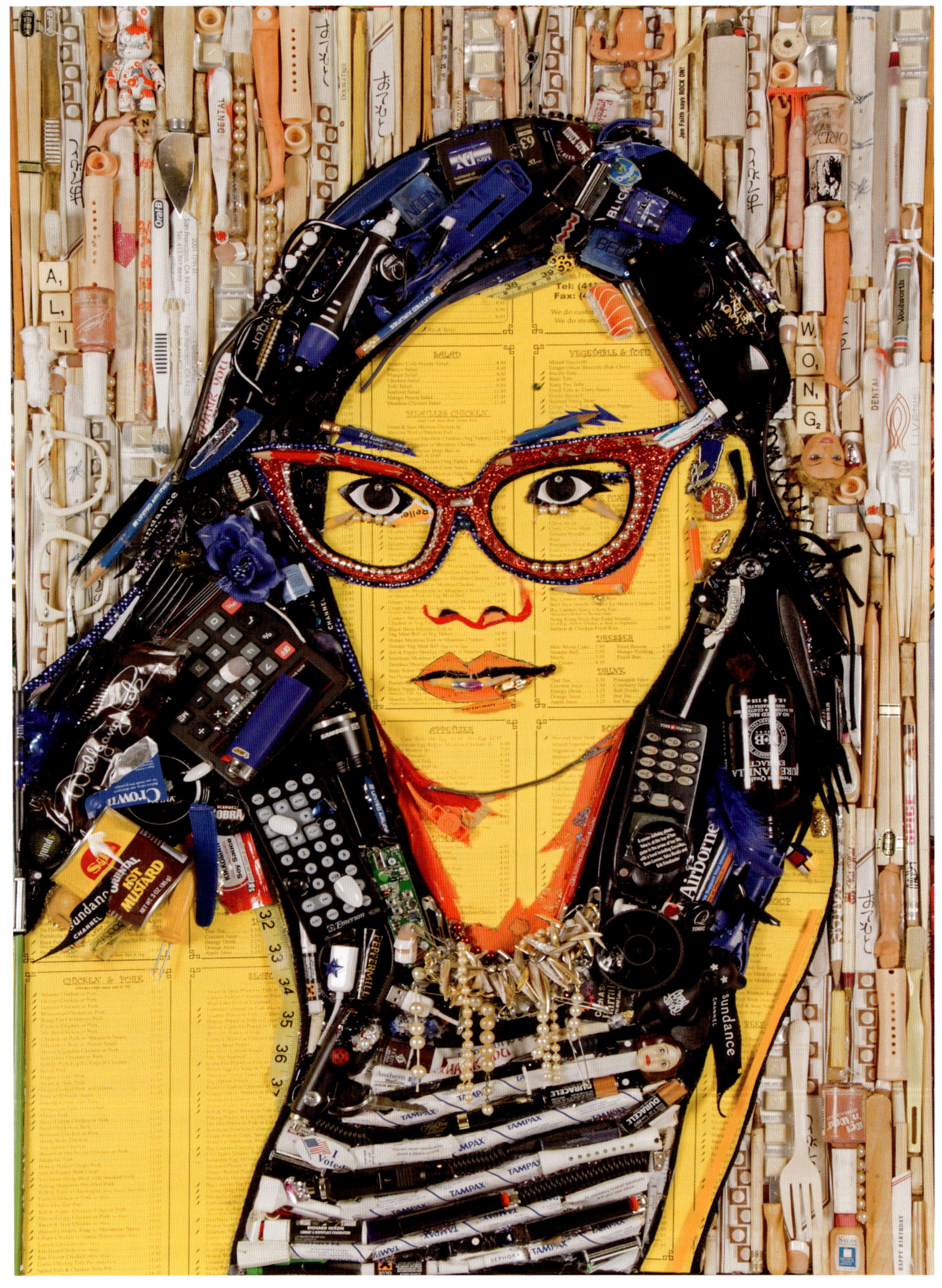

ALI WONG • Doll parts, calculators, chopsticks, restaurant menus, tampons, game tiles, 2017
Tour poster.

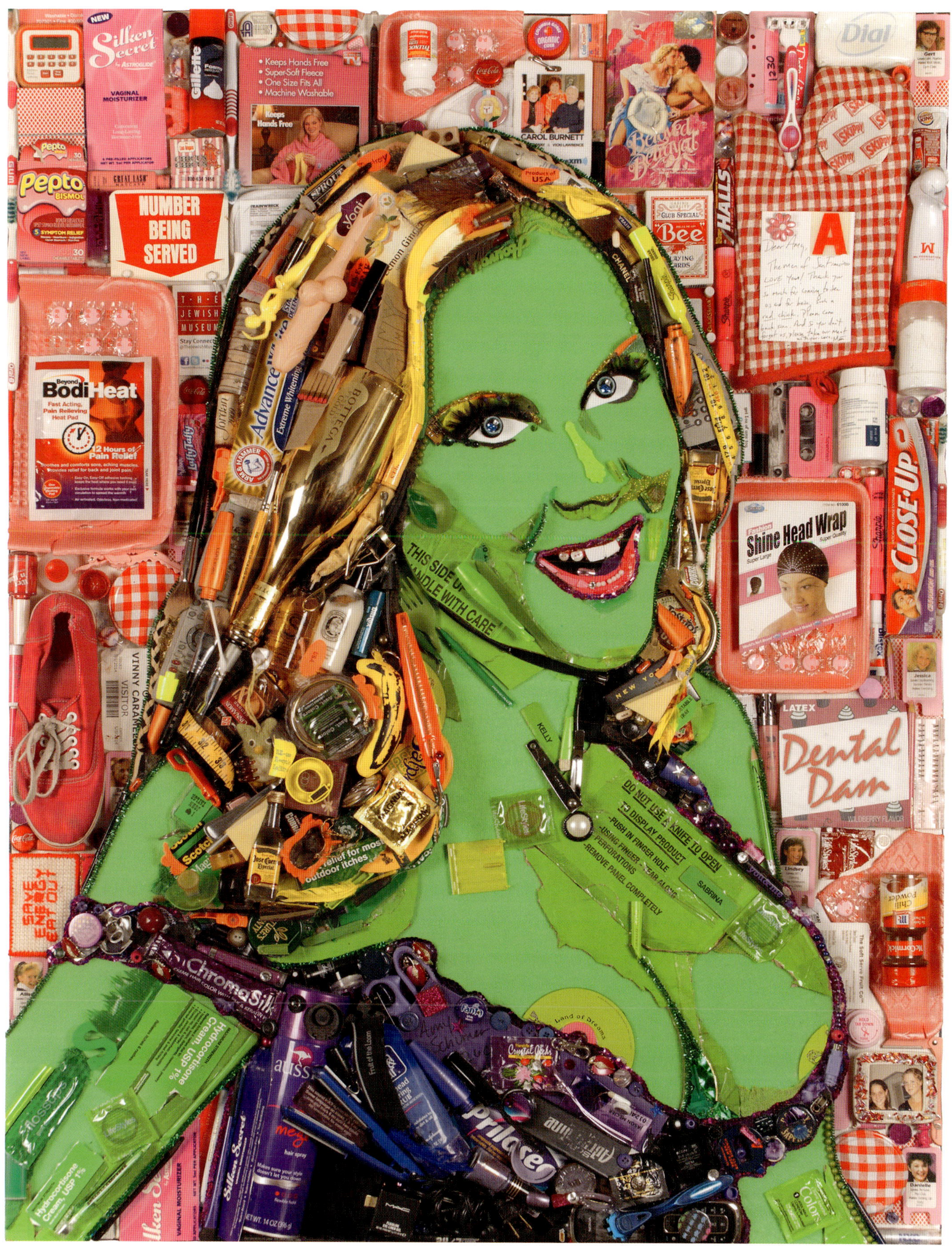

AMY SCHUMER • Dental dams, oven mitts, beauty products, condoms, antacid, romance paperback, wearable-blanket packaging, personal photo (Schumer's own junk), 2014

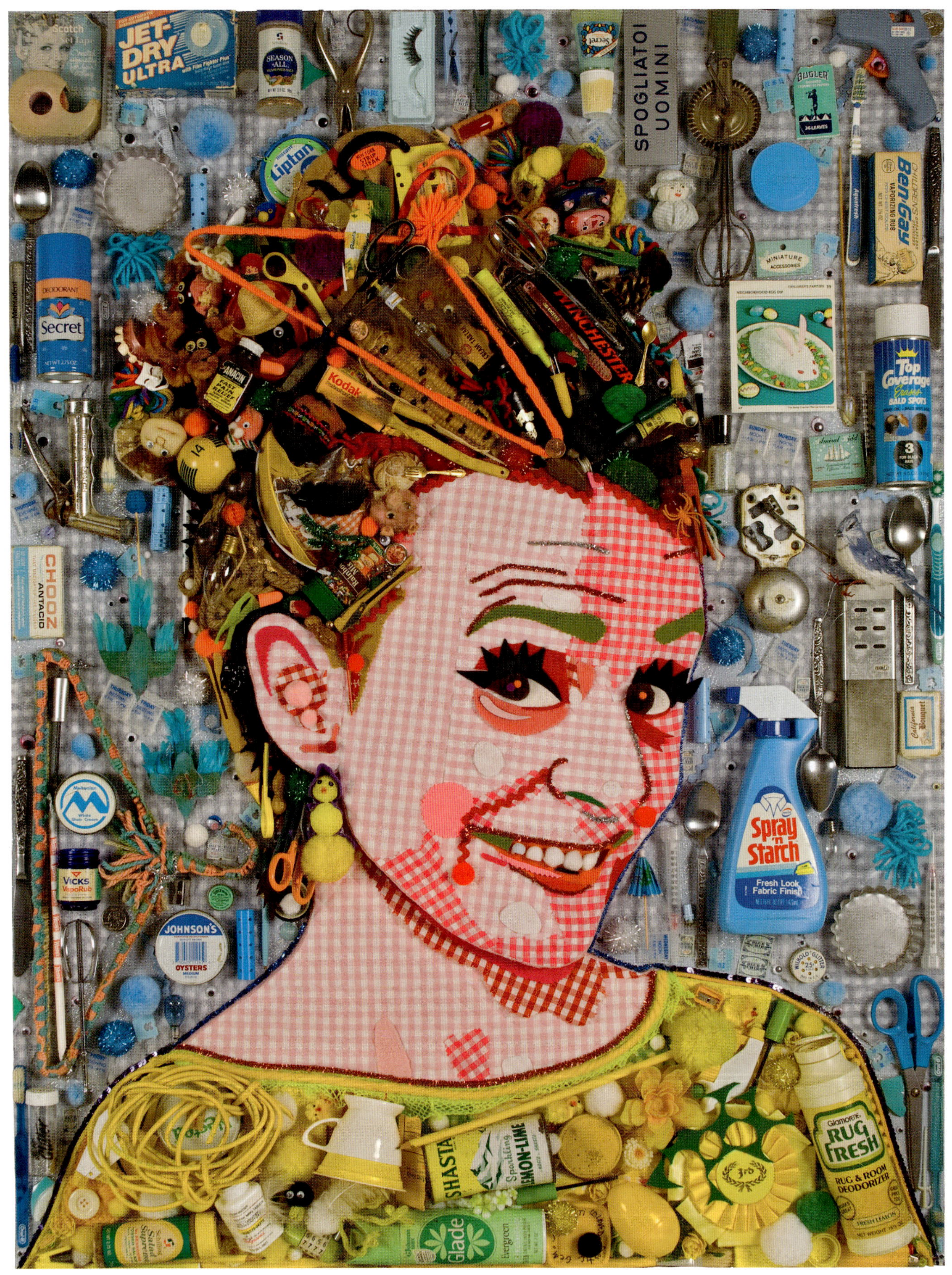

AMY SEDARIS • Cleaning supplies, cosmetics, household items, fabric, googly eyes (Sedaris's own junk and leftover supplies from her craft book), 2011

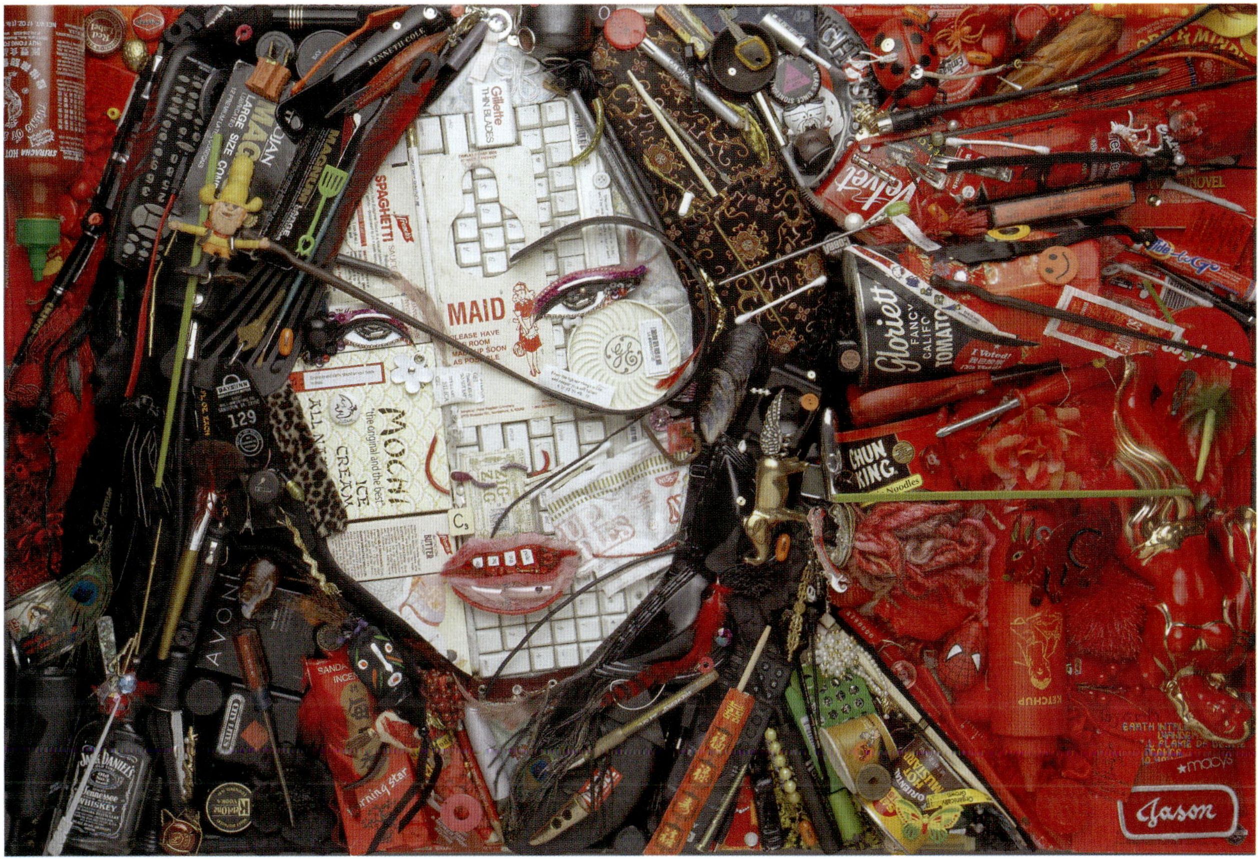

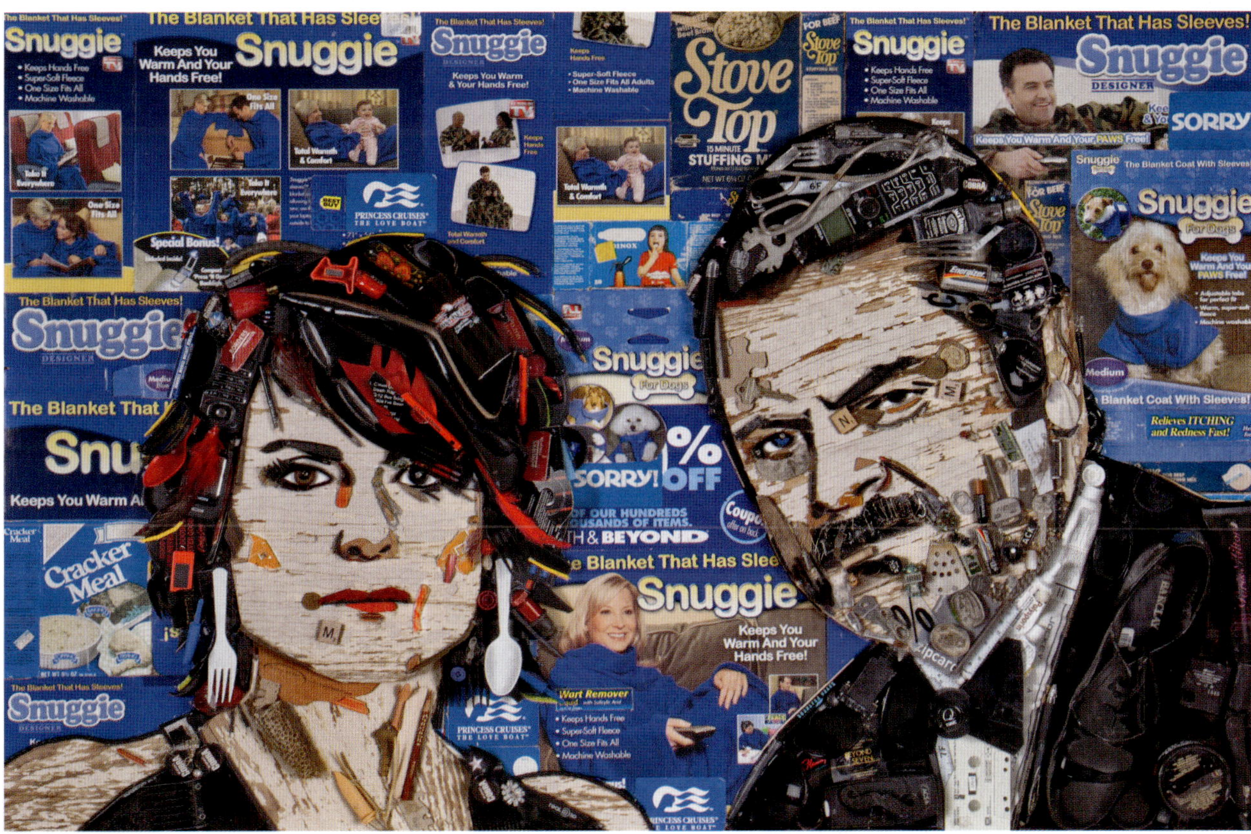

TOP: MARGARET CHO • Hot sauce, condoms, keyboard, mustard packaging, embroidered fabric, chopsticks, screwdrivers, 2008
Tour poster. Collection of Margaret Cho.

BOTTOM: MEGAN MULLALLY AND NICK OFFERMAN • Wearable-blanket packaging, weathered wood, board game tiles and cards, plastic utensils, shoes, sunglasses, 2015
Tour poster.

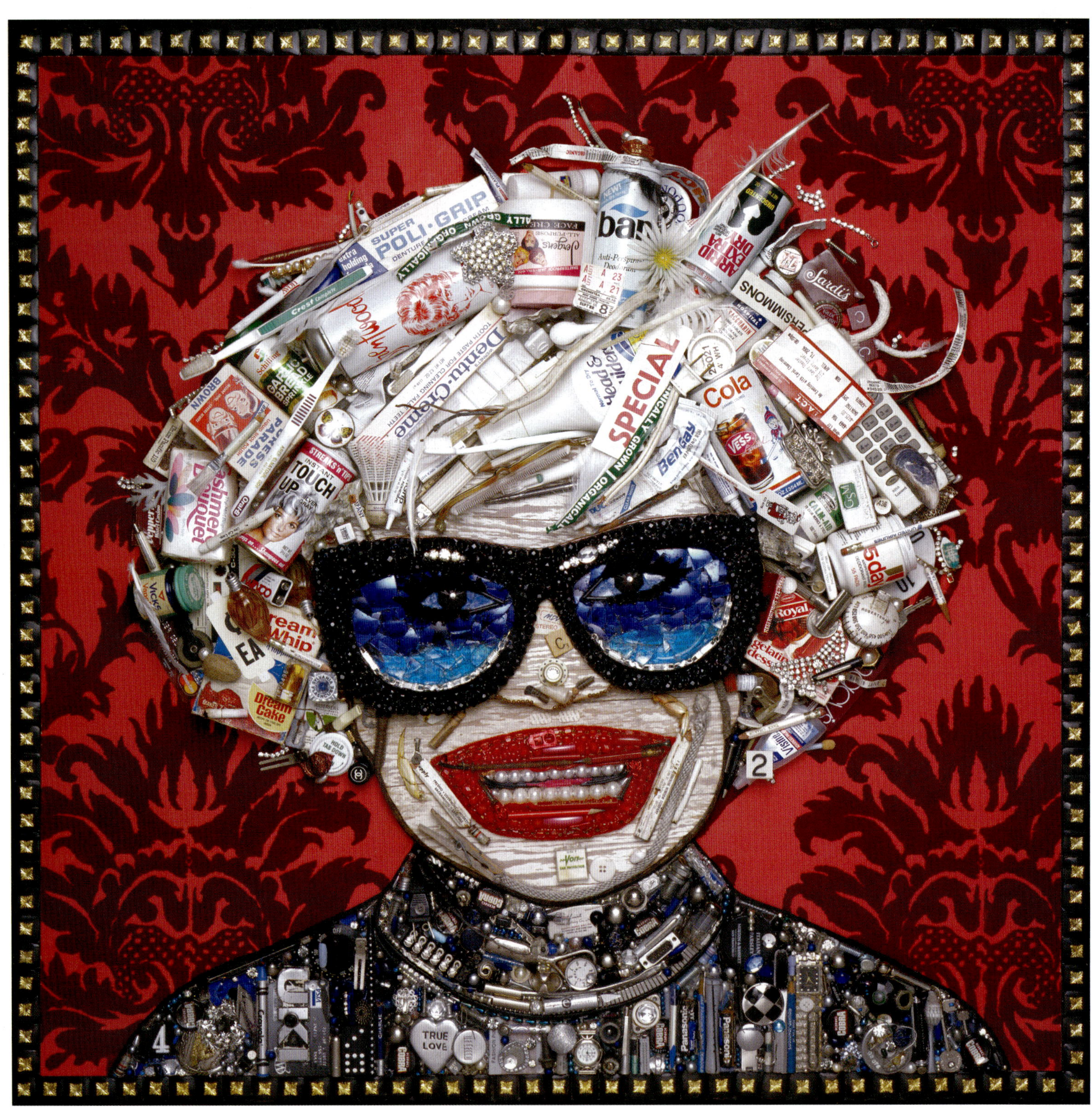

CAROL CHANNING • Jewelry, denture cream, hair products, theater ticket, velvet wallpaper, 2004

OPPOSITE: BARBRA STREISAND • Cassette and 8-track tapes, record sleeves, embroidery, feathers, corn cob holders, charge card, 2012

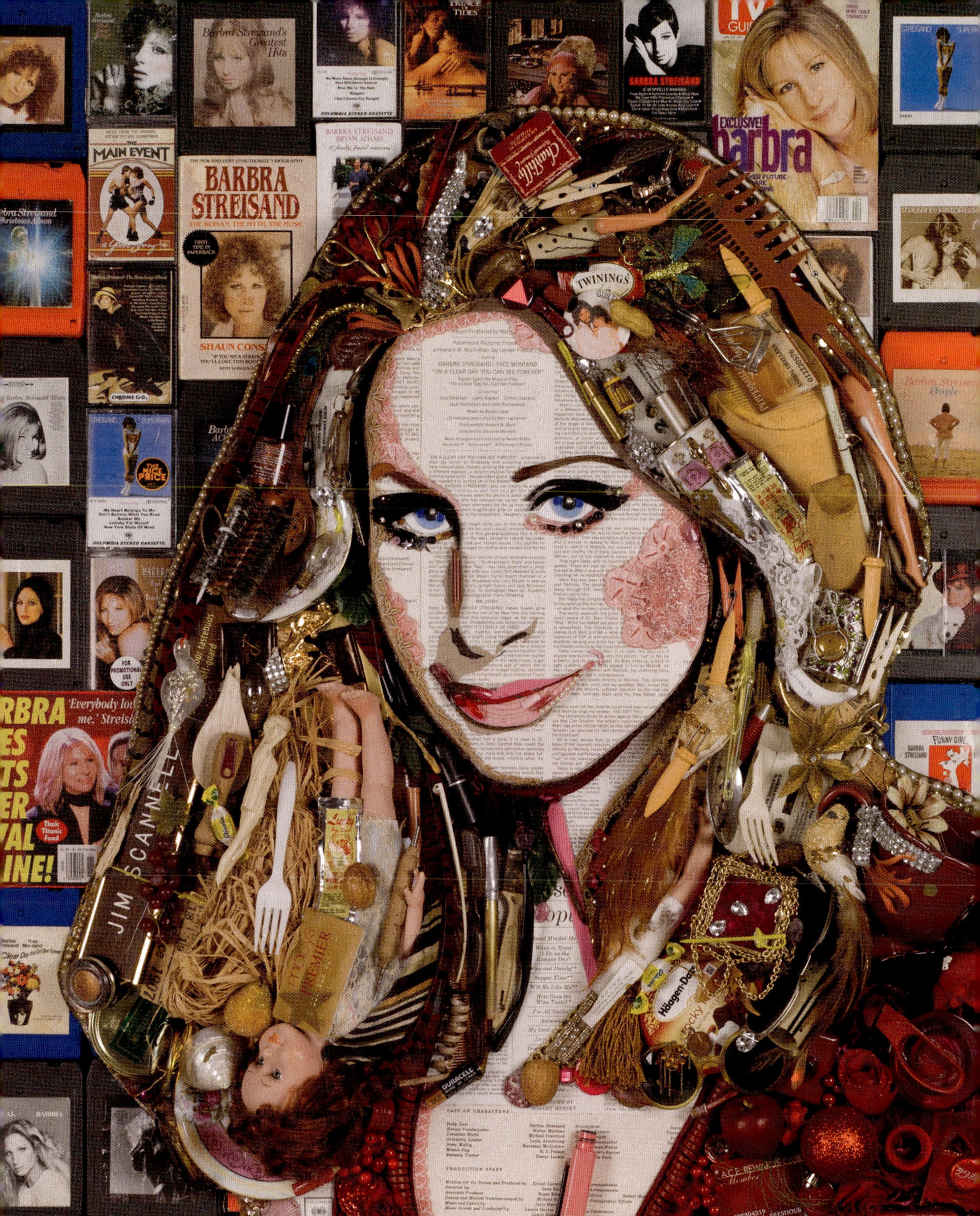

Barbra Streisand's Greatest Hits
COLUMBIA STEREO CASSETTE
BARBRA STREISAND
EXCLUSIVE!
barbra
THE MAIN EVENT
THE NEW AND VERY UNAUTHORIZED BIOGRAPHY
BARBRA STREISAND
THE WOMAN, THE MYTH, THE MUSIC
FIRST TIME IN PAPERBACK
BARBRA STREISAND
BRYAN ADAMS
Barbra Streisand
Christmas Album
STREISAND KRISTOFFERSON
CHROME CrO2
STREISAND SUPERMAN
THE NICE PRICE
COLUMBIA STEREO CASSETTE
TWININGS
BARBRA STREISAND / YVES MONTAND
"ON A CLEAR DAY YOU CAN SEE FOREVER"
Barbra Streisand
People
FOR PROMOTIONAL USE ONLY
'Everybody lo
me,' Streis
Their Titanic Feud
JIM SCANNELL
Lucky
macy's
PREMIER
Häagen-Dazs
DURACELL
FUNNY GIRL
CAST OF CHARACTERS
PRODUCTION STAFF
ACE REWARDS CLUB
Member

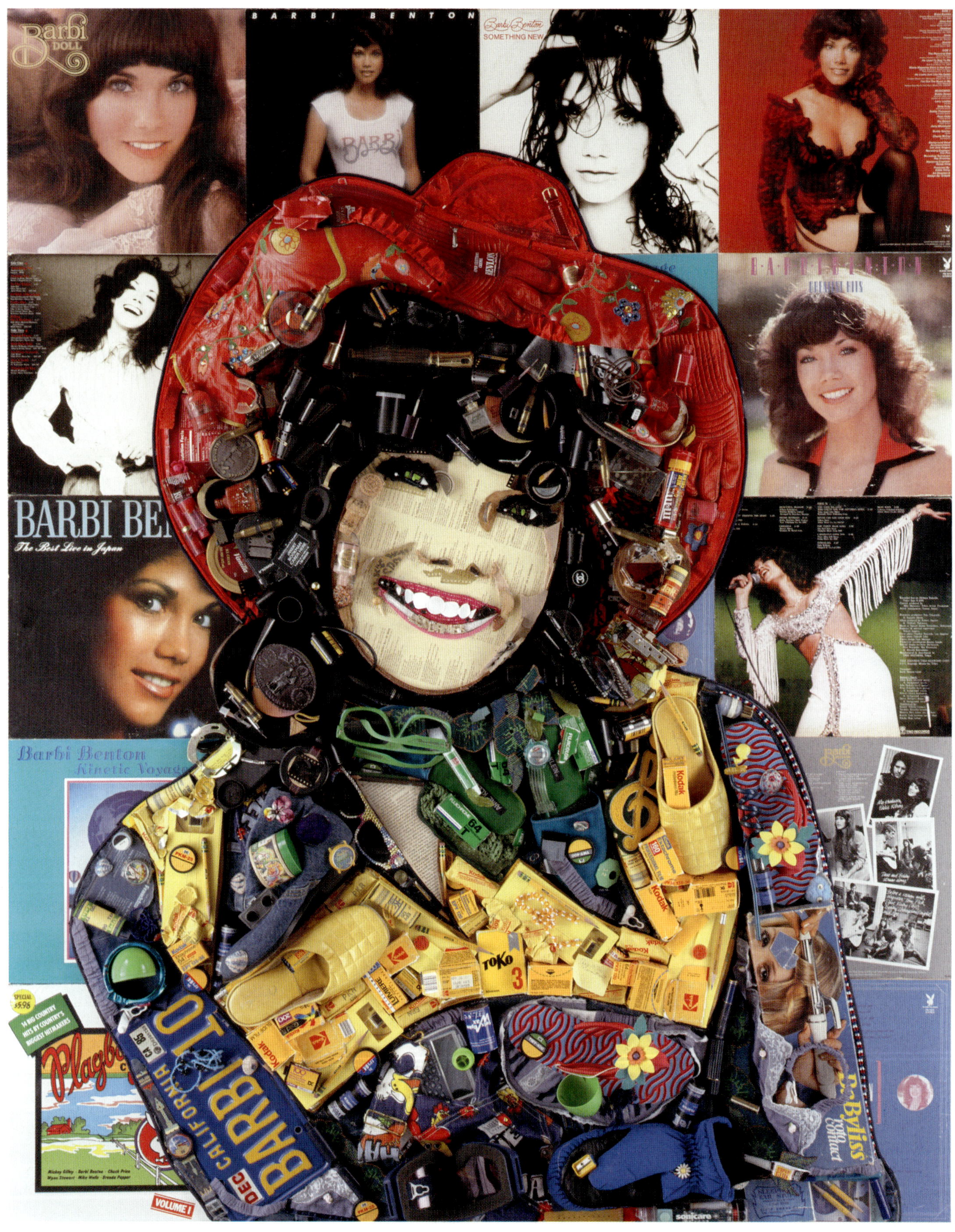

COUNTRY BARBIE • Record sleeves, film, personalized license plate, slippers, nail polish, *Hee-Haw* overalls (Benton's own junk), 2008
Collection of Barbie Benton.

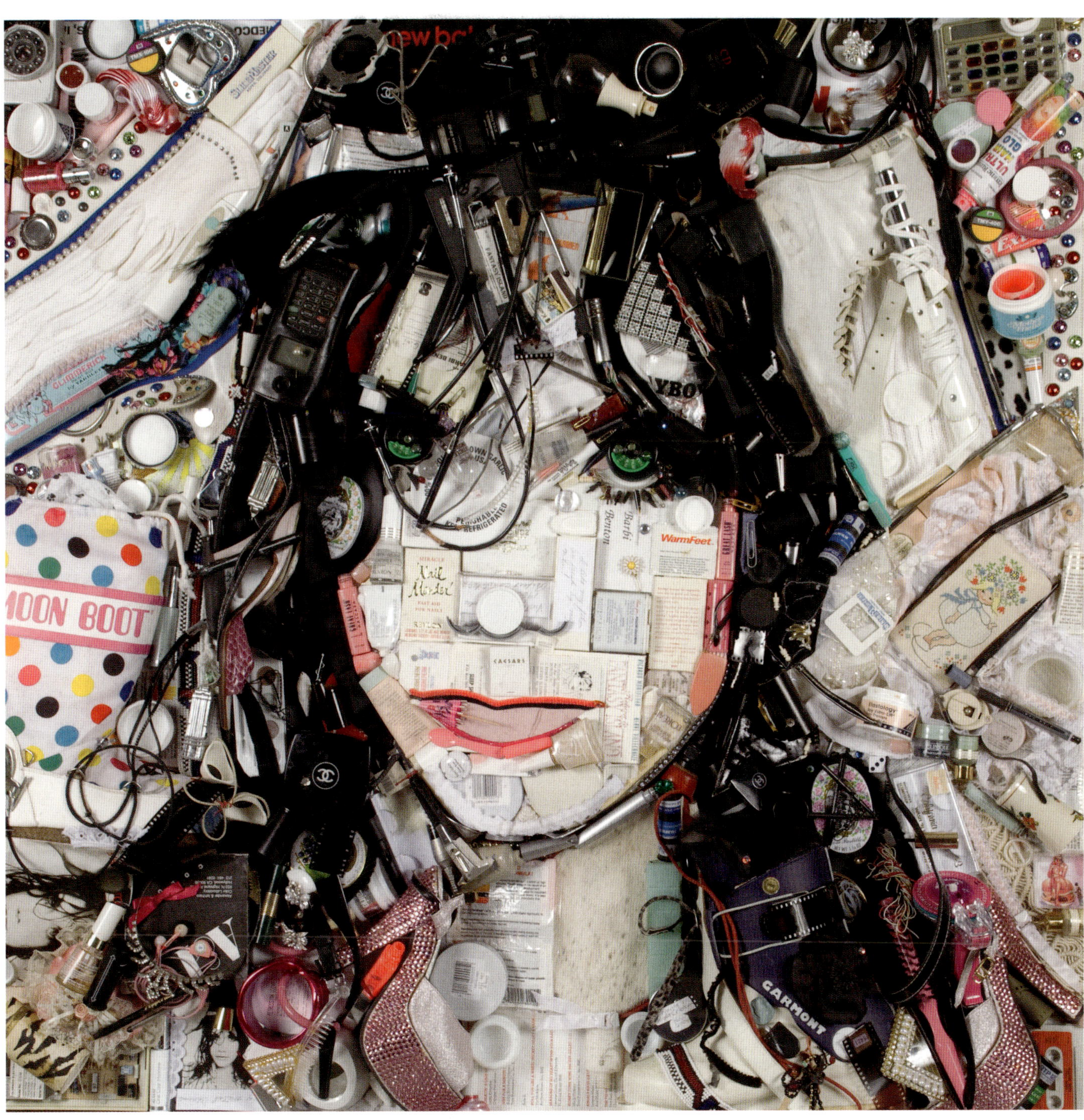

BARBIE BENTON • Cosmetics packaging, film, bedazzled items, cell phone, moon boot, ice skate, rhinestone platform shoes (Benton's own junk), 2006
Collection of Barbie Benton.

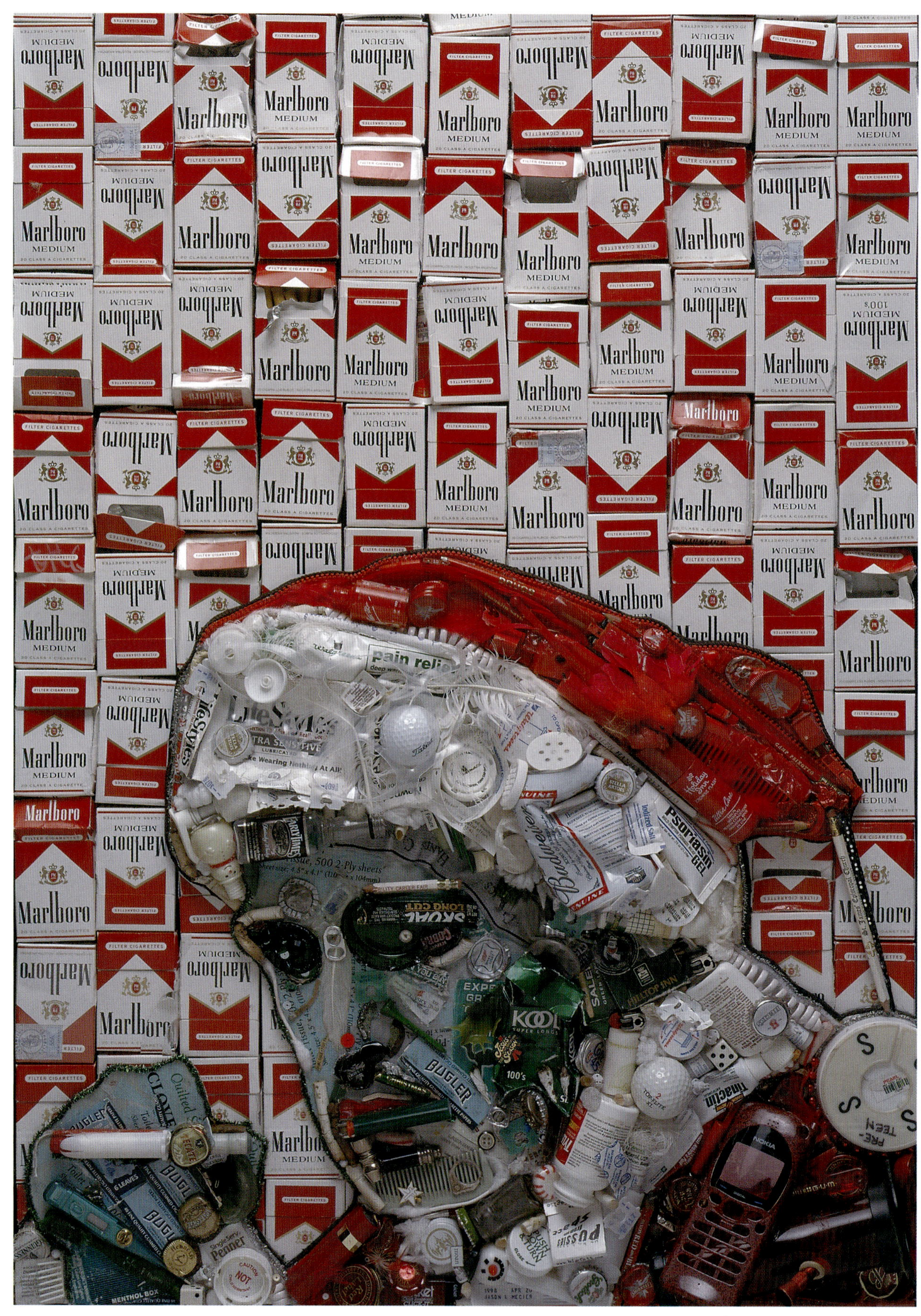

BAD SANTA • Cigarette boxes, rolling papers, condom wrapper, beer can, disposable lighters, pain relievers, bottle caps, bong, 2005

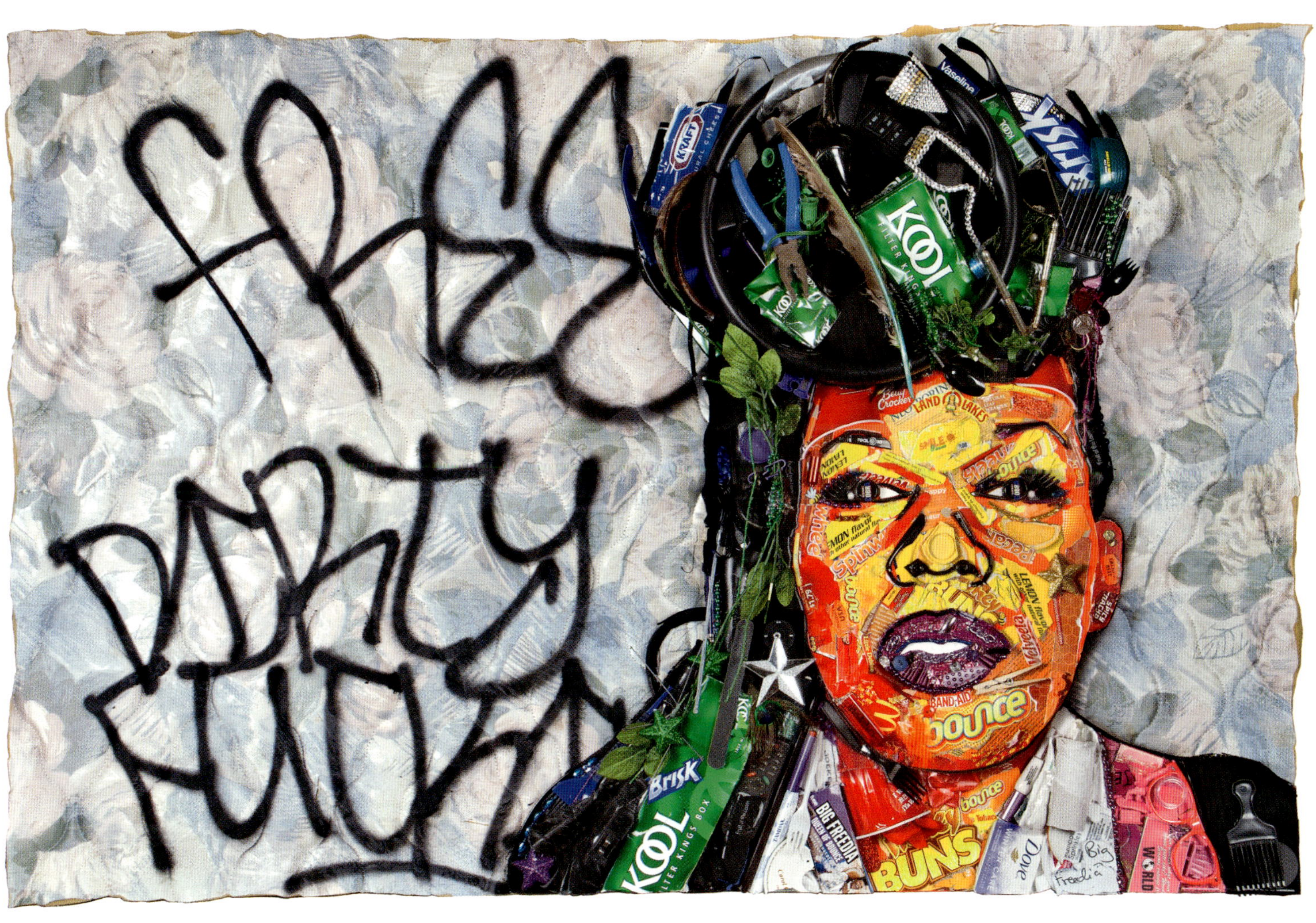

BIG FREEDIA • Mattress covering, food packaging, sunglasses, combs, cigarette boxes, stars, steering wheel, fabric softener, 2015

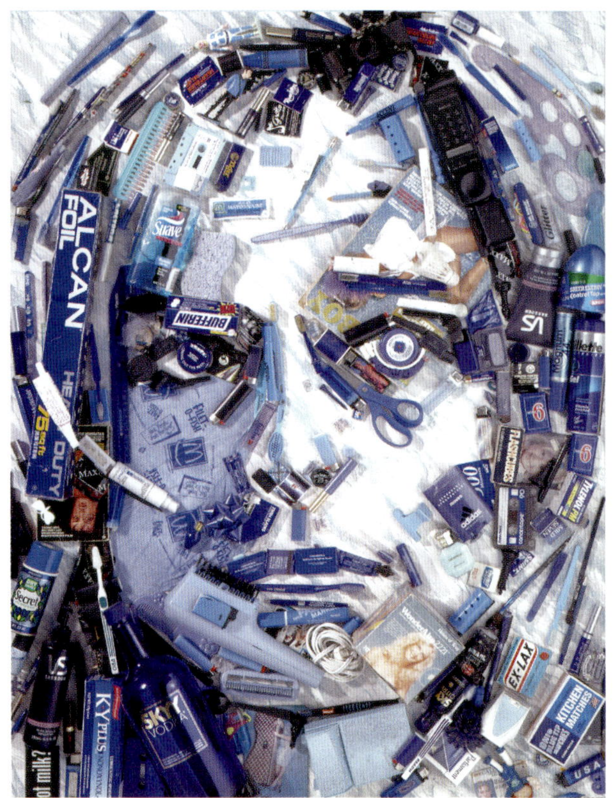

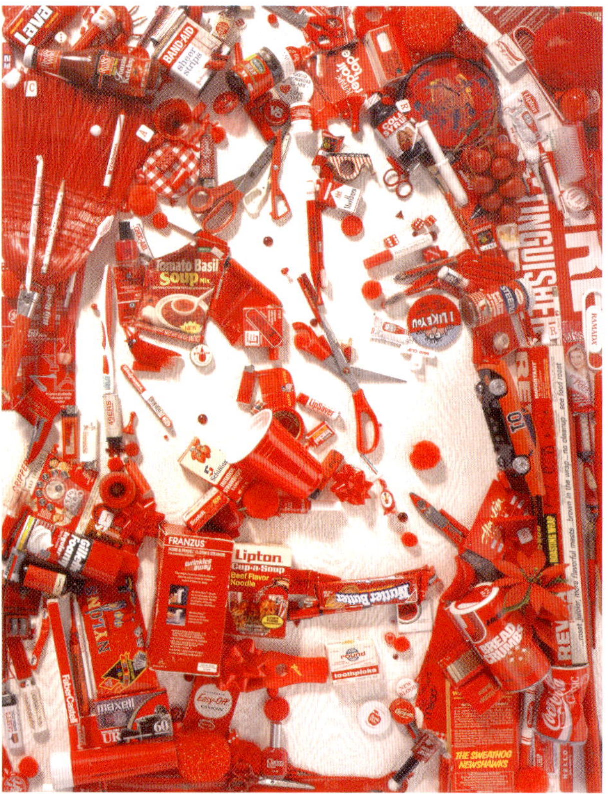

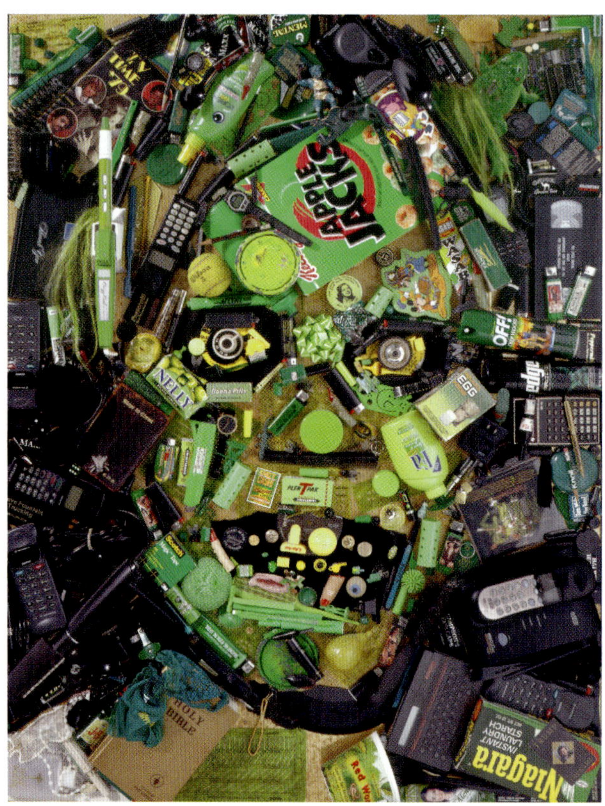

TOP LEFT: THE BURNING BED (FARRAH FAWCETT) • Matches, beauty and hygiene products, vodka bottle, fast-food wrapper, magazine, 2002

One of my first junk pieces, part of a monochrome series.

TOP RIGHT: CARRIE (SISSY SPACEK) • Red and white found objects, soup, ketchup, scissors, nail polish, bows, matches, 2002

BOTTOM: THE EXORCIST (LINDA BLAIR) • Bible, cell phones, plastic toys, panties, disposable lighters, videotapes, cereal box, 2002

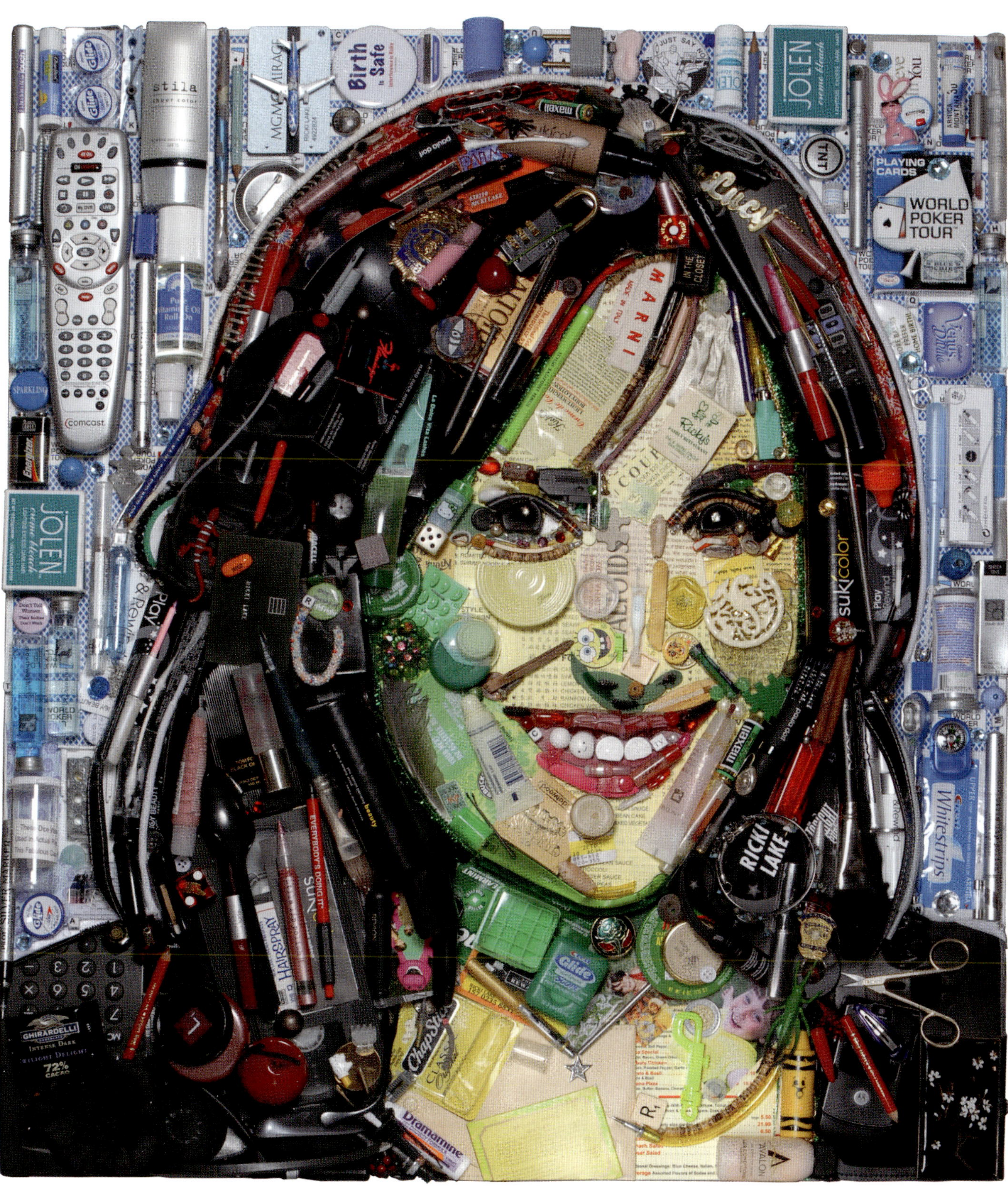

RICKI LAKE • Cosmetics and personal-care items, remote control, playing cards, family photos, take-out menus, (Lake's own junk), 2009

Collection of Ricki Lake.

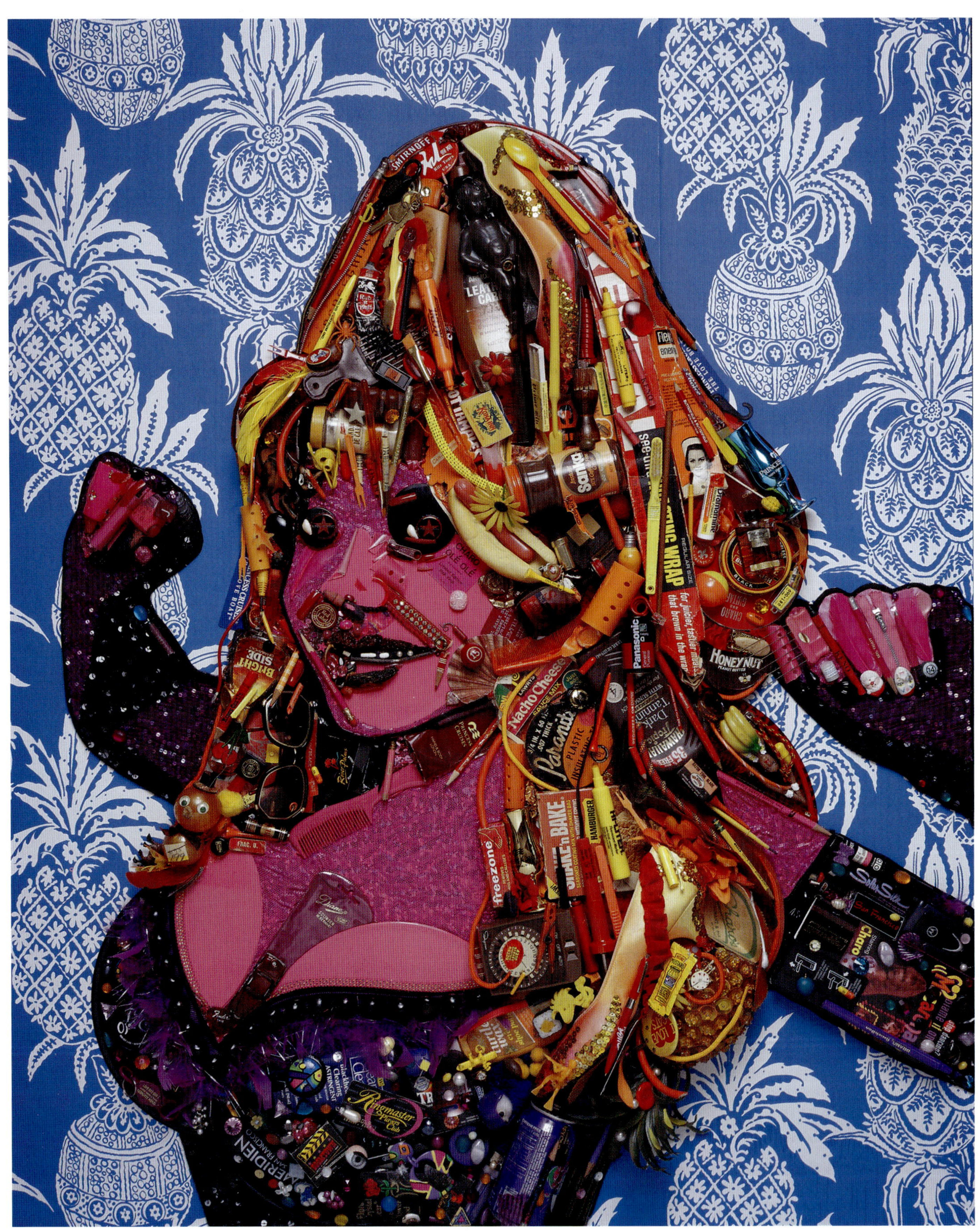

CHARO • Fabric, feathers, hair curlers, highlight markers, plastic fruit, 2008

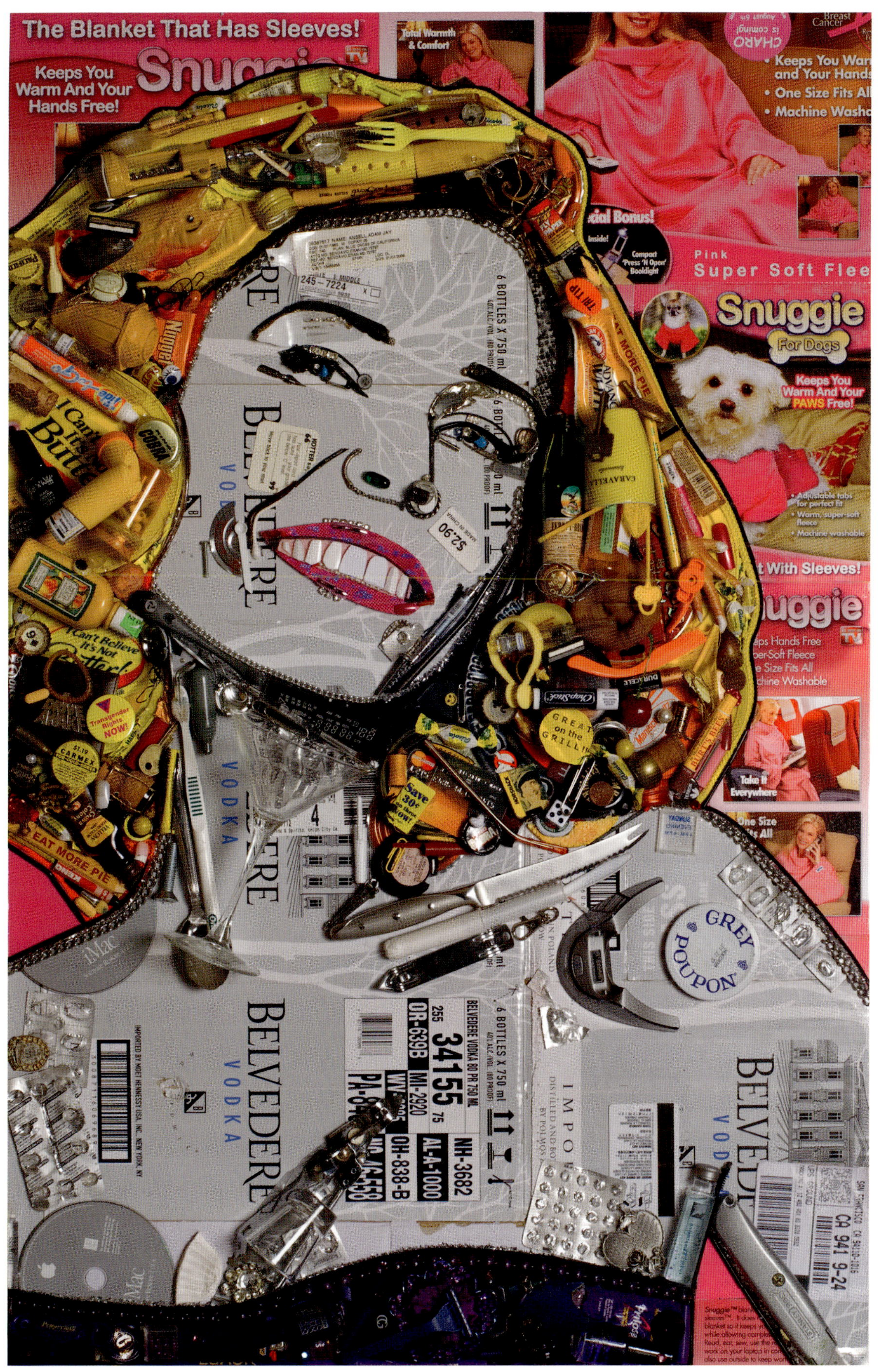

CHELSEA HANDLER • Vodka packaging, wearable-blanket packaging, bottle openers, knives, nail polish, pill packaging, 2010

Tour poster.

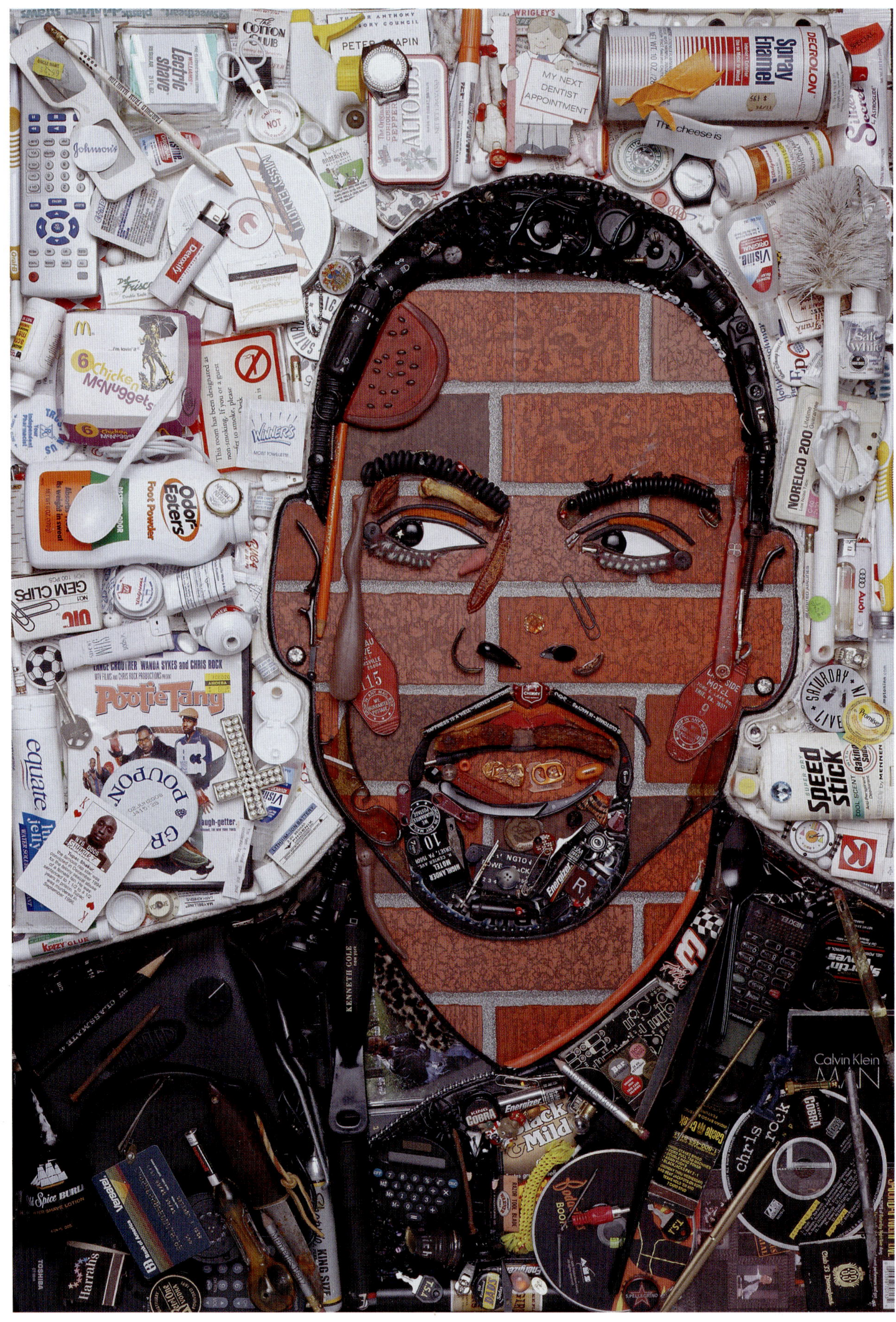

CHRIS ROCK • Brick wall contact paper, DVD case, eye drops, hotel room keys, matchbooks, doll leg, 2008
Tour Poster.

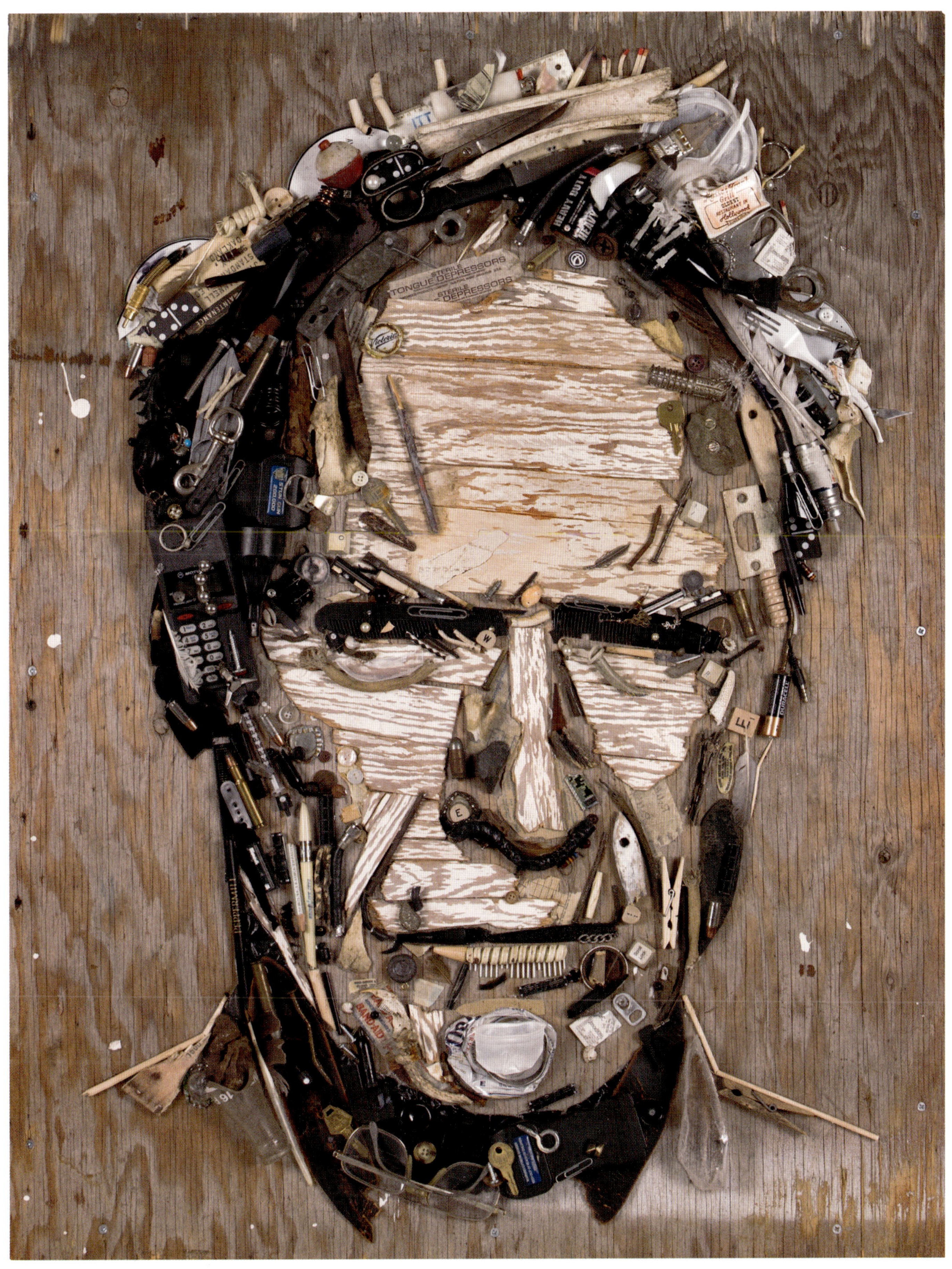

CLINT EASTWOOD • Wood, nails, bullets, bone, leather scraps, stun gun, 2012

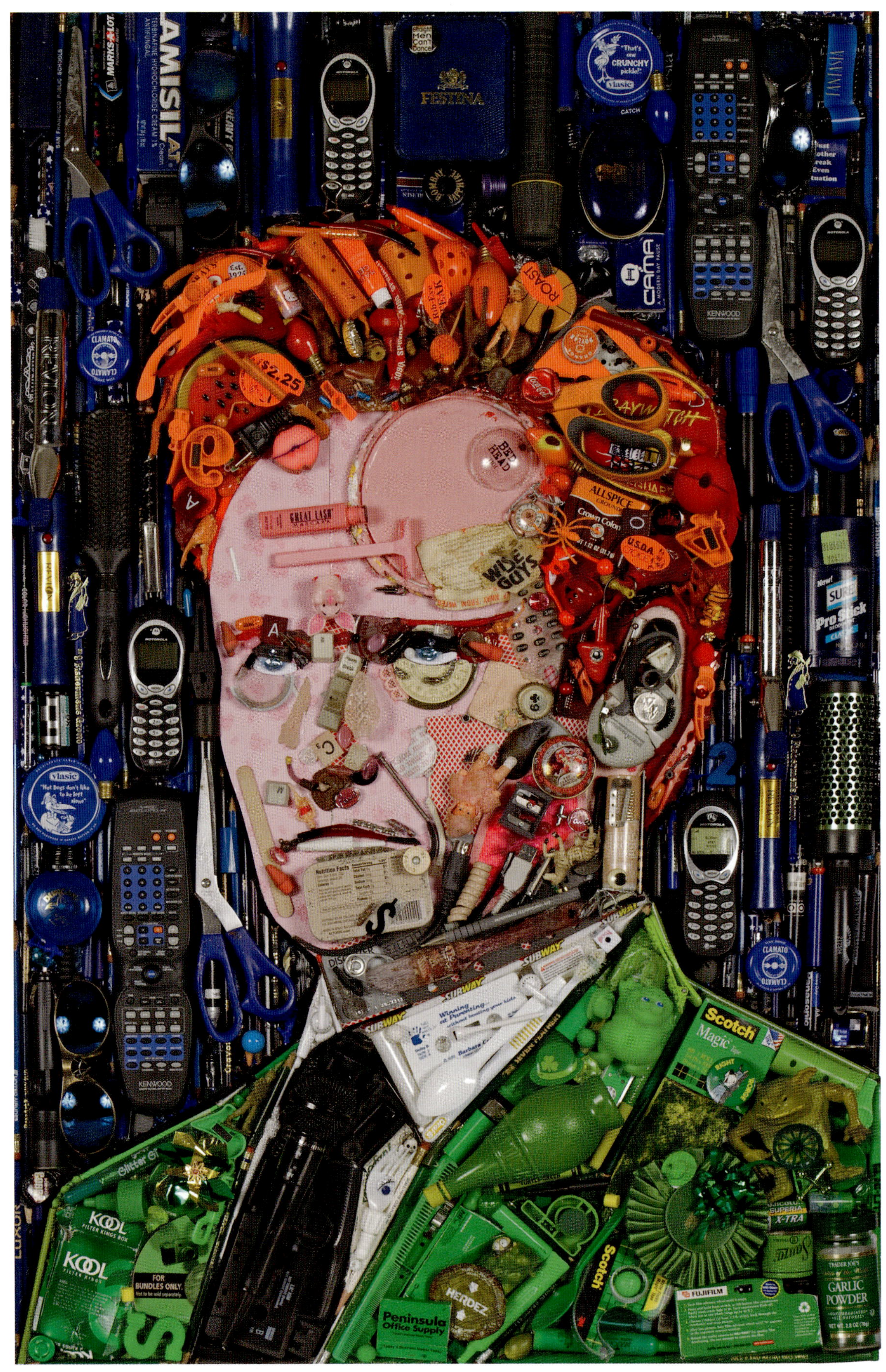

CONAN O'BRIEN • Cell phones, remote controls, pencils and pens, scissors, supermarket stickers, curling irons, microphone, 2010

Tour poster.

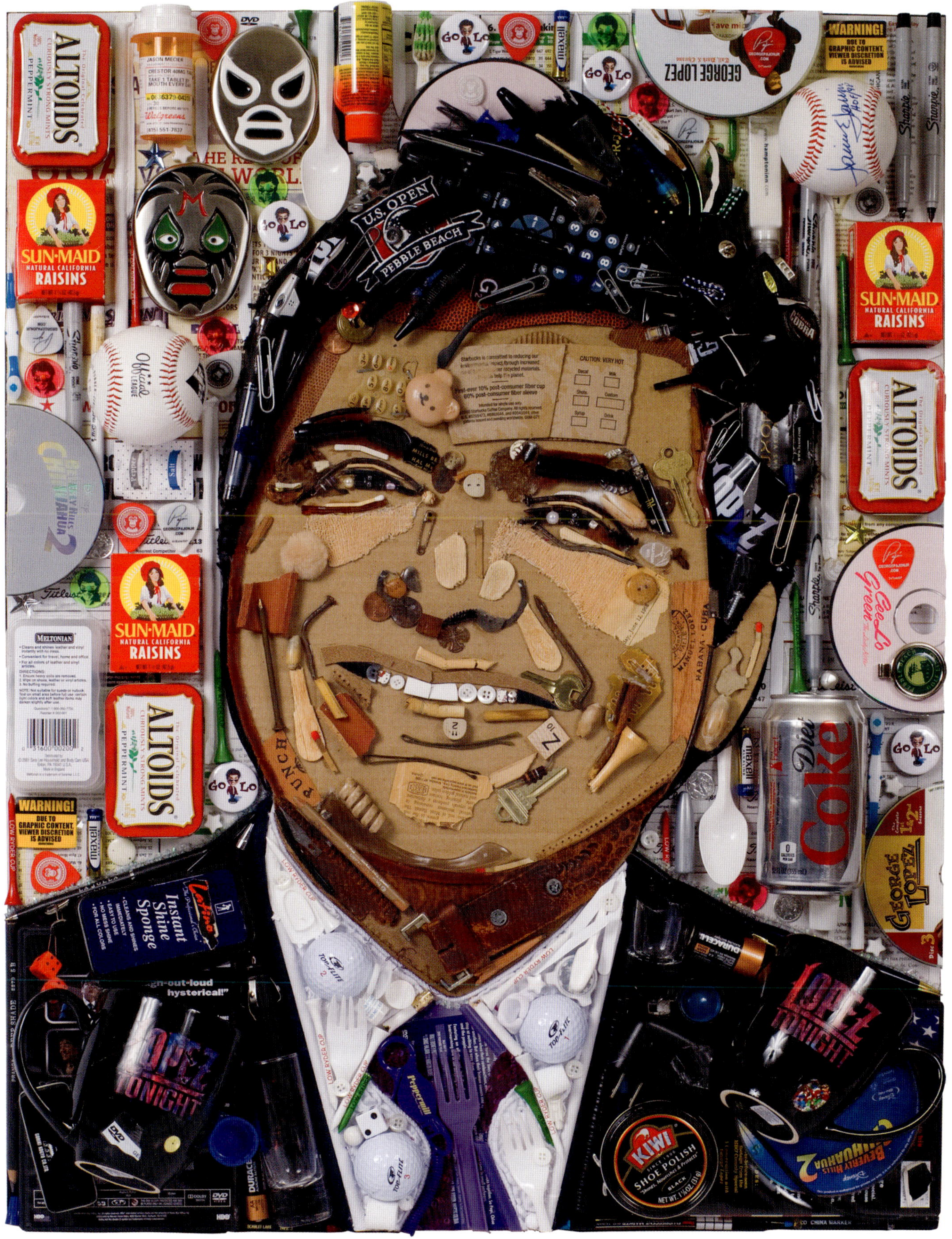

GEORGE LOPEZ • Golf balls, breath mints, DVDs, coffee mug, prescription bottle, raisins, pens, buttons (Lopez's own junk), 2011

Margaret Cho commissioned me to make this, and she presented it to George on his show.

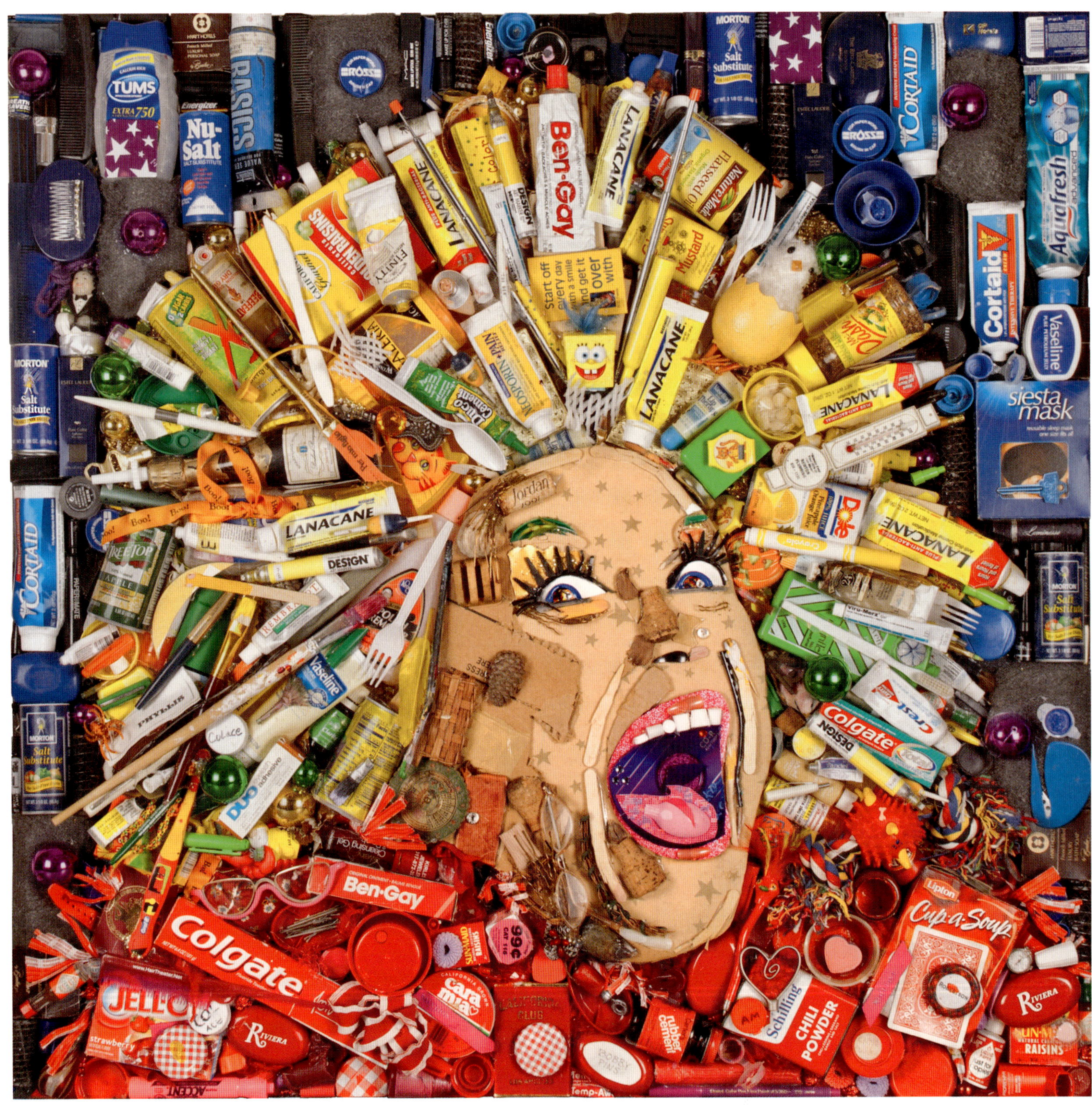

PHYLLIS DILLER • Cosmetics and personal-care items, kitchen goods, pens, holiday decorations, mini Champagne bottle (Diller's own trash), 2015

OPPOSITE, TOP: PHYLLIS DILLER • Jewelry, denture cream, pill container, watches, spice bottles (Diller's own junk), 2015

OPPOSITE, BOTTOM: PHYLLIS DILLER (GOLD) • Cosmetics and personal-care items, kitchen goods, wallpaper, jewelry, handwritten notes, pine cones, (Diller's own junk), 2006
Collection of Rosie O'Donnell.

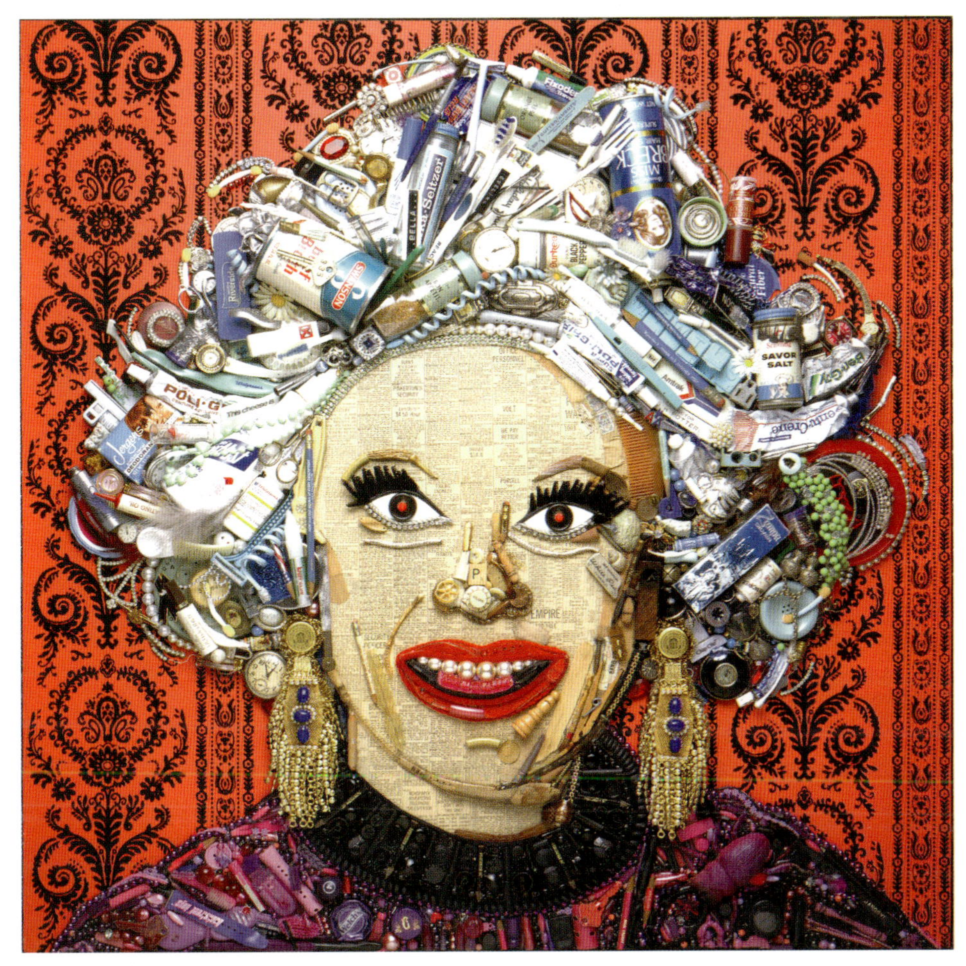
SAVOR
SALT

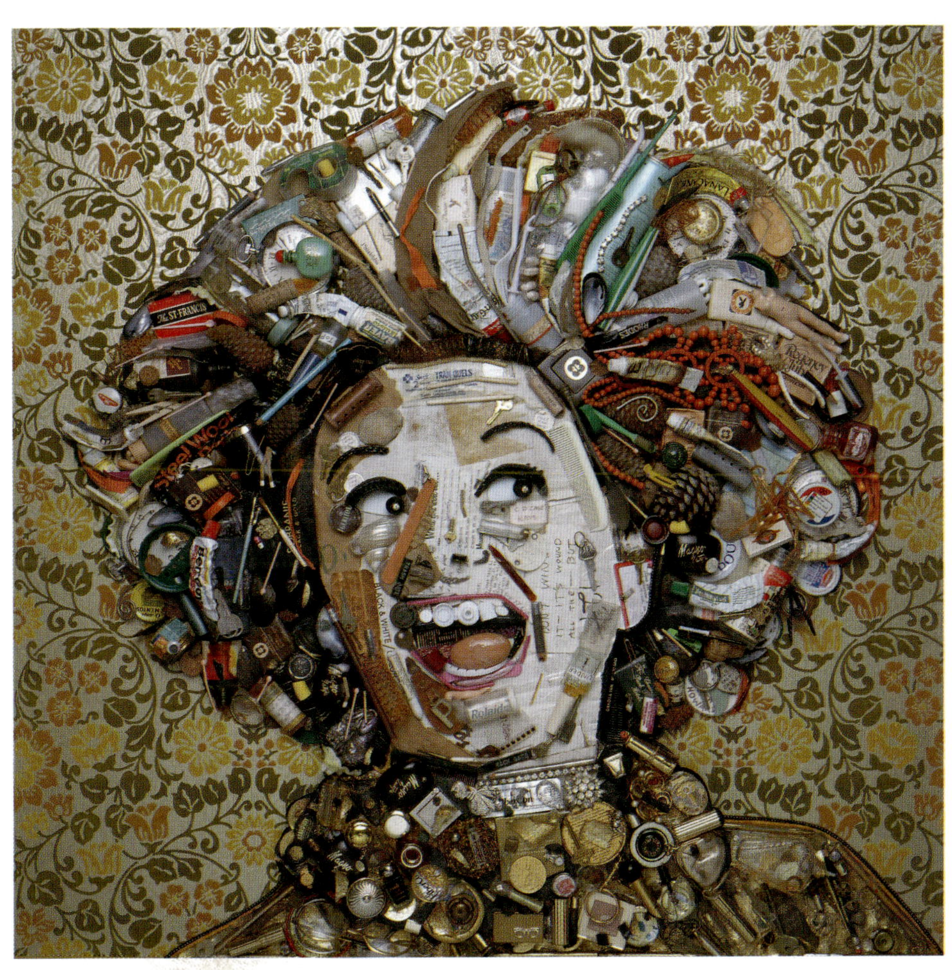

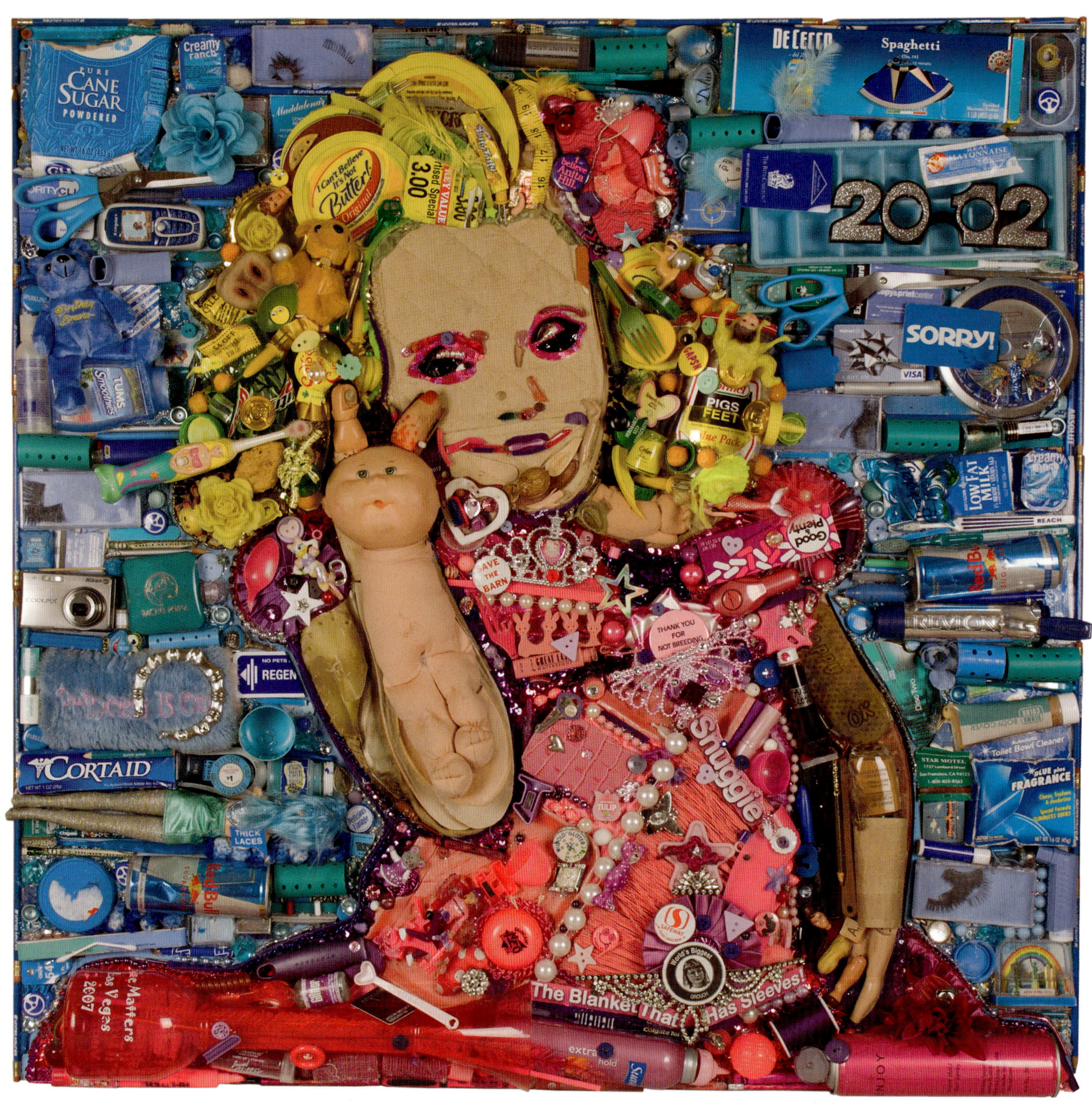

HONEY BOO BOO • Dolls, jewelry, stuffed animals, plastic bric-a-brac, energy drink cans, cheese balls, hairspray, curlers, 2012
Collection of TLC network.

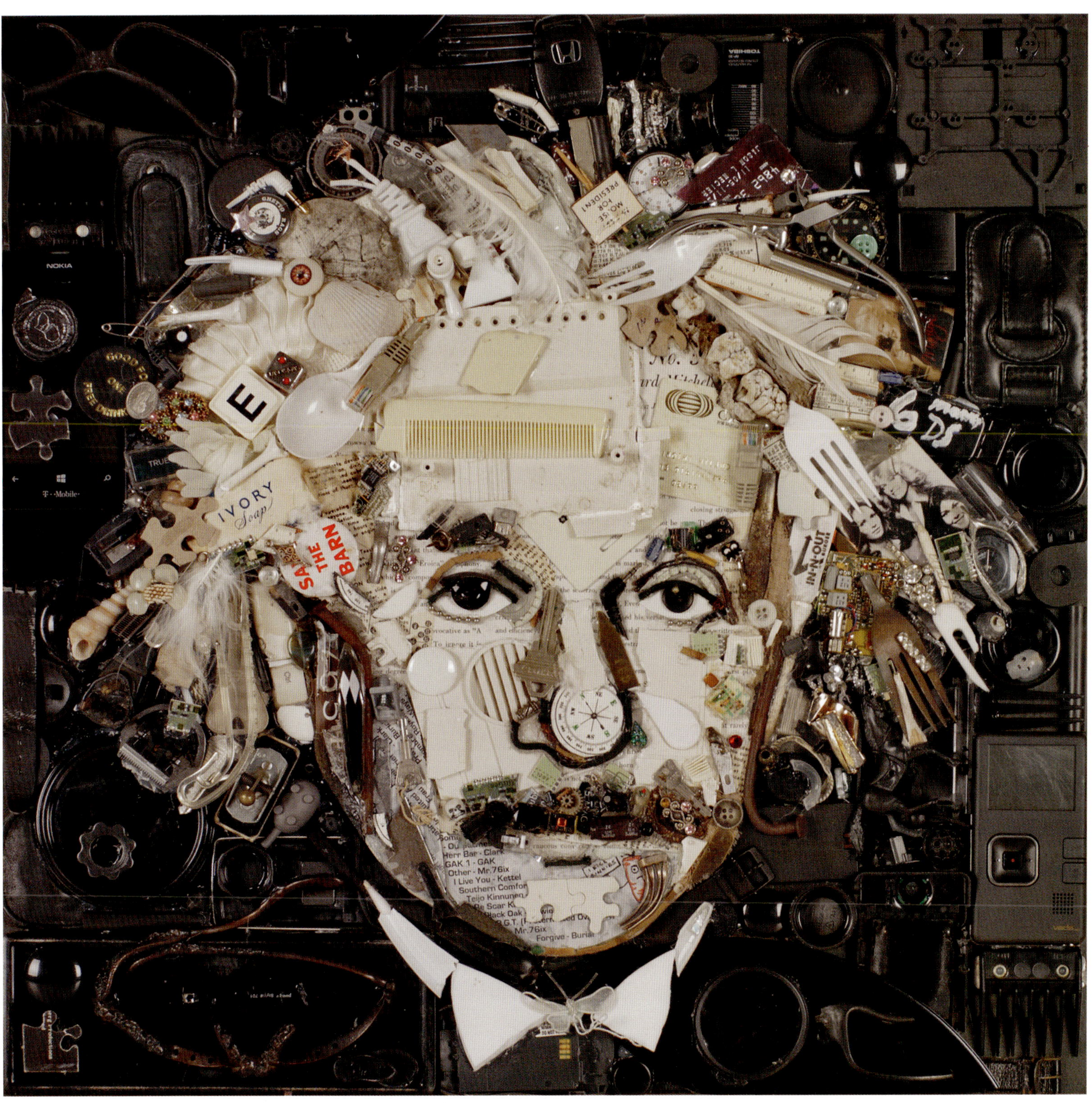

ALBERT EINSTEIN • Puzzle pieces, electronics, comb, feathers, compass face, 2014
This was featured in the James Franco movie *Why Him?* I managed to sneak *Charlie's Angels* into his hair.

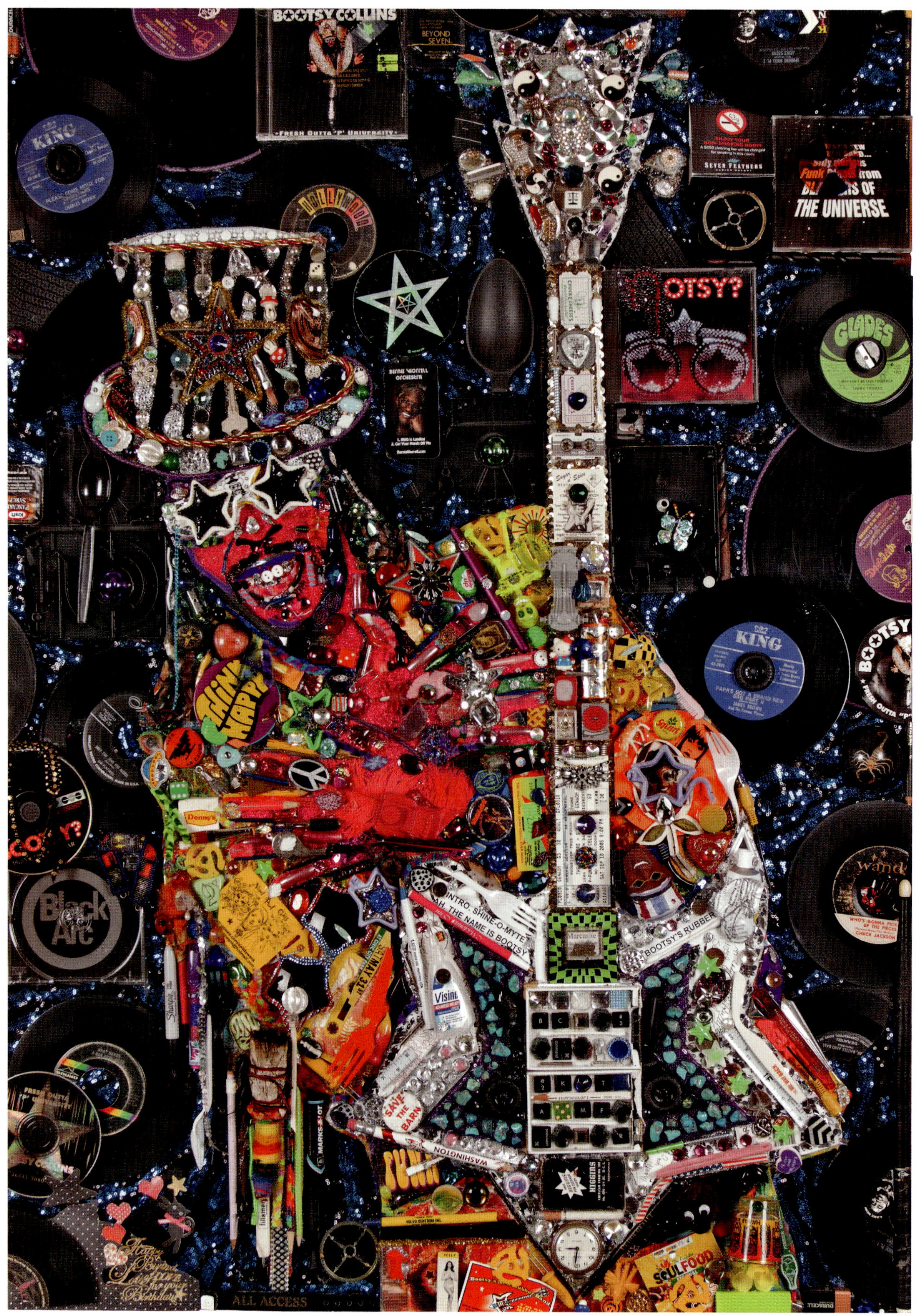

BOOTSY COLLINS • CDs, vinyl records, buttons, crystals, jewelry, sequins (Collins' own junk), 2016

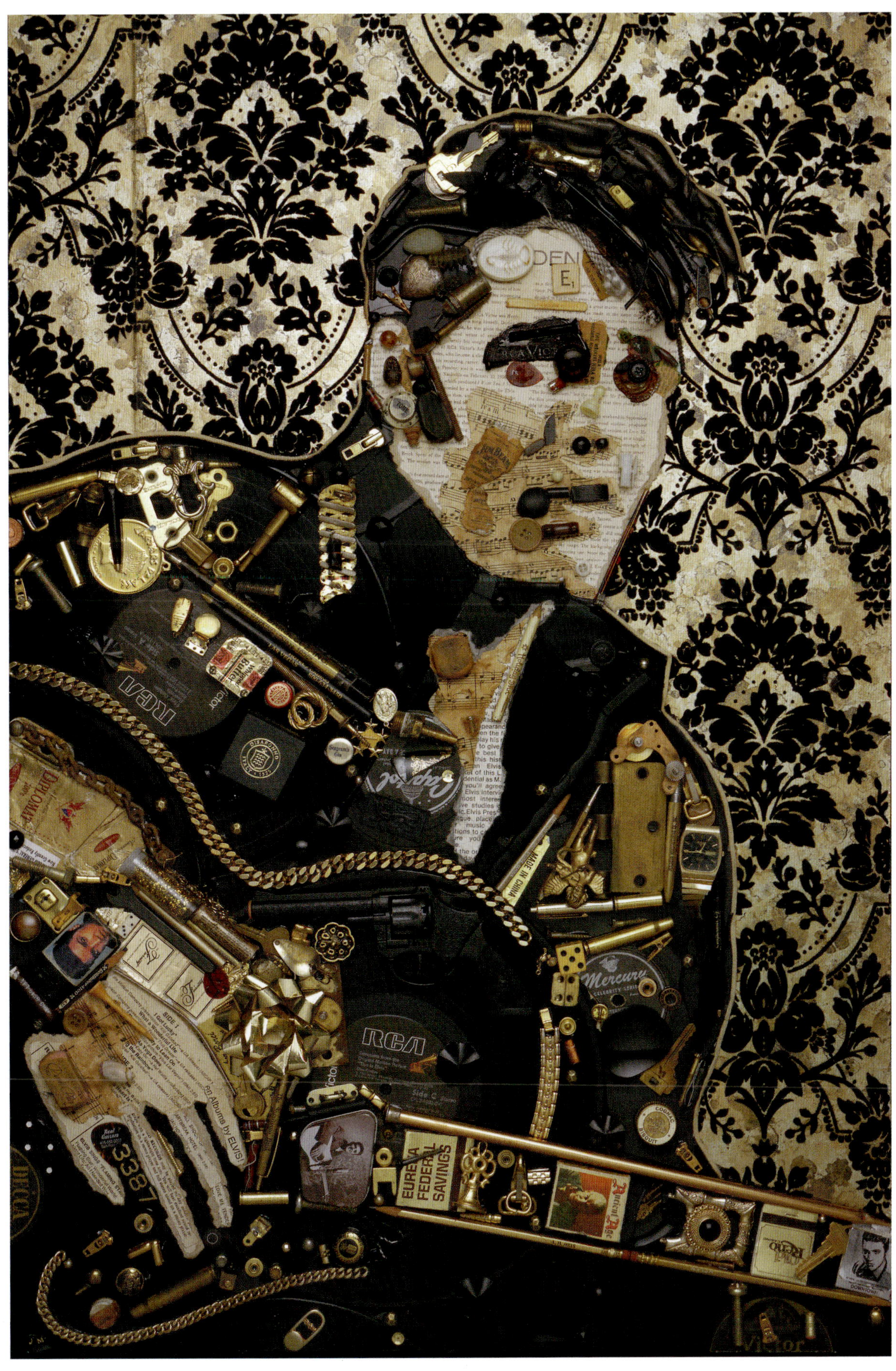

ELVIS PRESLEY • Vinyl records, bullets, velvet wallpaper, chains and bracelets, sheet music, casino medallion, 2003

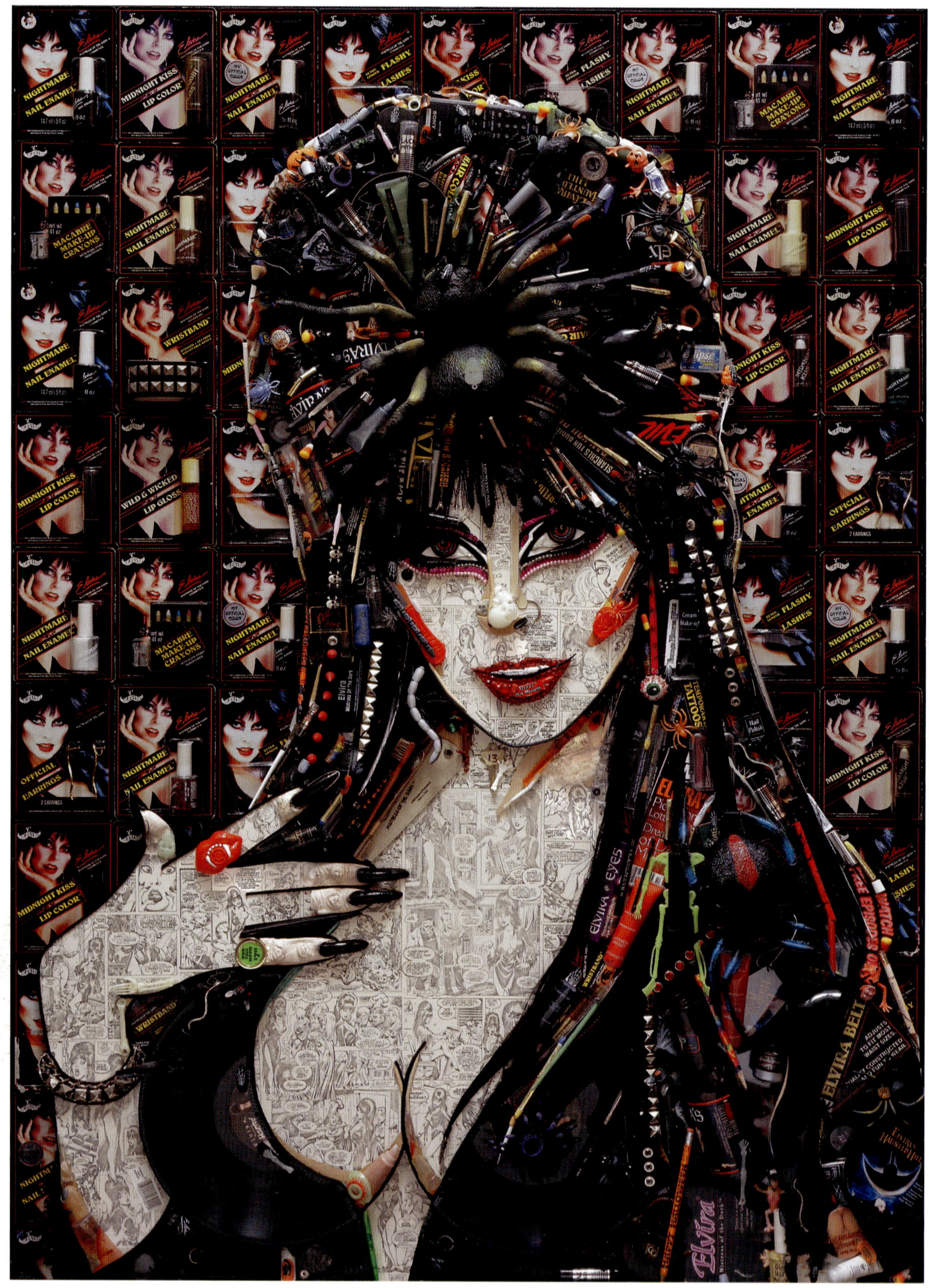

ELVIRA • Cosmetics, comics, vinyl records, studded wristbands, rubber and plastic spiders (Elvira's own junk), 2007
Collection of Elvira, Mistress of the Dark.

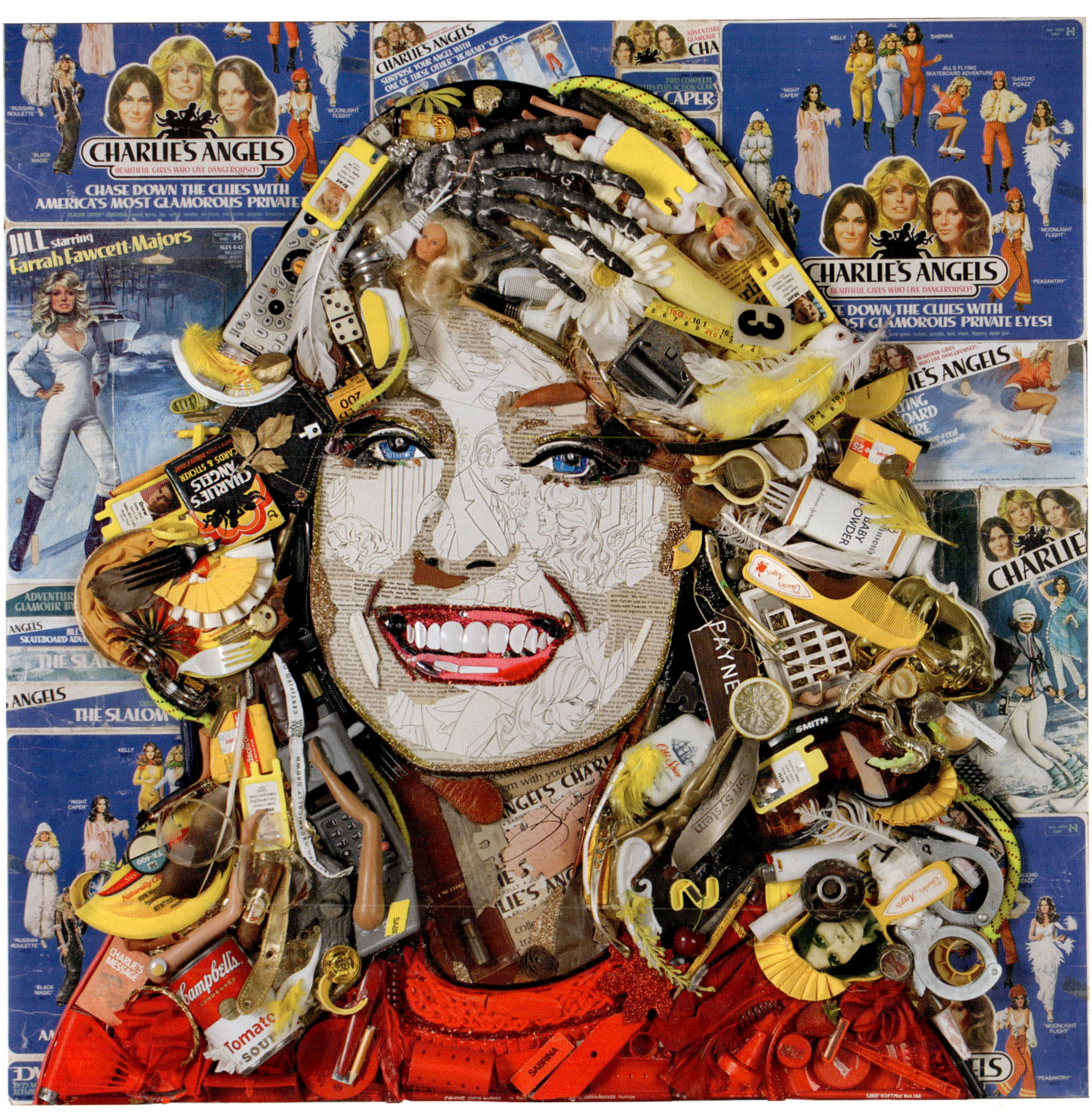

JILL (*CHARLIE'S ANGELS*) • Toy packaging, doll and doll parts, feathers, trading cards, film, 2014

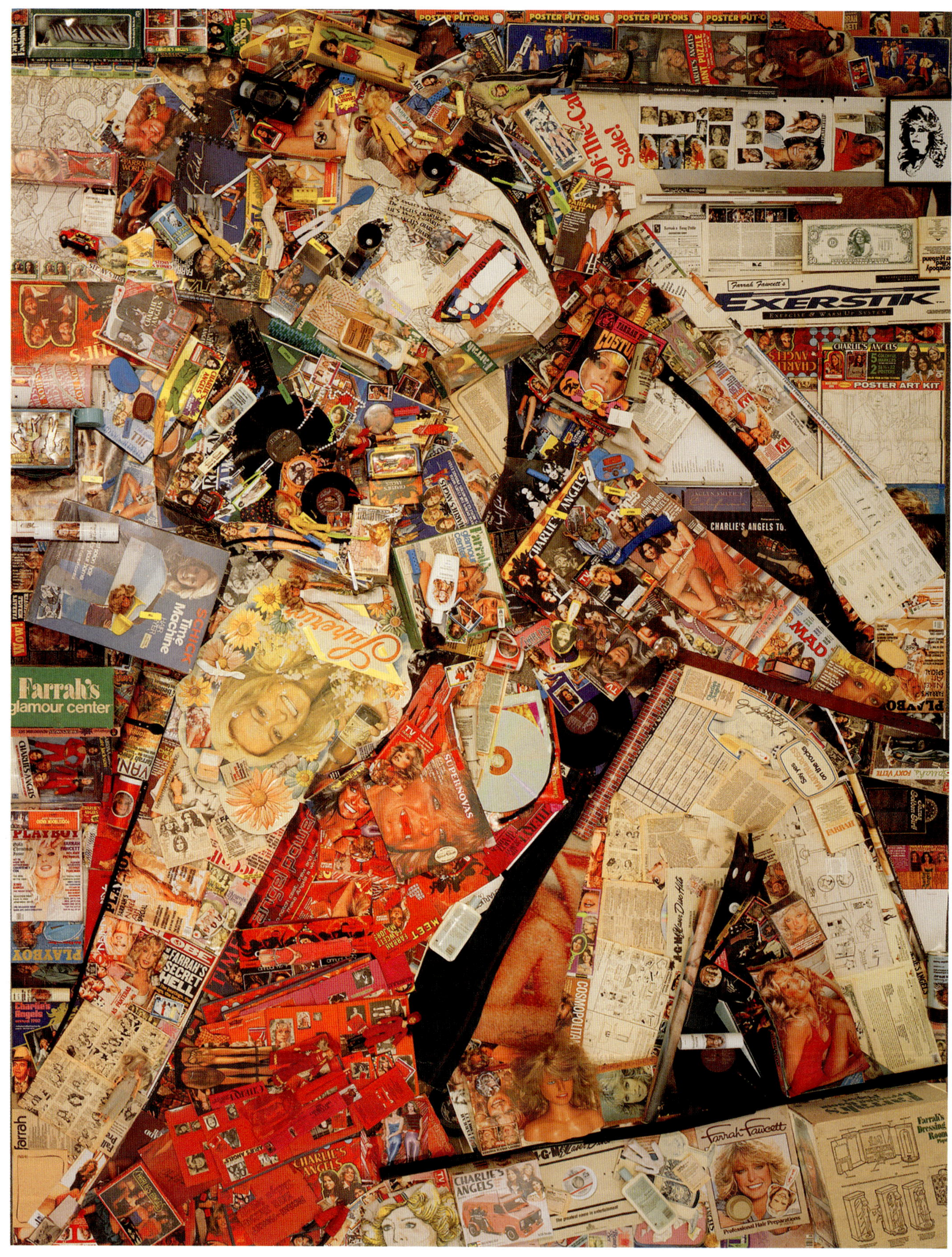

FARRAH FAWCETT • Magazines, posters, dolls, vinyl records, beauty products, 2014

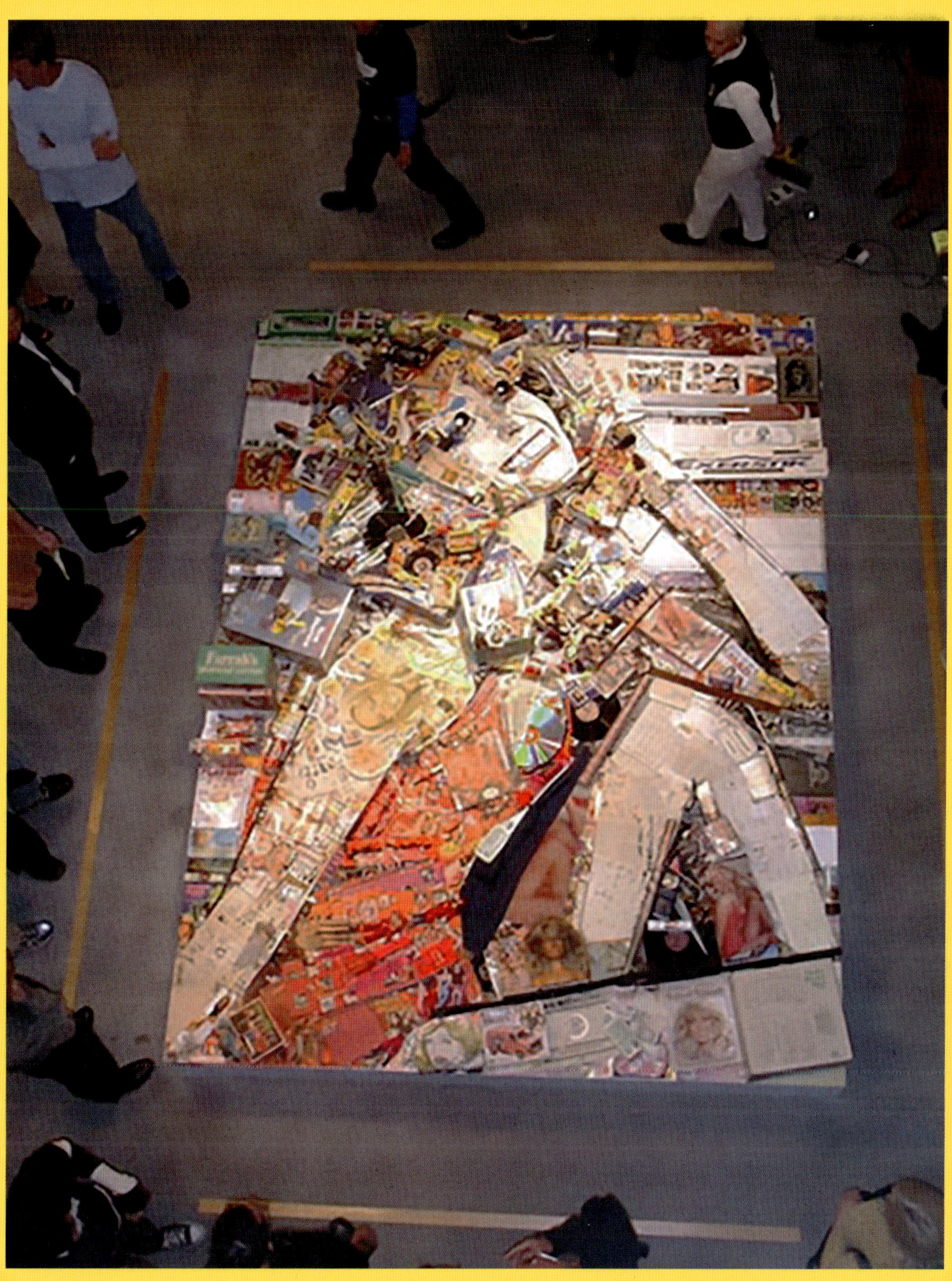

Here is the piece installed at the Yerba Buena Center for the Arts in San Francisco. It measured 9 x 12 feet and was best viewed from this perspective on an upper balcony. I later made posters of the piece and met Farrah, who autographed one for me.

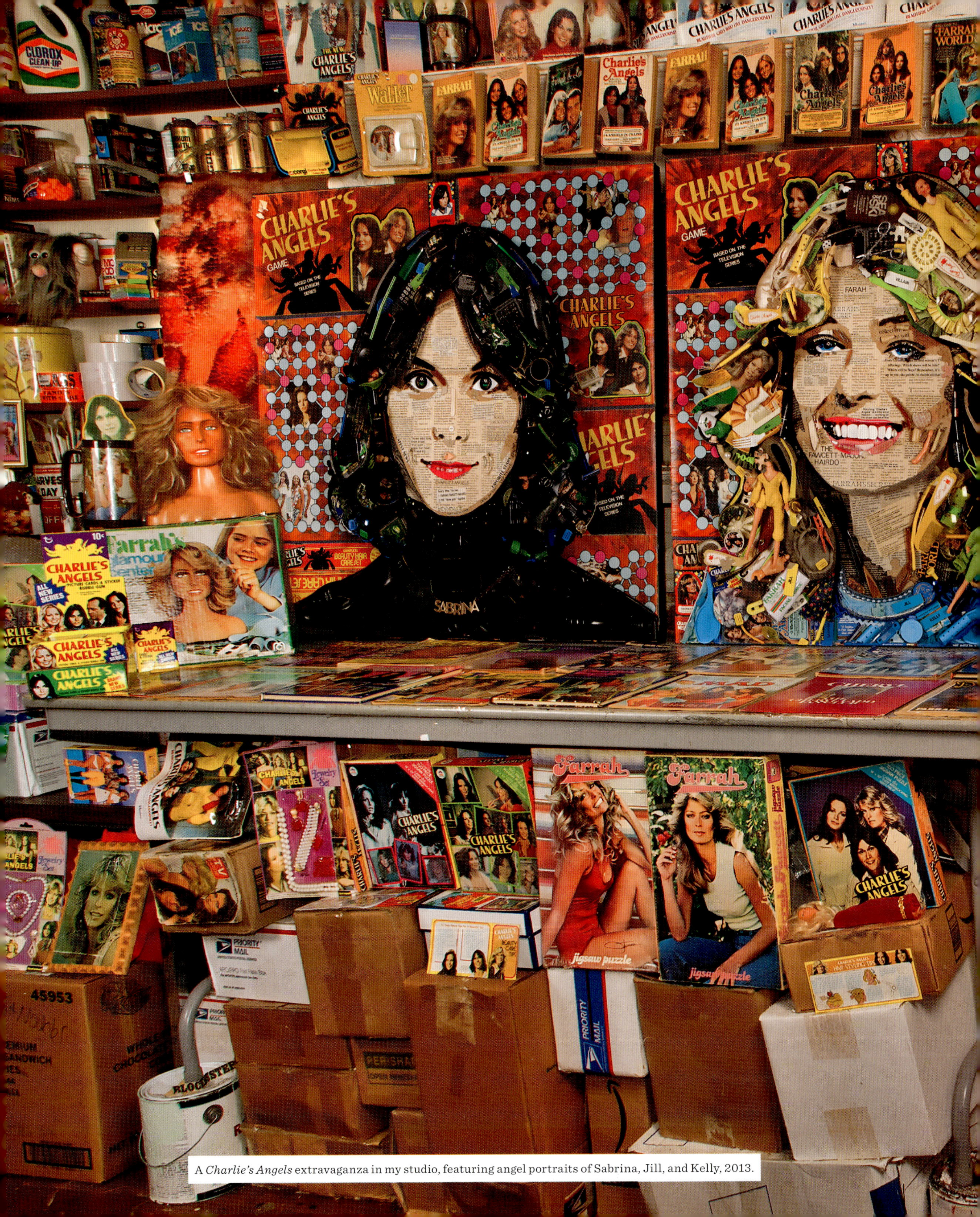

A *Charlie's Angels* extravaganza in my studio, featuring angel portraits of Sabrina, Jill, and Kelly, 2013.

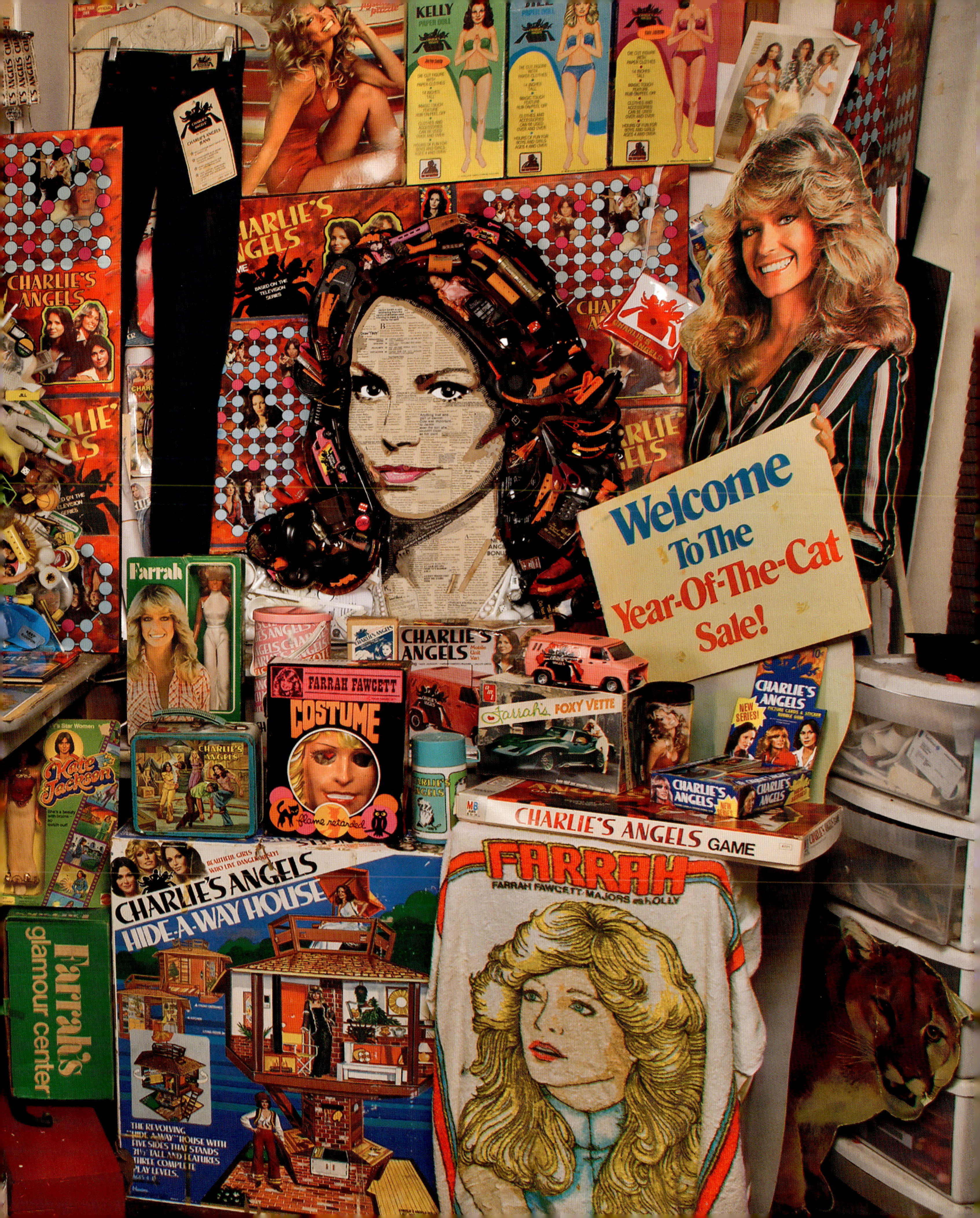
Welcome
To The
Year-Of-The-Cat
Sale!
CHARLIE'S ANGELS
FARRAH FAWCETT
COSTUME
Farrah
CHARLIE'S ANGELS GAME
FARRAH
FARRAH FAWCETT-MAJORS as JILL
CHARLIE'S ANGELS
HIDE-A-WAY HOUSE
Farrah's glamour center
Kate Jackson
Farrah's FOXY VETTE
KELLY
PAPER DOLL

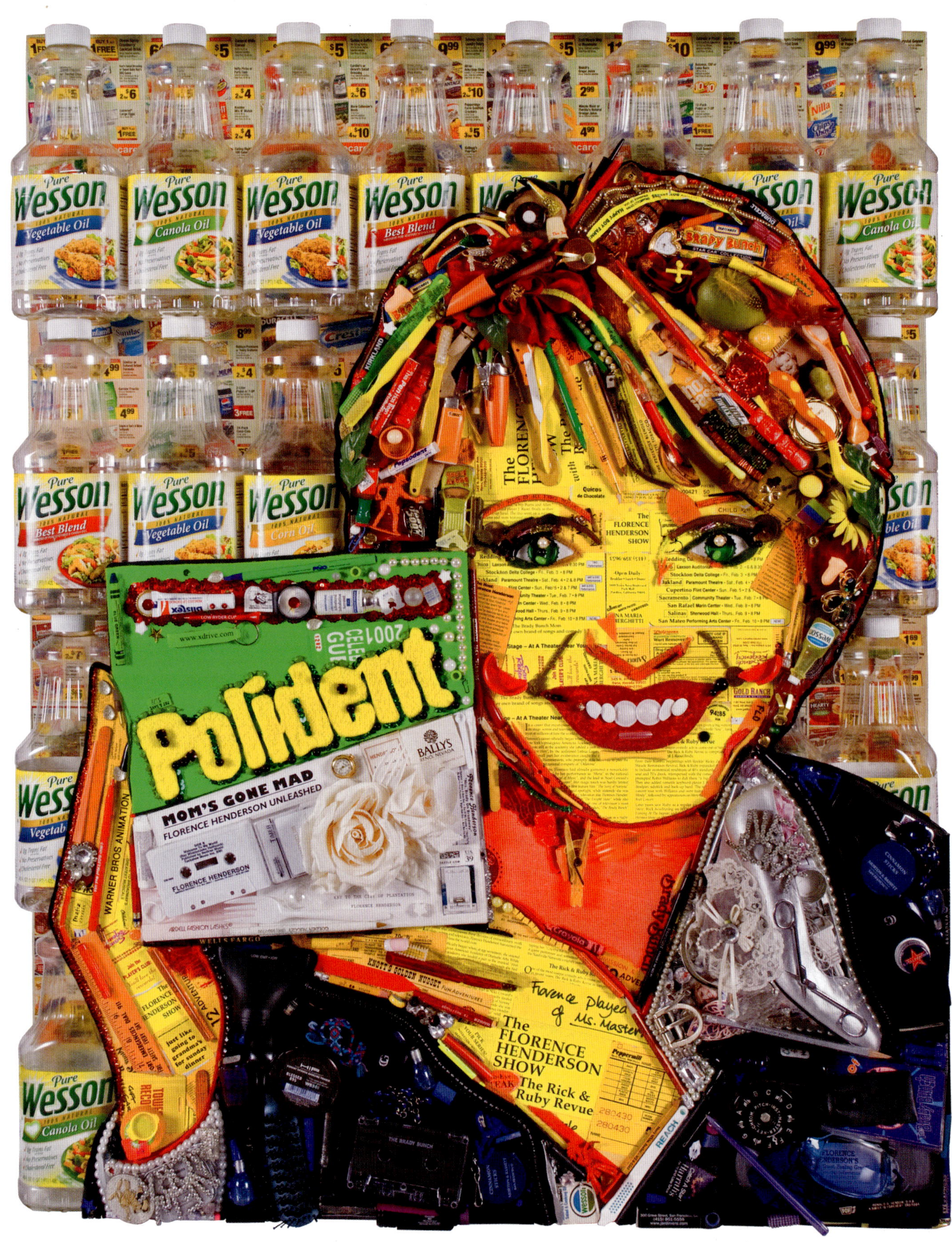

FLORENCE HENDERSON • Cooking oil bottles, theatrical notices, cassette tapes, jewelry, bottle caps, toothbrushes (Henderson's own junk), 2011

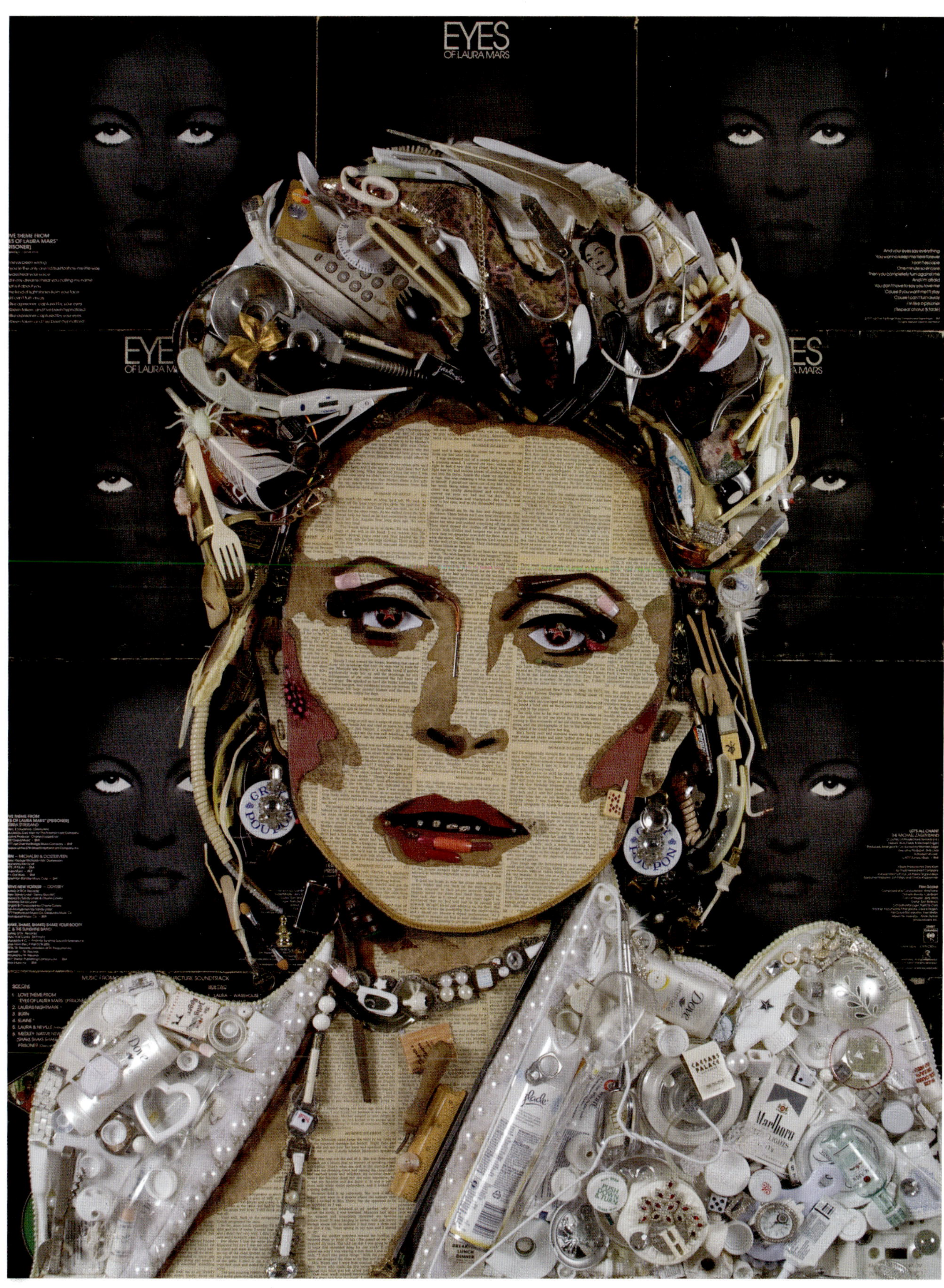

FAYE DUNAWAY • Record sleeves, book pages, cigarettes, beauty products, glass stems, jewelry, wire hangers, 2010

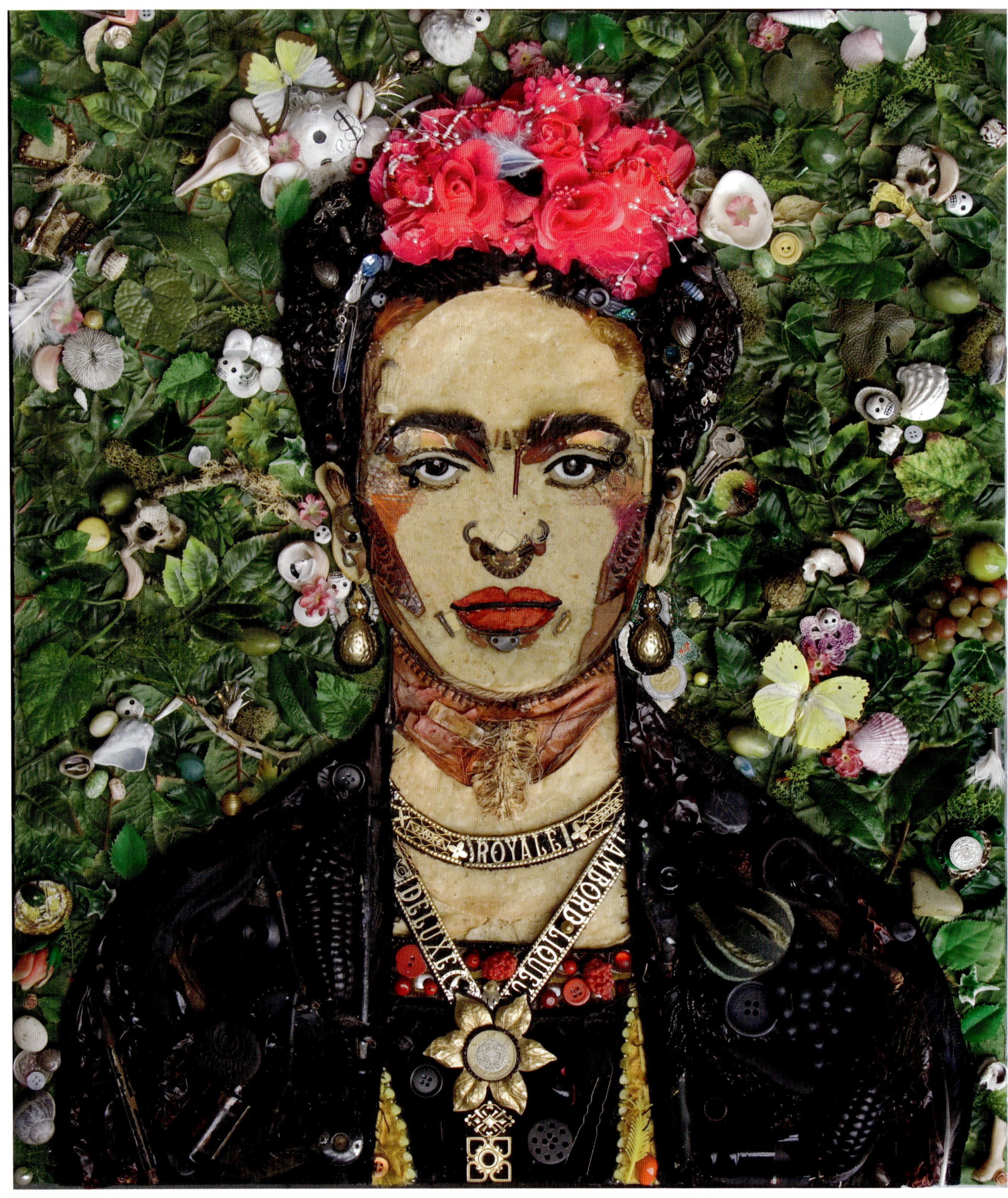

FRIDA KAHLO • Plastic leaves and flowers, shells, plastic butterflies, buttons, crafted skulls, 2010

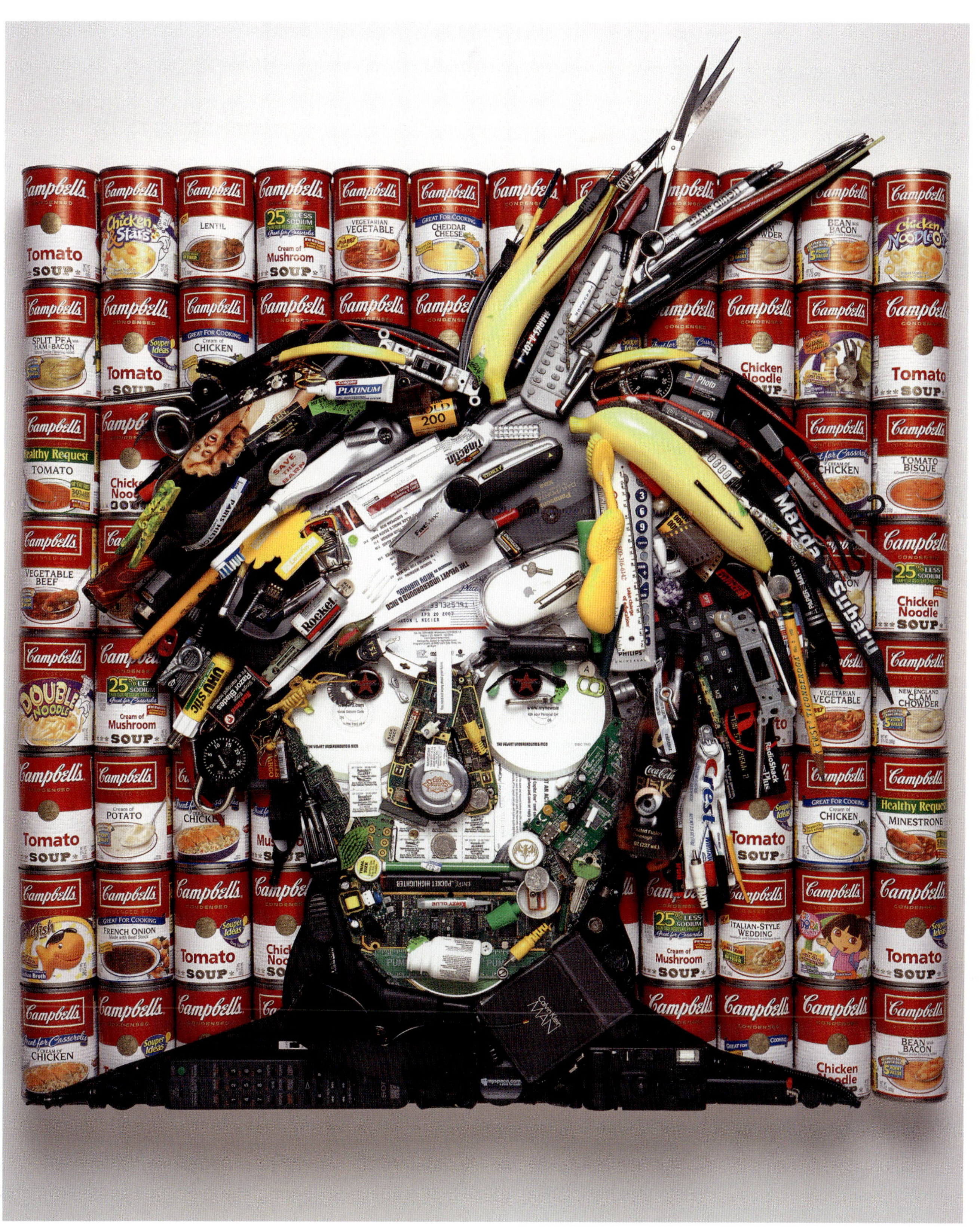

ANDY WARHOL • Soup cans, bananas, computer and cell phone parts, film rolls, silver ink pen, 2007

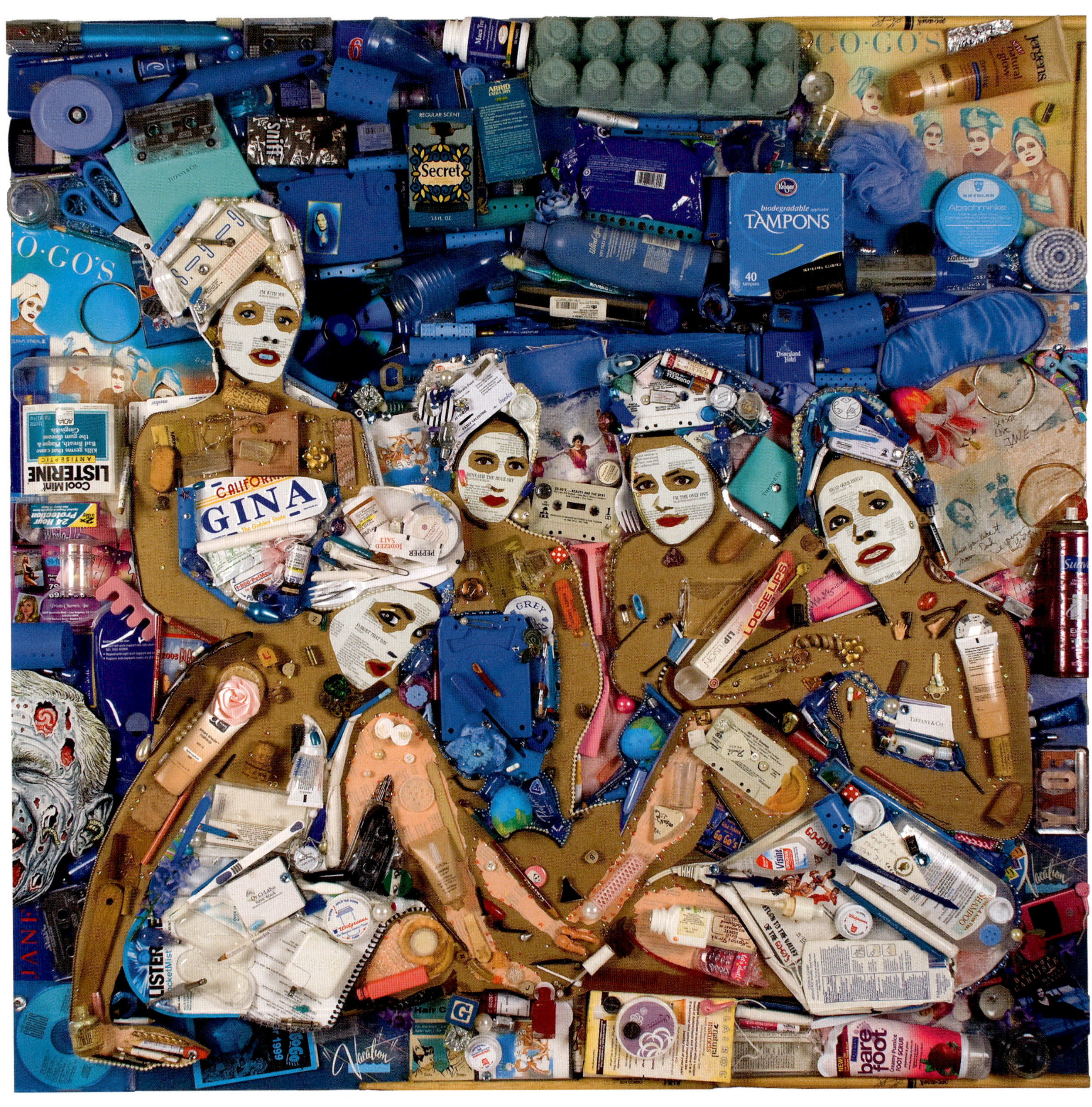

THE GO-GO'S • Record sleeves, cassette tapes, beauty supplies, jewelry, egg carton, tampons, sleep mask (the band's own junk), 2011

Tour poster.

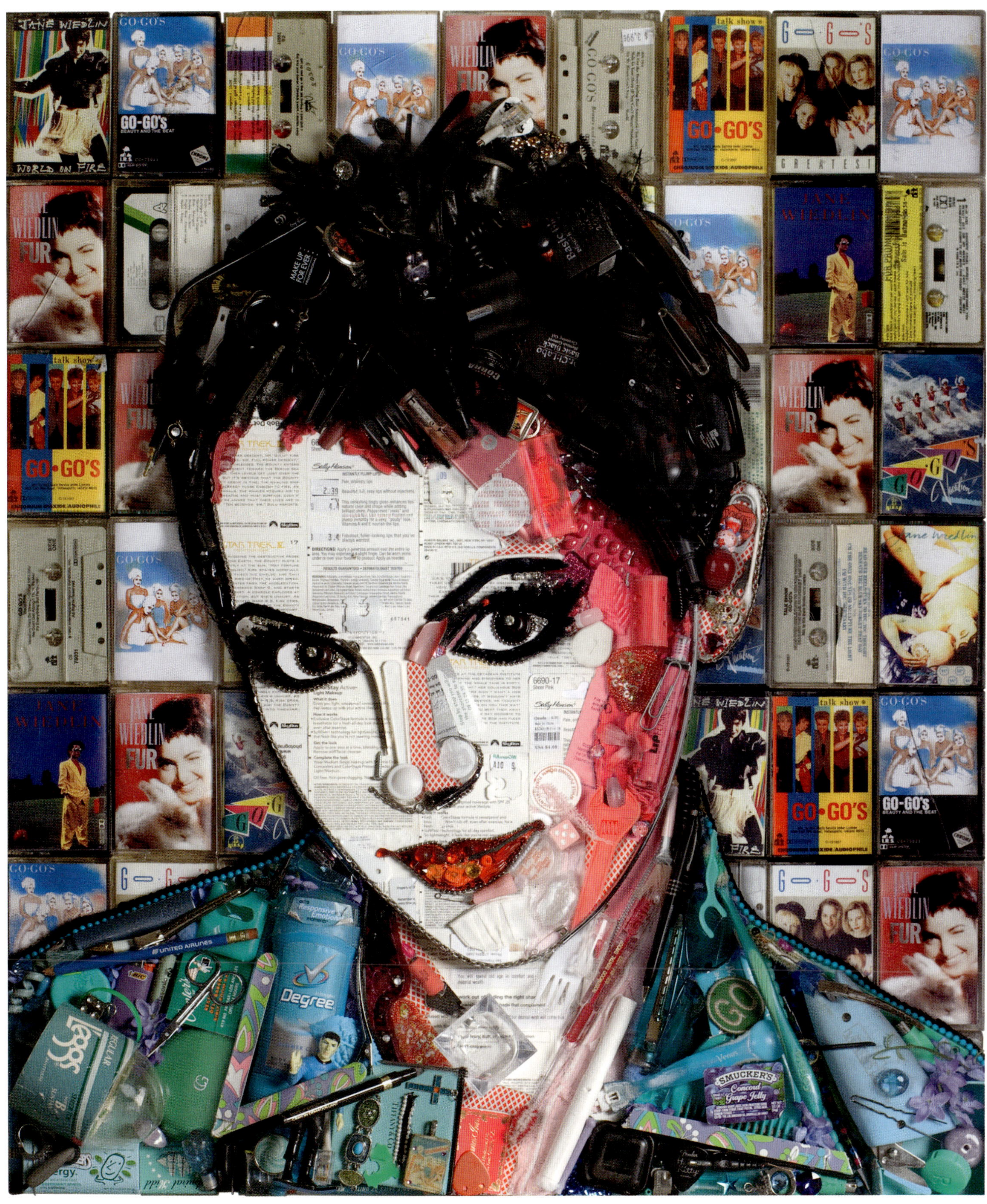

JANE WIEDLIN • Cassette tapes, hair dye, guitar picks, beauty supplies, flashbulb, figurine (Wiedlin's own junk), 2010

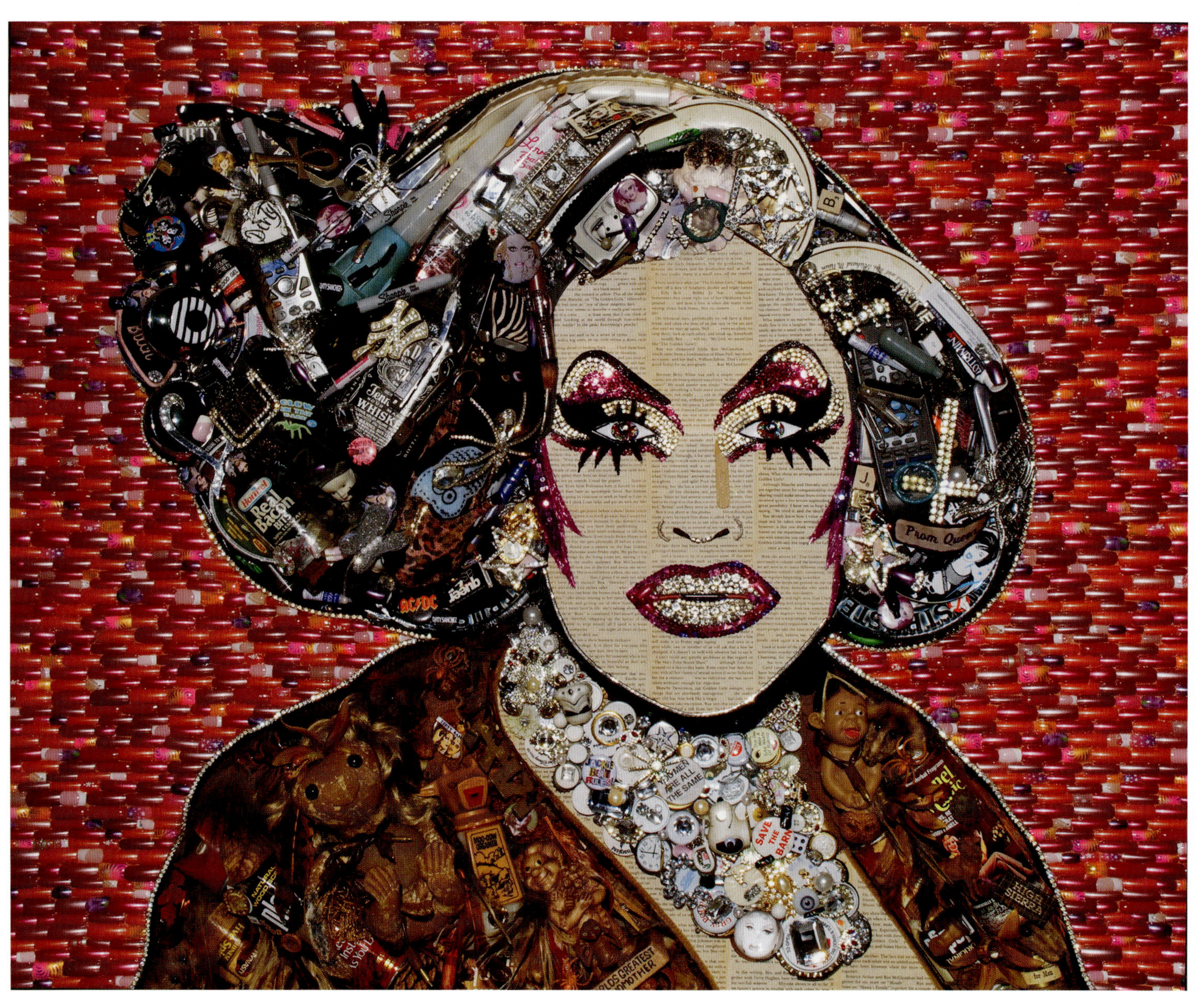

JACKIE BEAT • Plastic nails, rhinestones, jewelry, pinbacks, stuffed animals (Beat's own junk), 2009
Collection of Jackie Beat

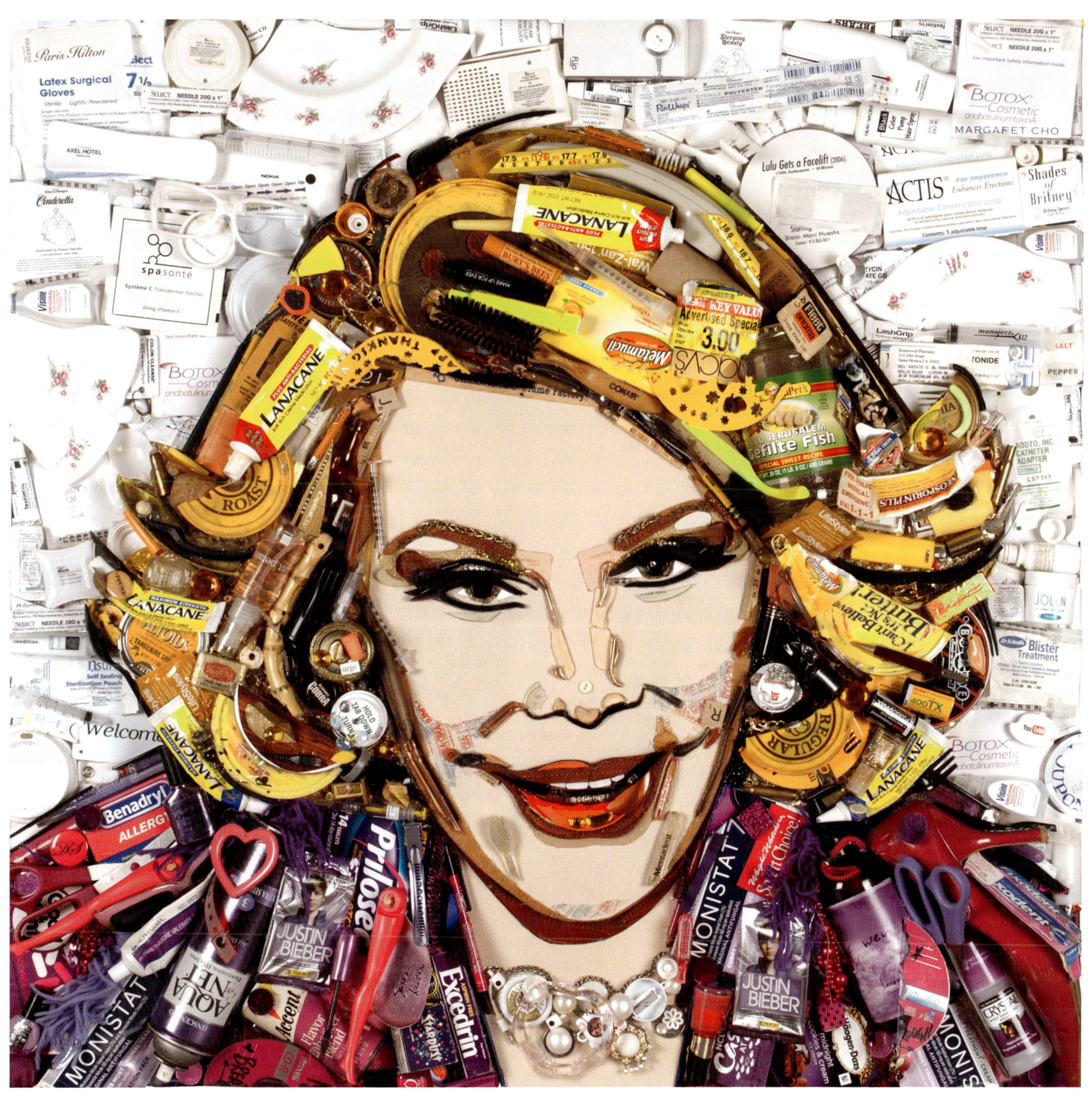

JOAN RIVERS • Skin cream and pain reliever packaging, hair spray, CDs, scissors, broken plate, gefilte fish, 2014

I made this one primarily from leftovers of other comedians' junk portraits (Phyllis Diller, Margaret Cho, Rosie O'Donnell, Ricki Lake). Collection of Margaret Cho.

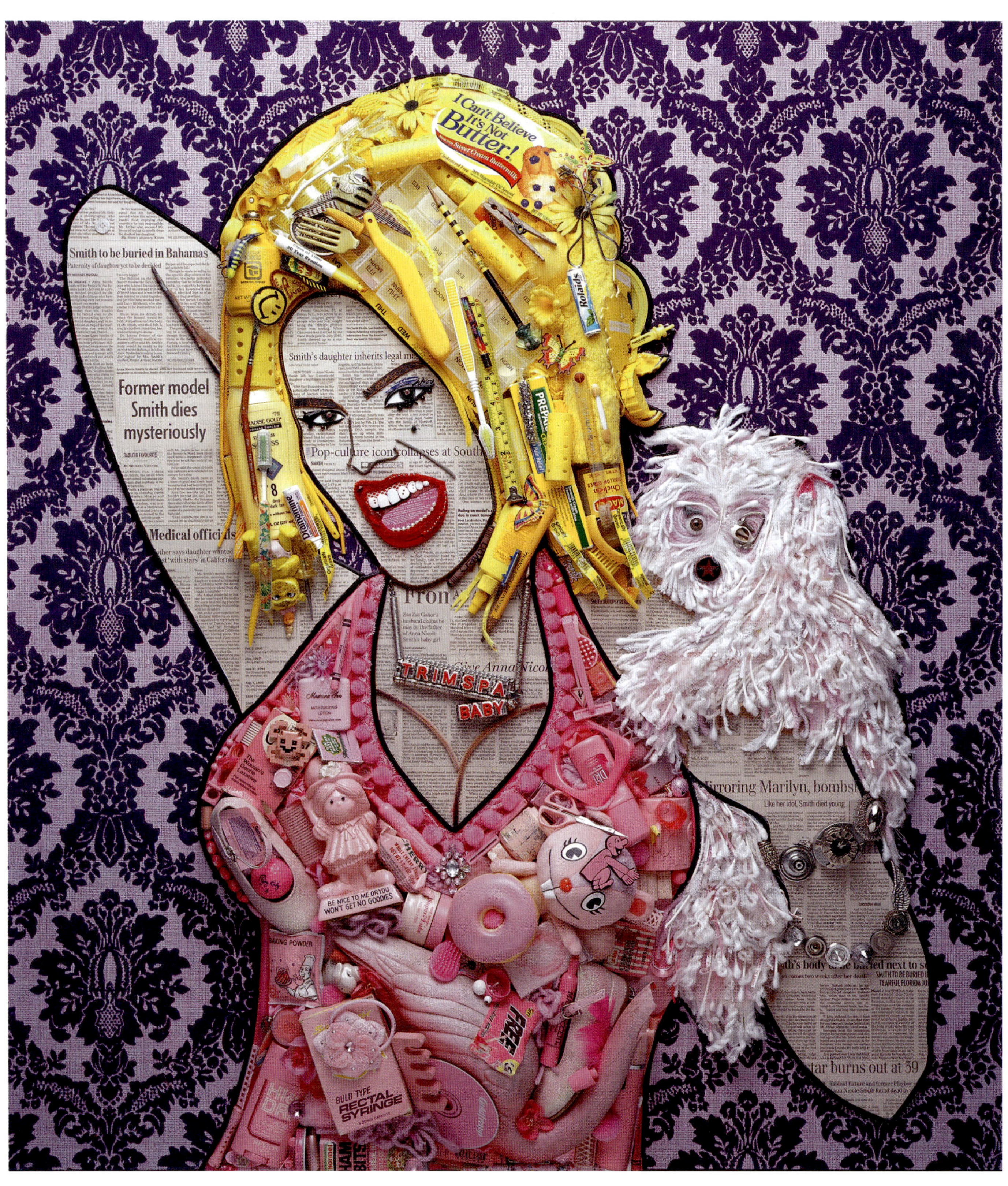

ANNA NICOLE SMITH • Pink plastic toys, newspaper clippings, wallpaper, yarn, hygiene products, jewelry, lipstick impression, 2008

The lipstick kiss on toilet paper is hers (a friend of mine did her makeup a long time ago).
In the collection of the Ripley's Believe It or Not! museum in Niagra Falls.

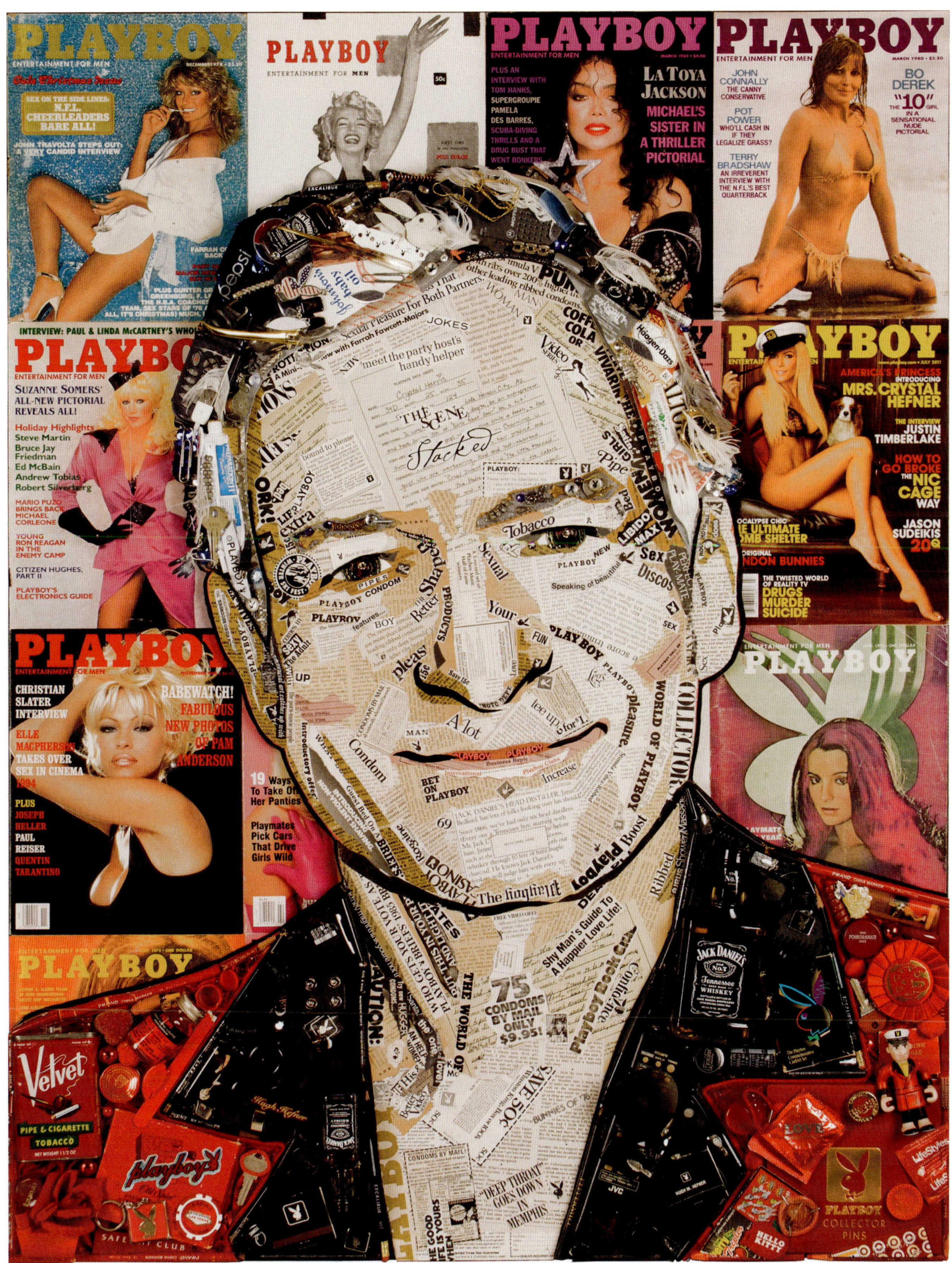

HUGH HEFNER • Magazine covers and clippings, liquor bottles, condoms, cigarette packaging, matchbooks, figurine (Hefner's own junk), 2013

Hefner's wife Crystal commissioned me to make this for his birthday. Collection of Hugh Hefner.

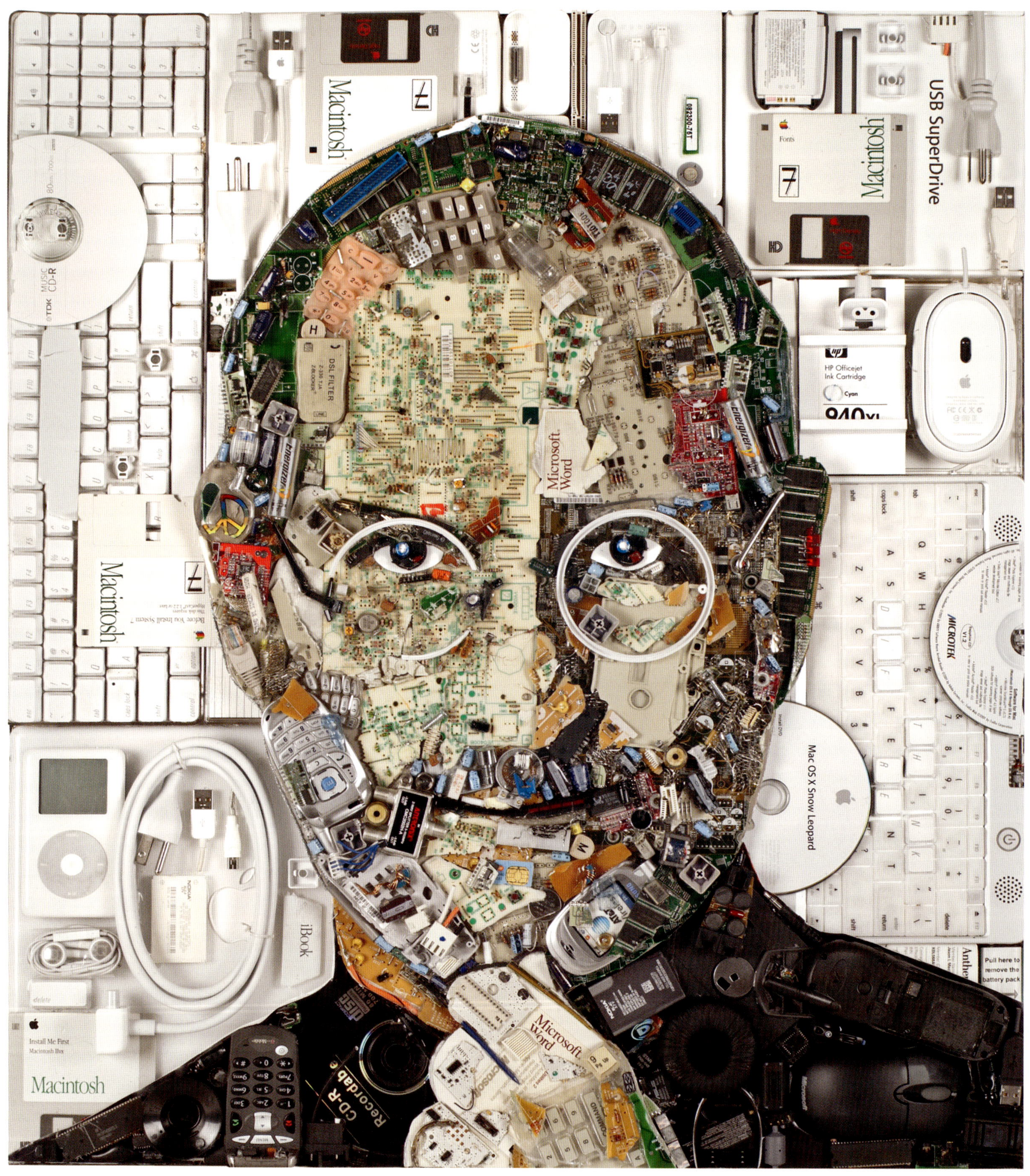

STEVE JOBS • Computer products, circuit boards, electronic items, e-waste, peace symbol, 2014

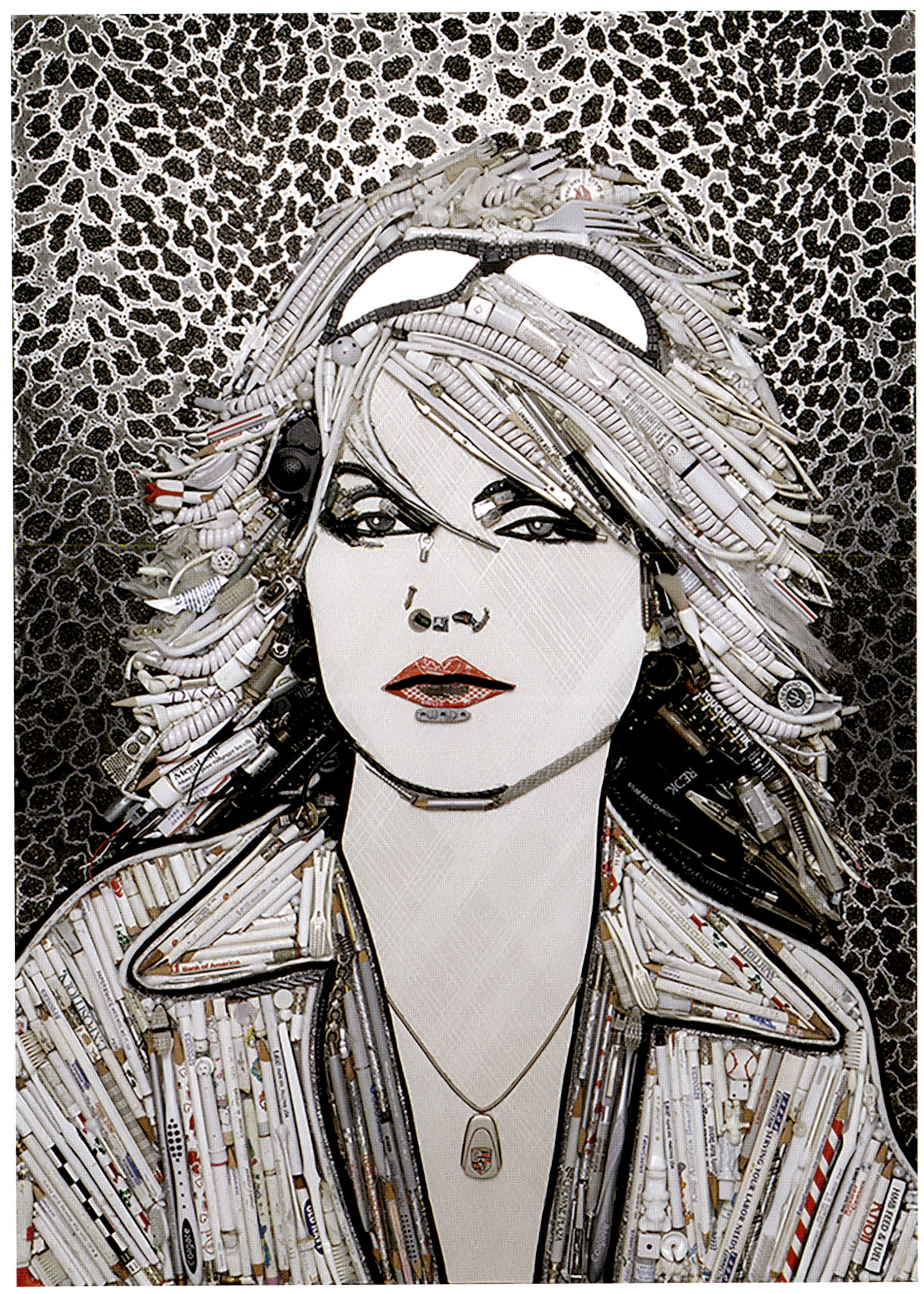

DEBBIE HARRY • Telephone cords, pencils, toothbrushes, patterned wallpaper, 2005

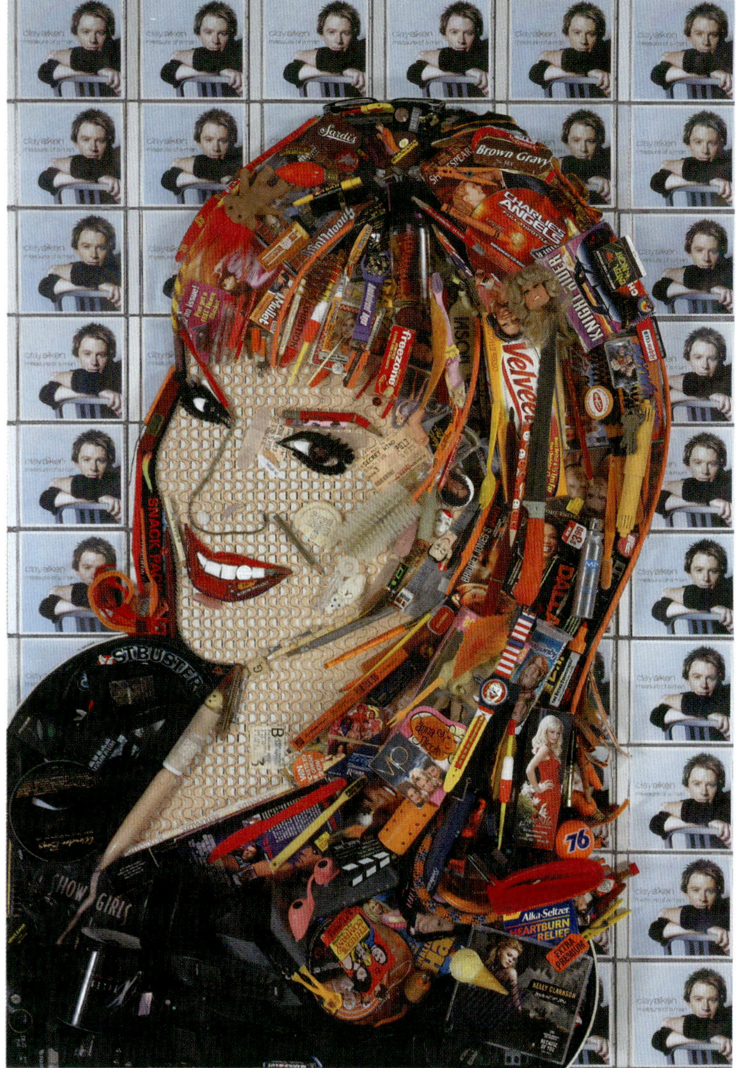

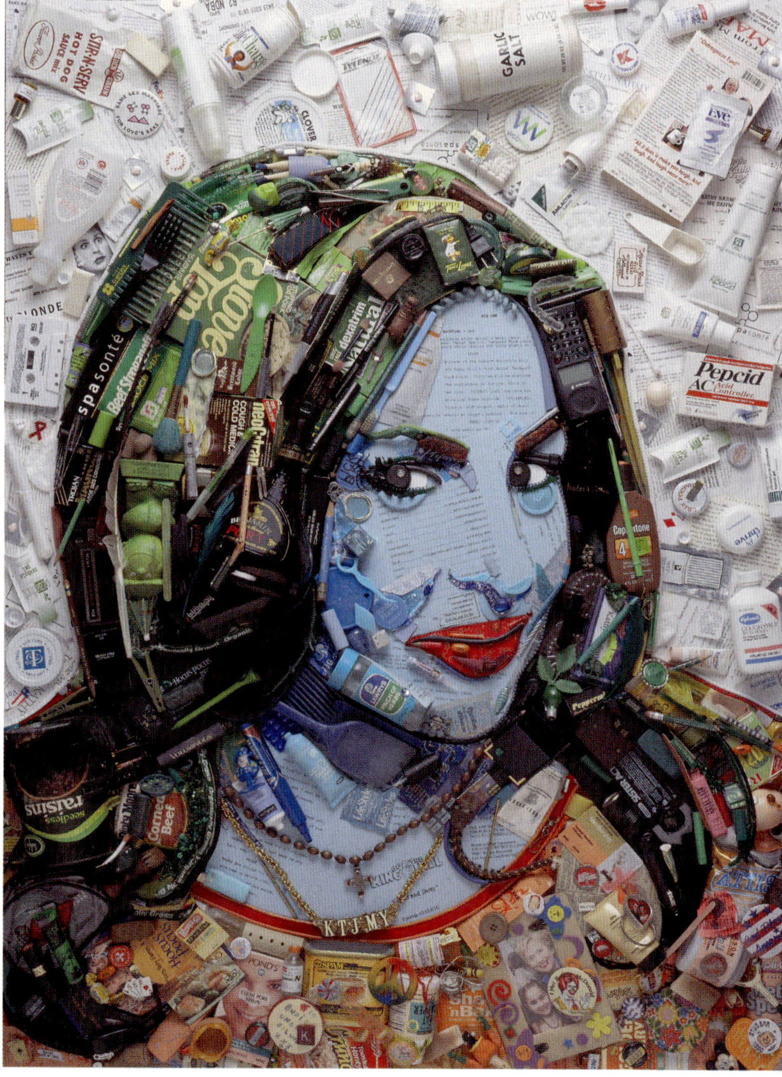

LEFT: KATHY GRIFFIN • CDs and DVDs, trading cards, cell phone, doll head, watch, 2006

Tour poster.

RIGHT: KATHY NAJIMY • Necklace, food packaging, inspirational figurine, script pages, liquor bottle, health care products, pinbacks (Najimy's own junk), 2007

Collection of Kathy Najimy.

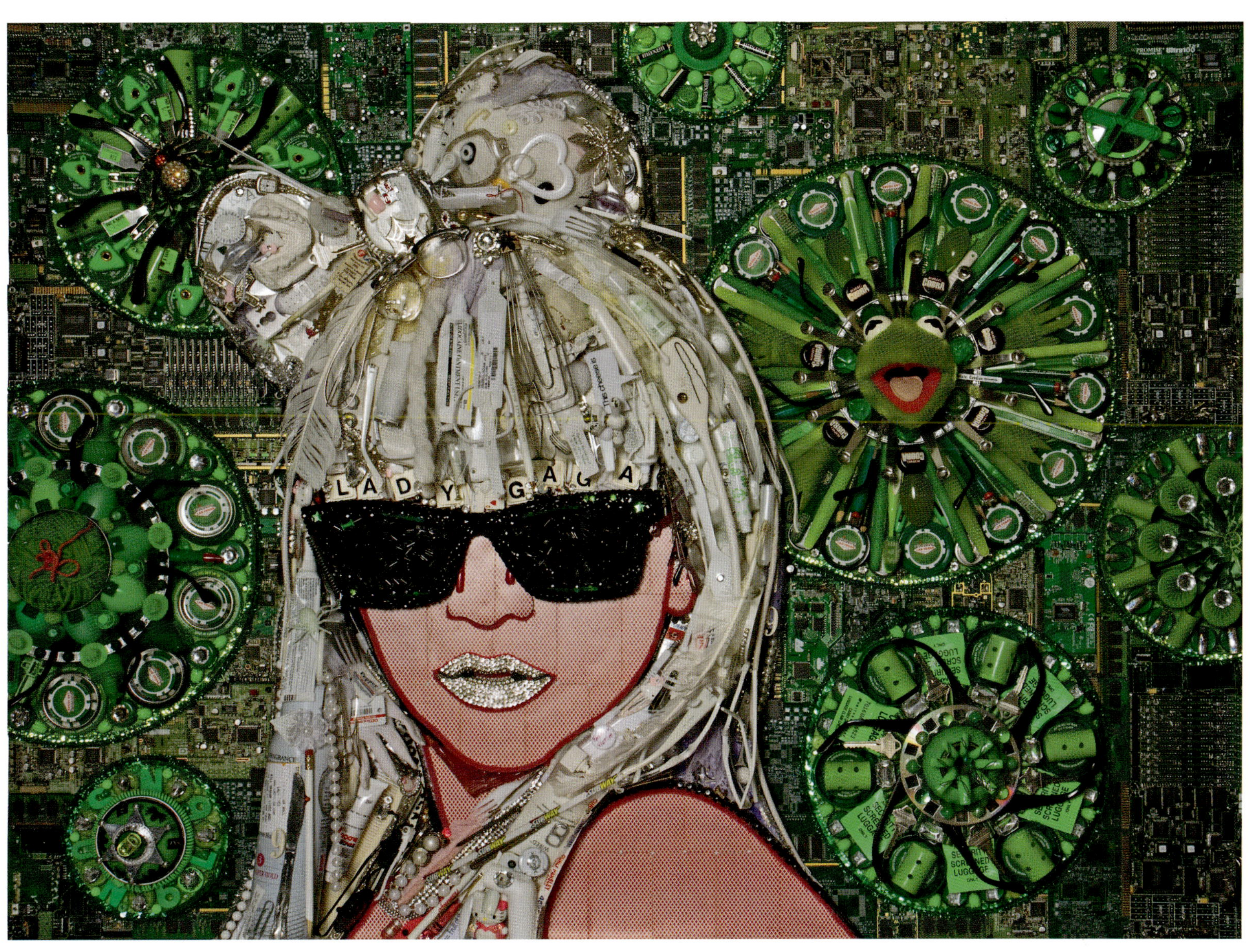

LADY GAGA • Poker chips, luggage stickers, pens, toothbrushes, circuit boards, keys, jewelry, rhinestones, frog head, 2011

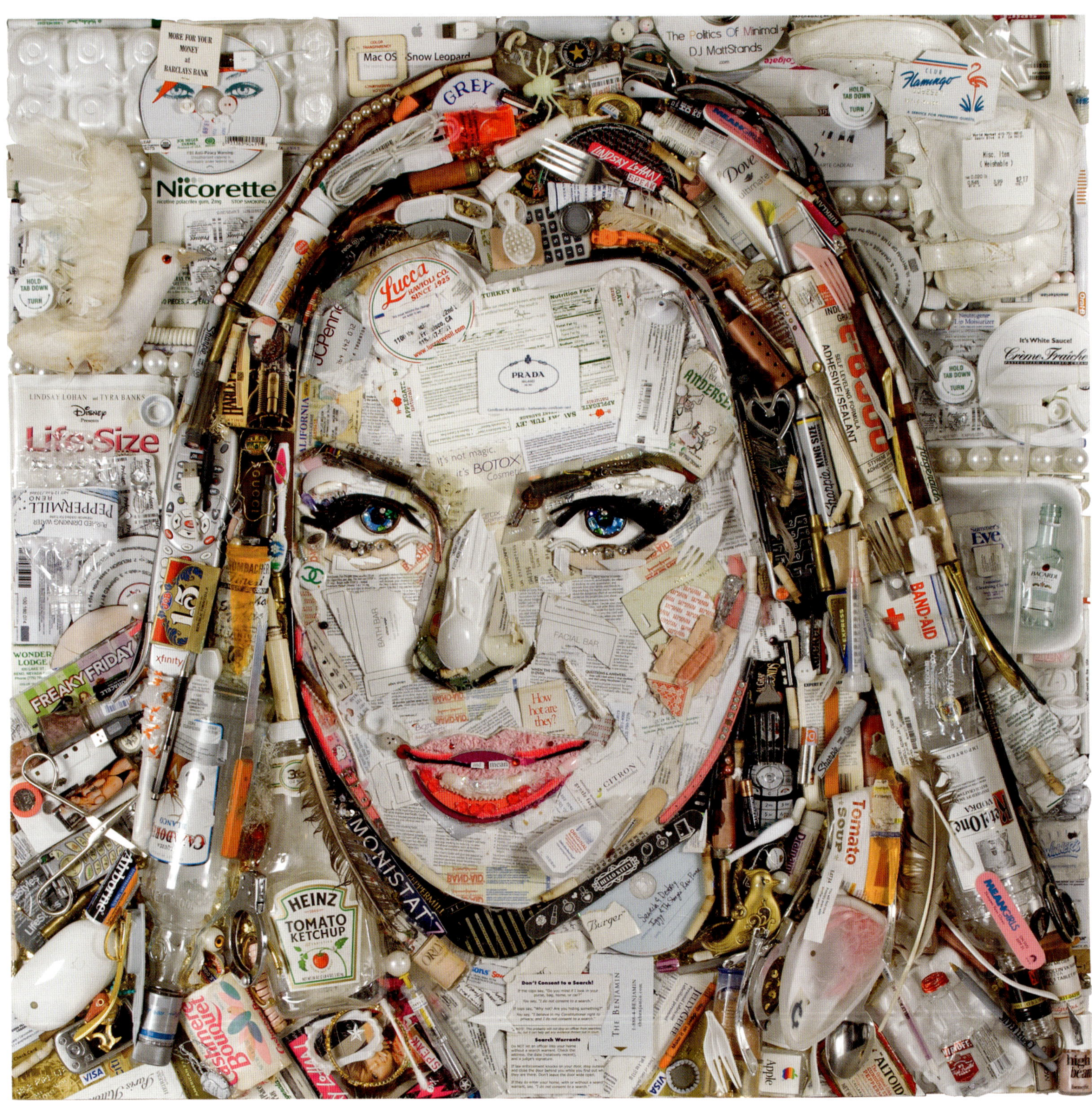

LINDSAY LOHAN • Liquor bottles, credit cards, DVDs and CDs, remote controls, hygiene products, smoking cessation gum, dove, 2013

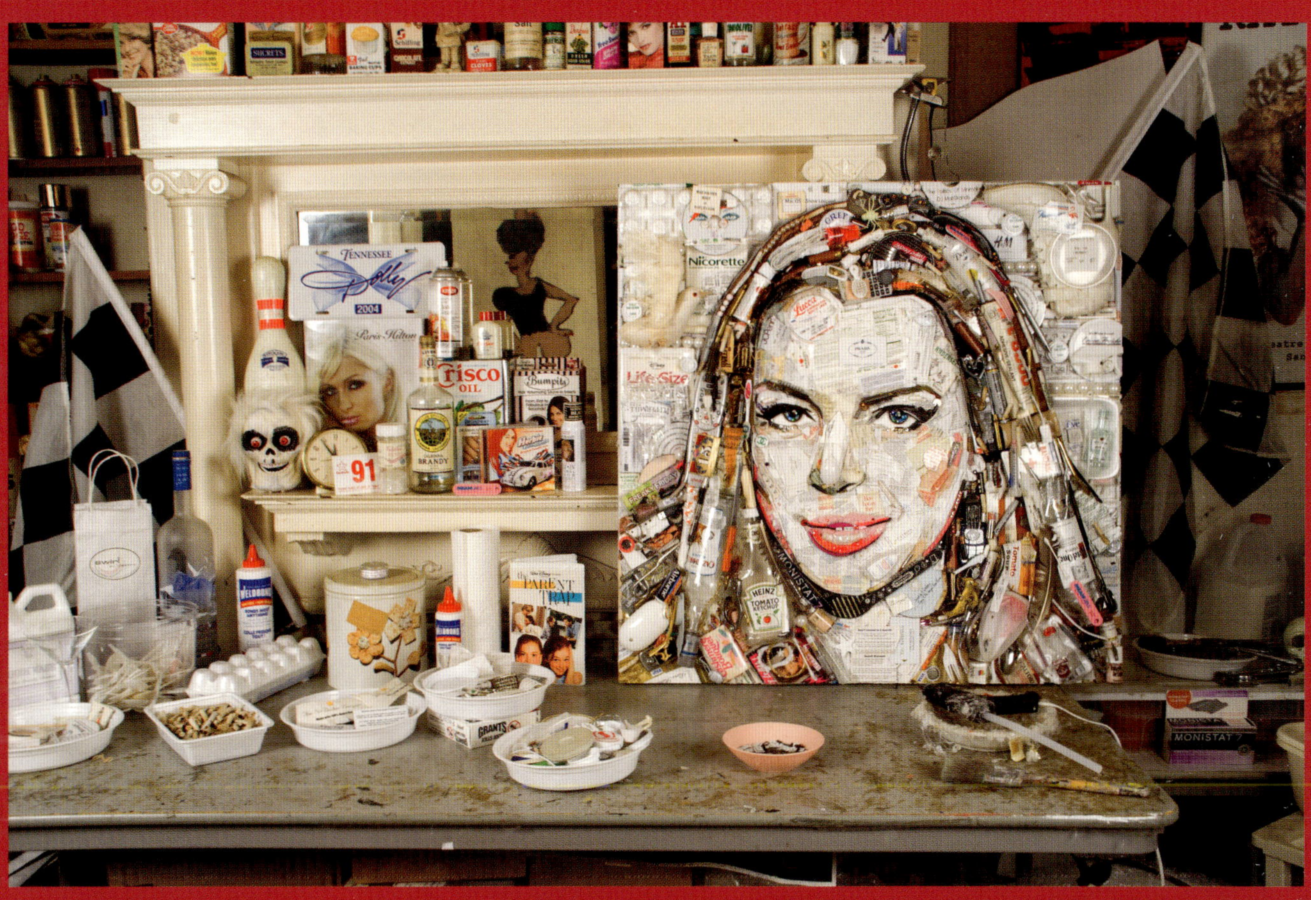

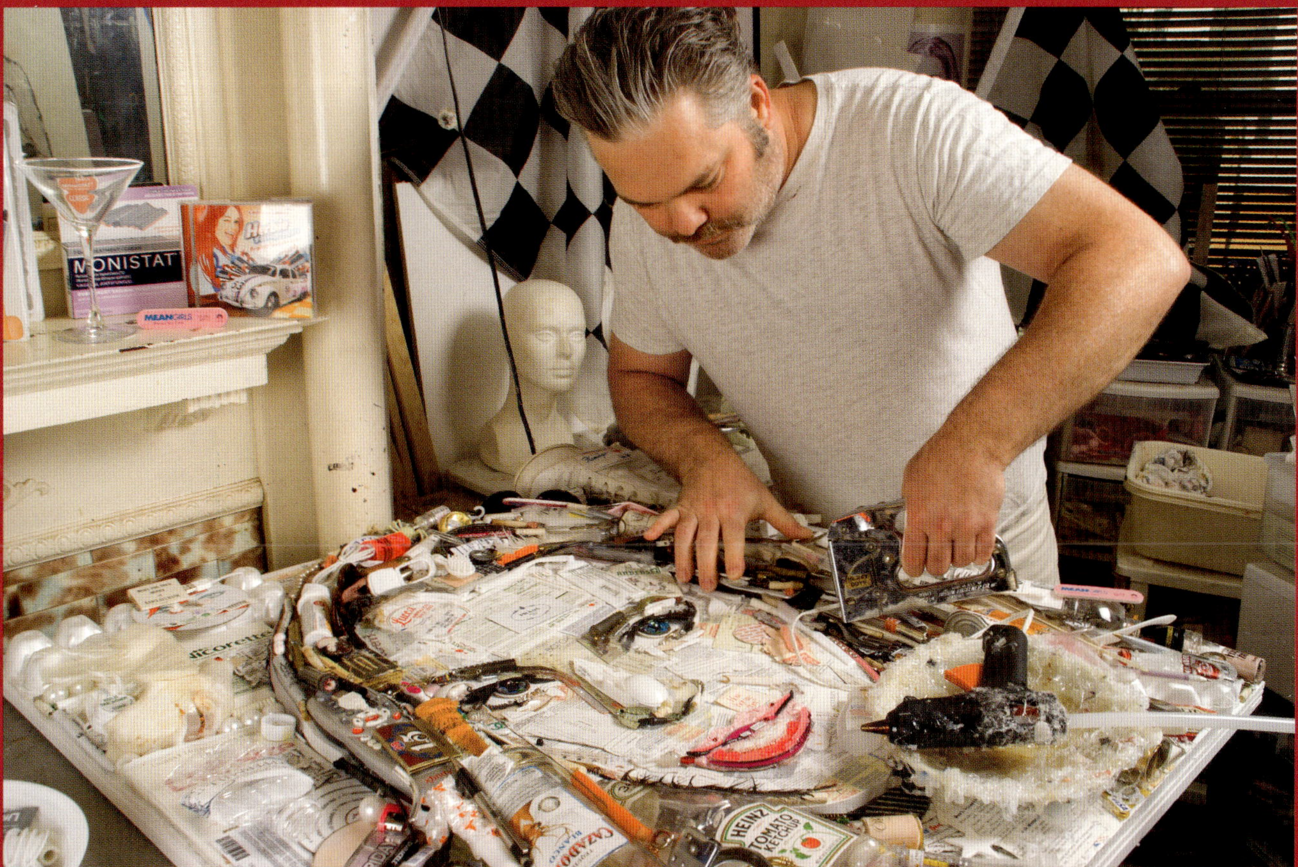

TOP: In my studio.

BOTTOM: In process.

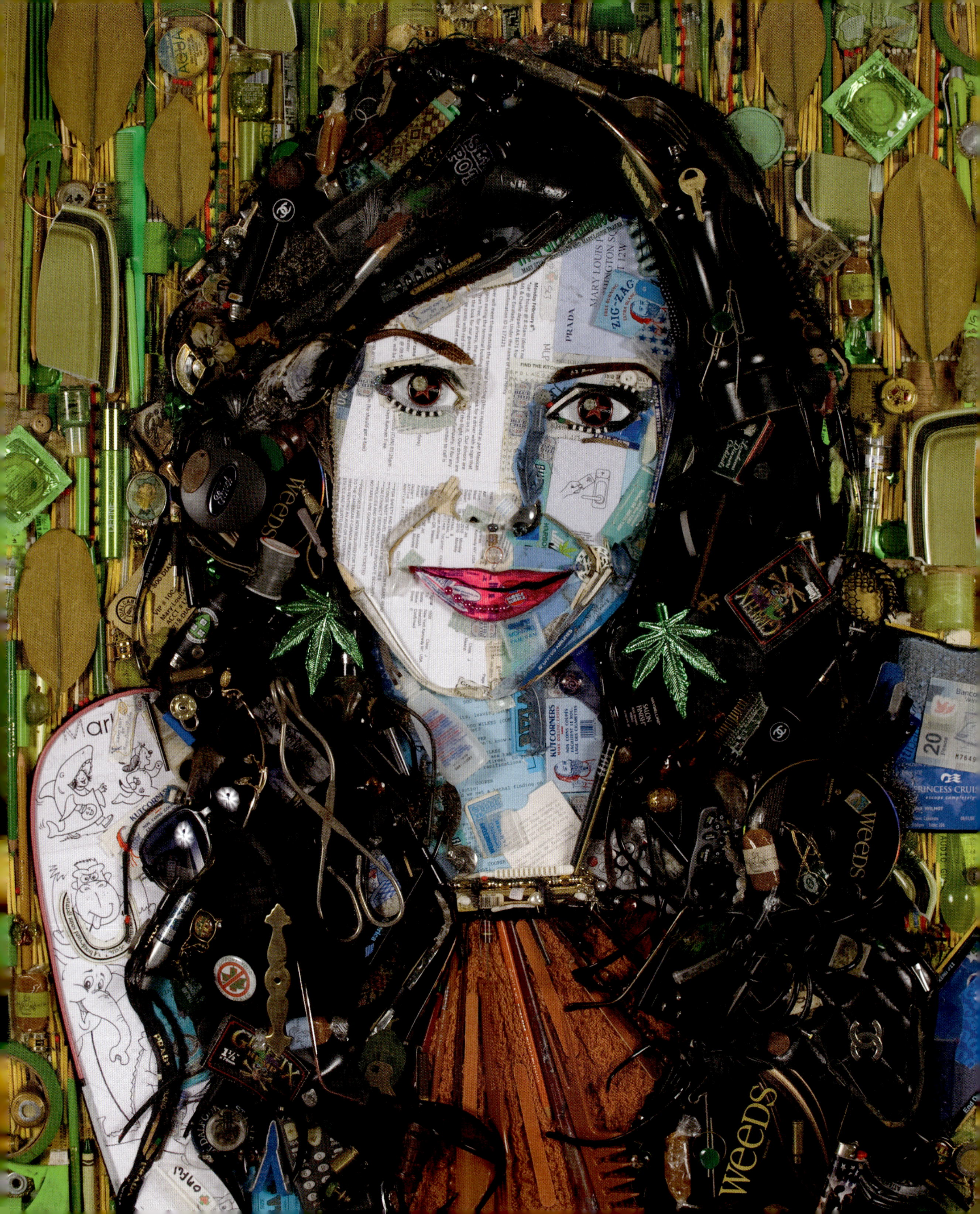

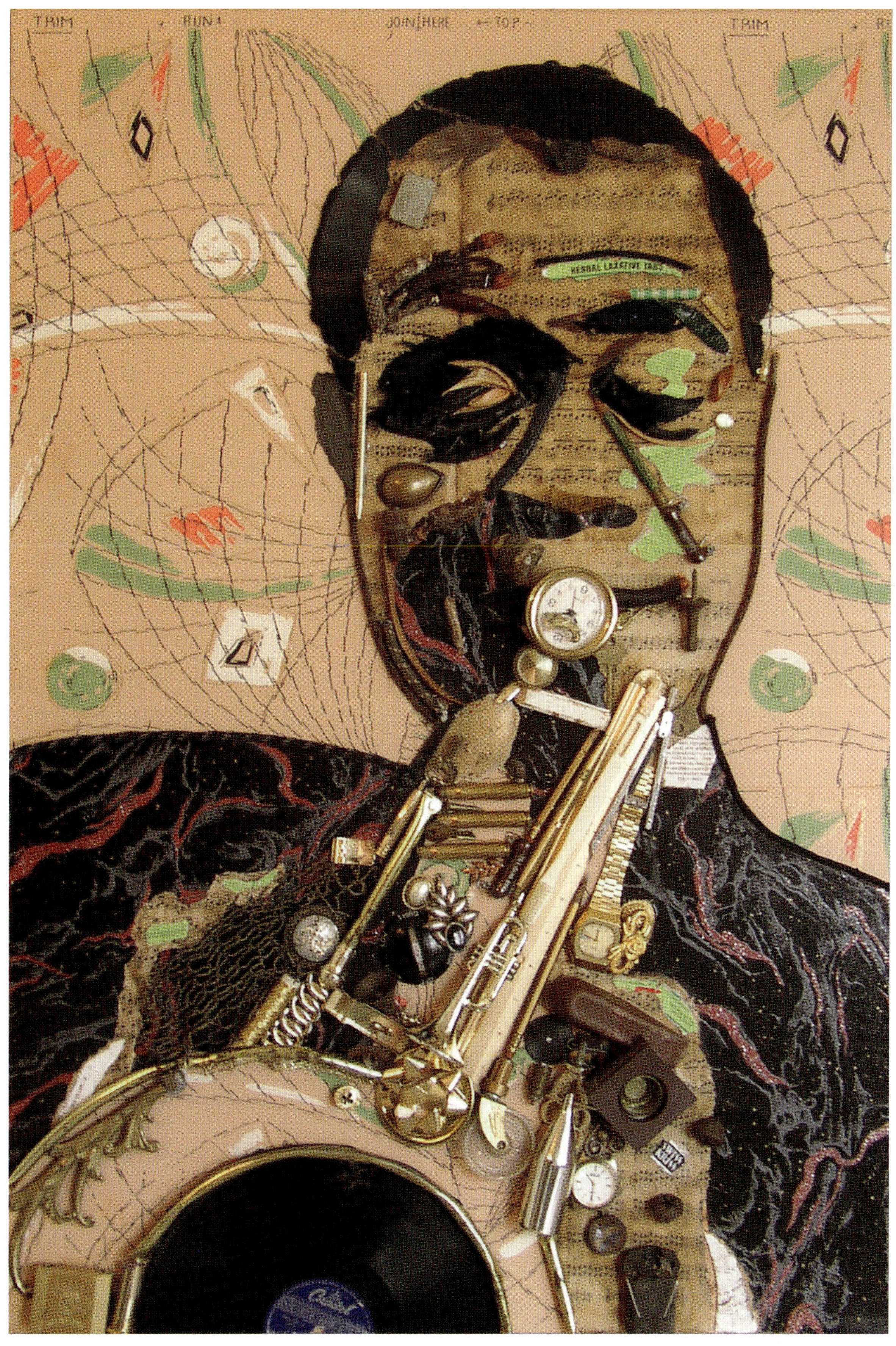

OPPOSITE: MARY LOUISE PARKER • Rolling papers, eye drops, DVDs, plastic leaves, matches, designer logo items, script pages, sunglasses (Parker's own junk), 2010

LOUIS ARMSTRONG • Sheet music, shellac record, wallpaper, timepieces, plastic trumpet, 2003

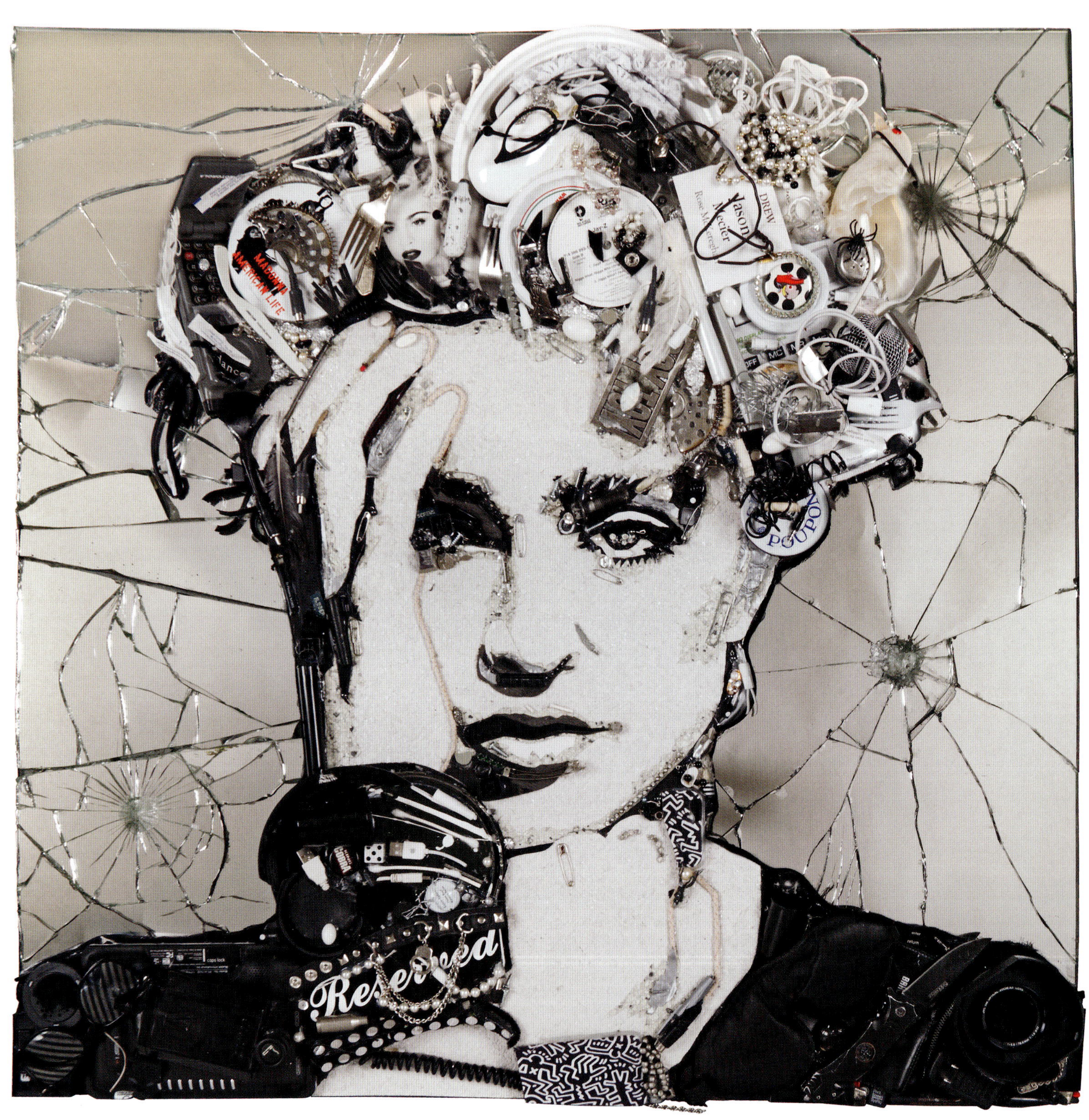

MADONNA • CDs, broken mirror, camera lens, lace, jewelry, microphone, pocket knife, 2018

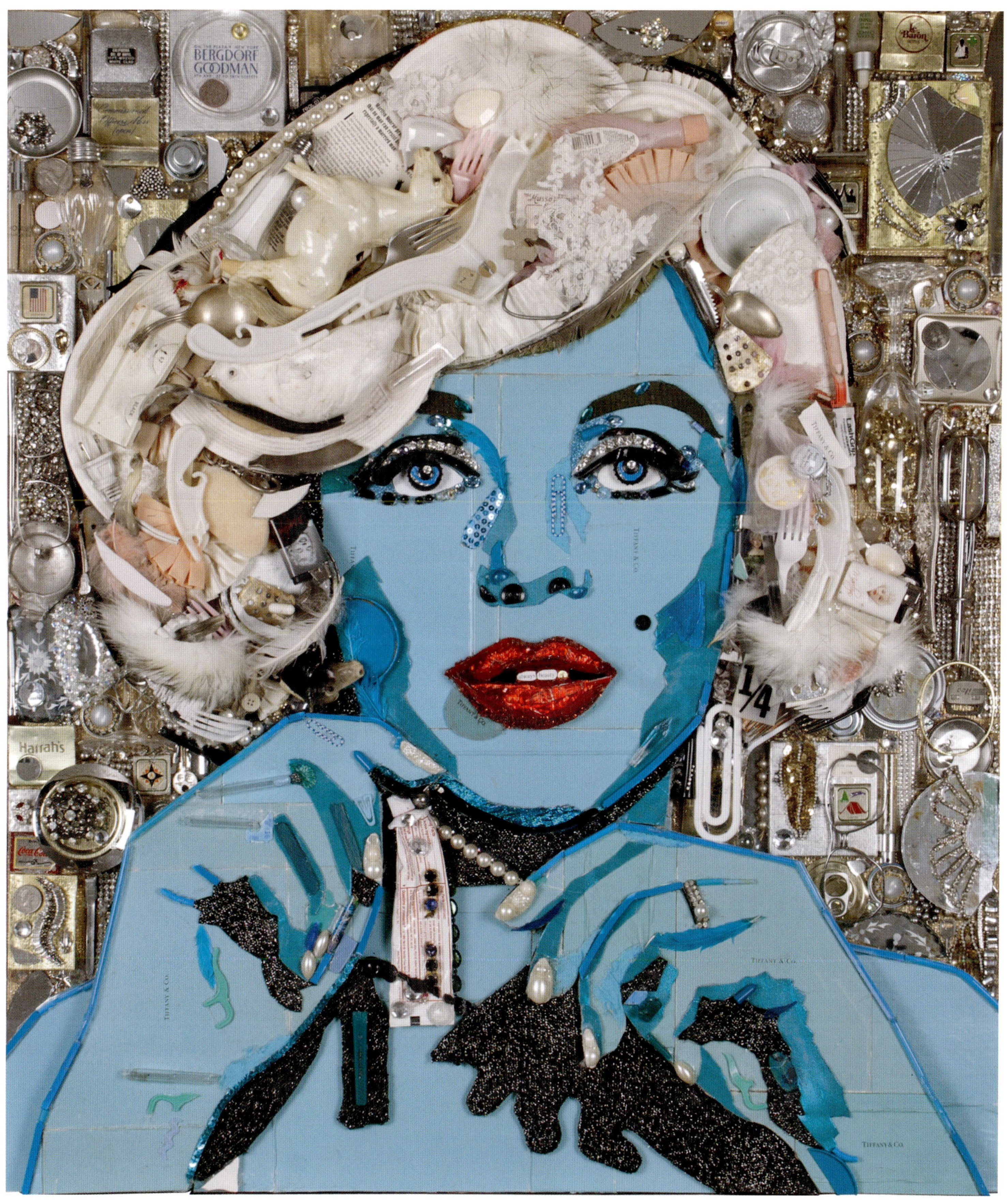

MARILYN MONROE • Jewelry, feathers, paper clips, plastic horse, lace, disposable lighter, 2015

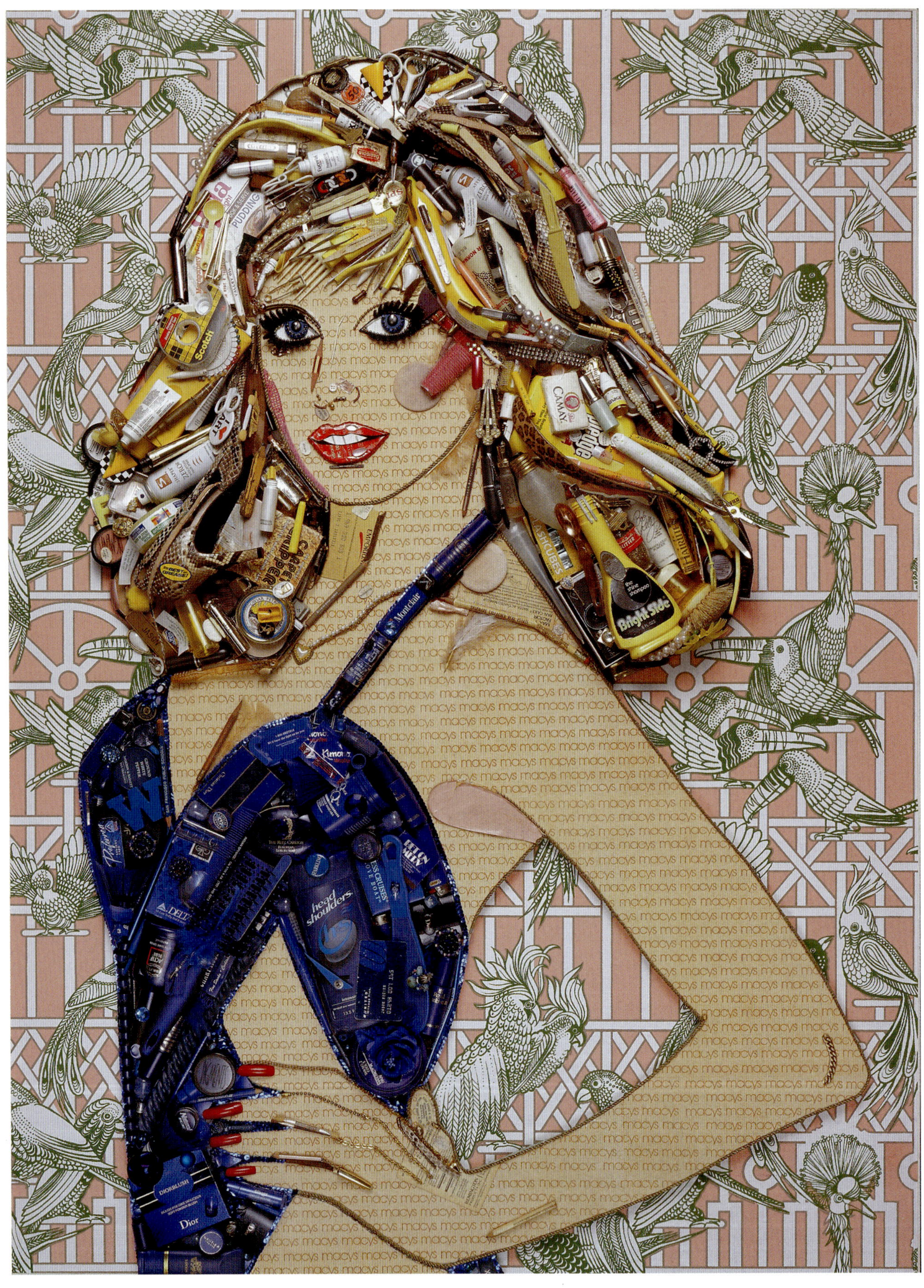

MORGAN FAIRCHILD • Cosmetics and personal care items, wallpaper, department store wrapping, jewelry, shoes, artificial nails (Fairchild's own junk), 2007

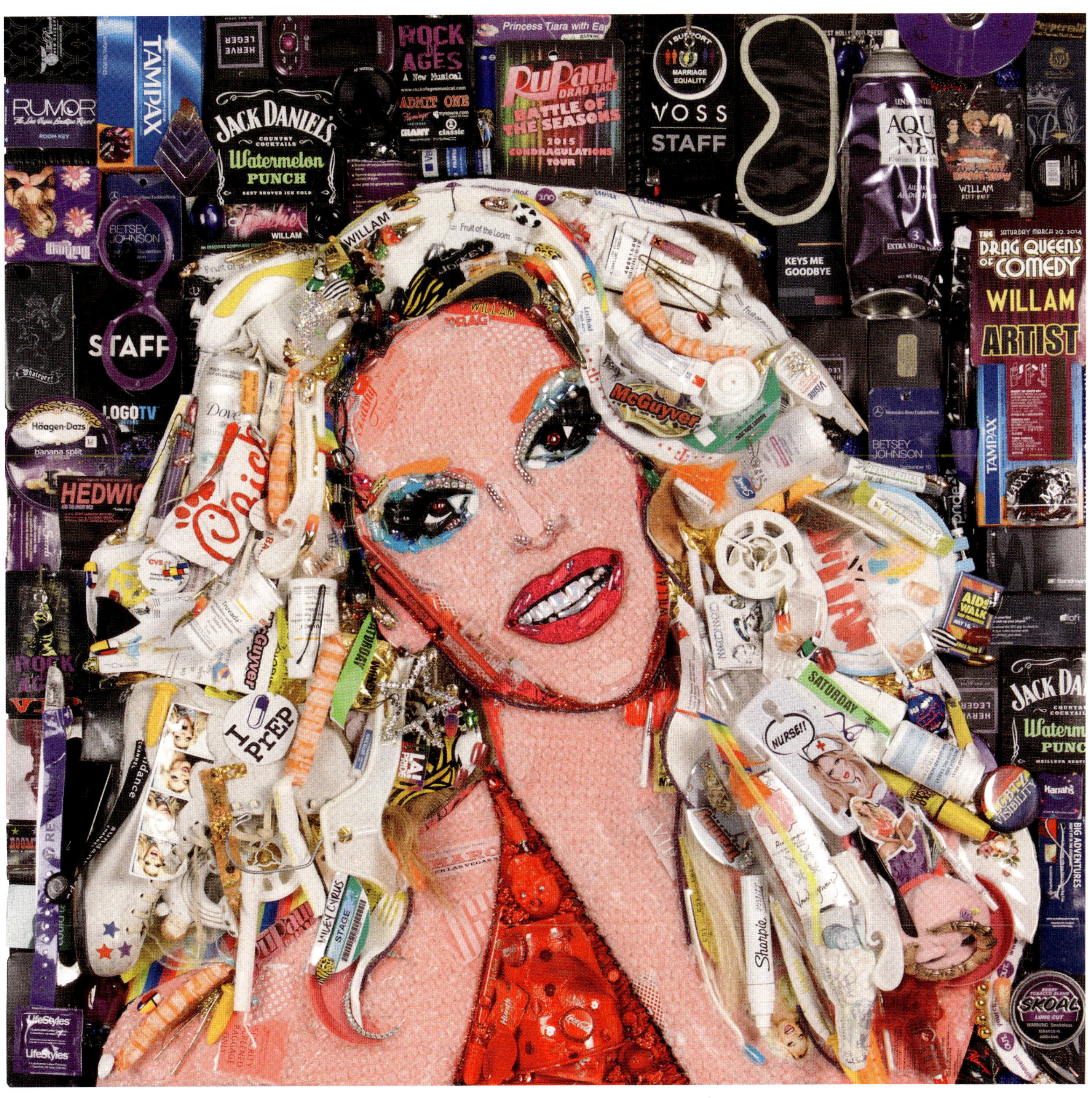

WILLAM • Sequins, sunglasses, stage passes, sleep mask, photobooth strip, liquor packaging, cosmetics, hairspray (Willam's own junk), 2018

Collection of Willam.

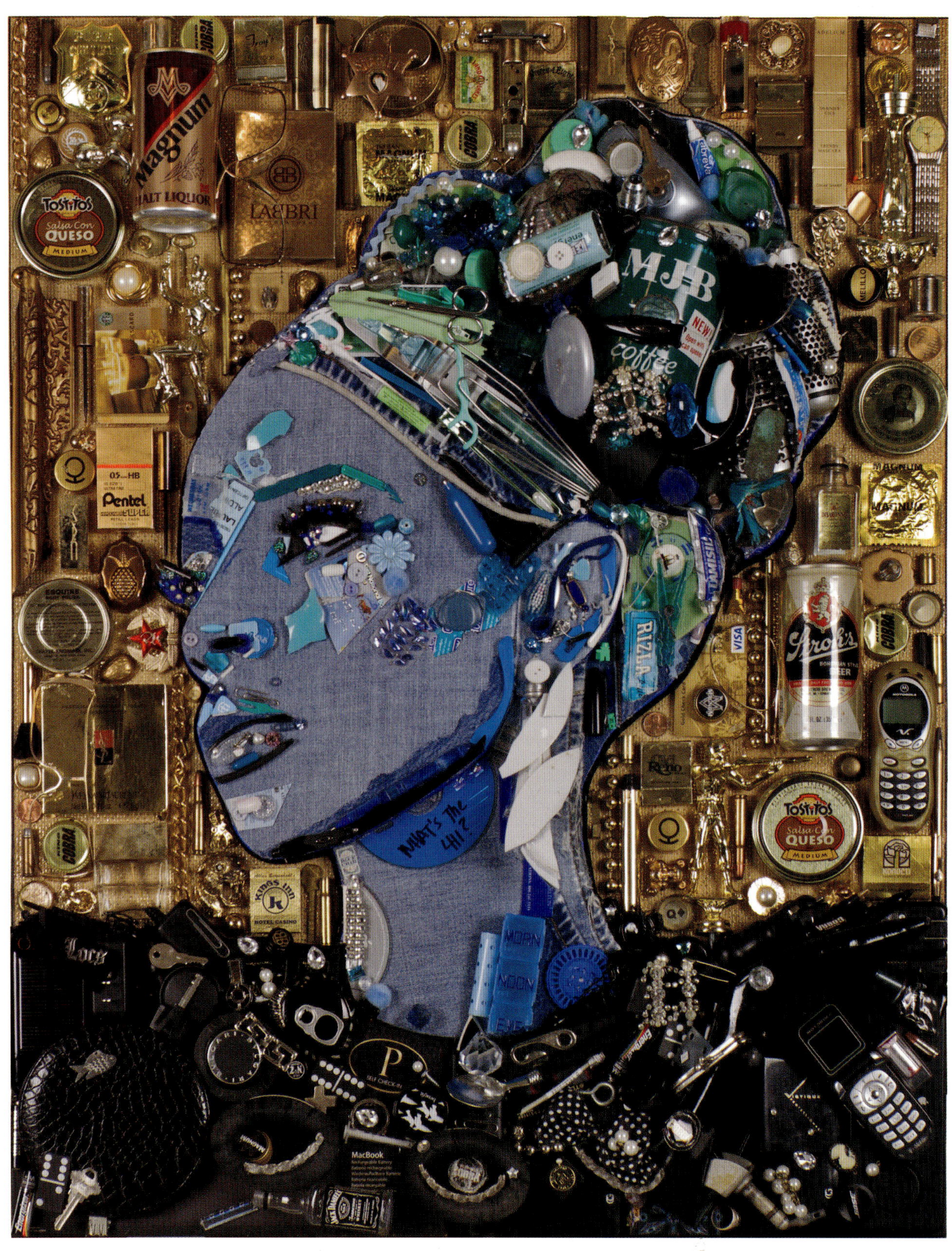

MARY J. BLIGE • Jewelry, cosmetics, credit cards, beer cans, trophy tops, coffee can, denim, 2012

OPPOSITE: MISSY ELLIOTT • Crushed cosmetics and cosmetics packaging, 2004

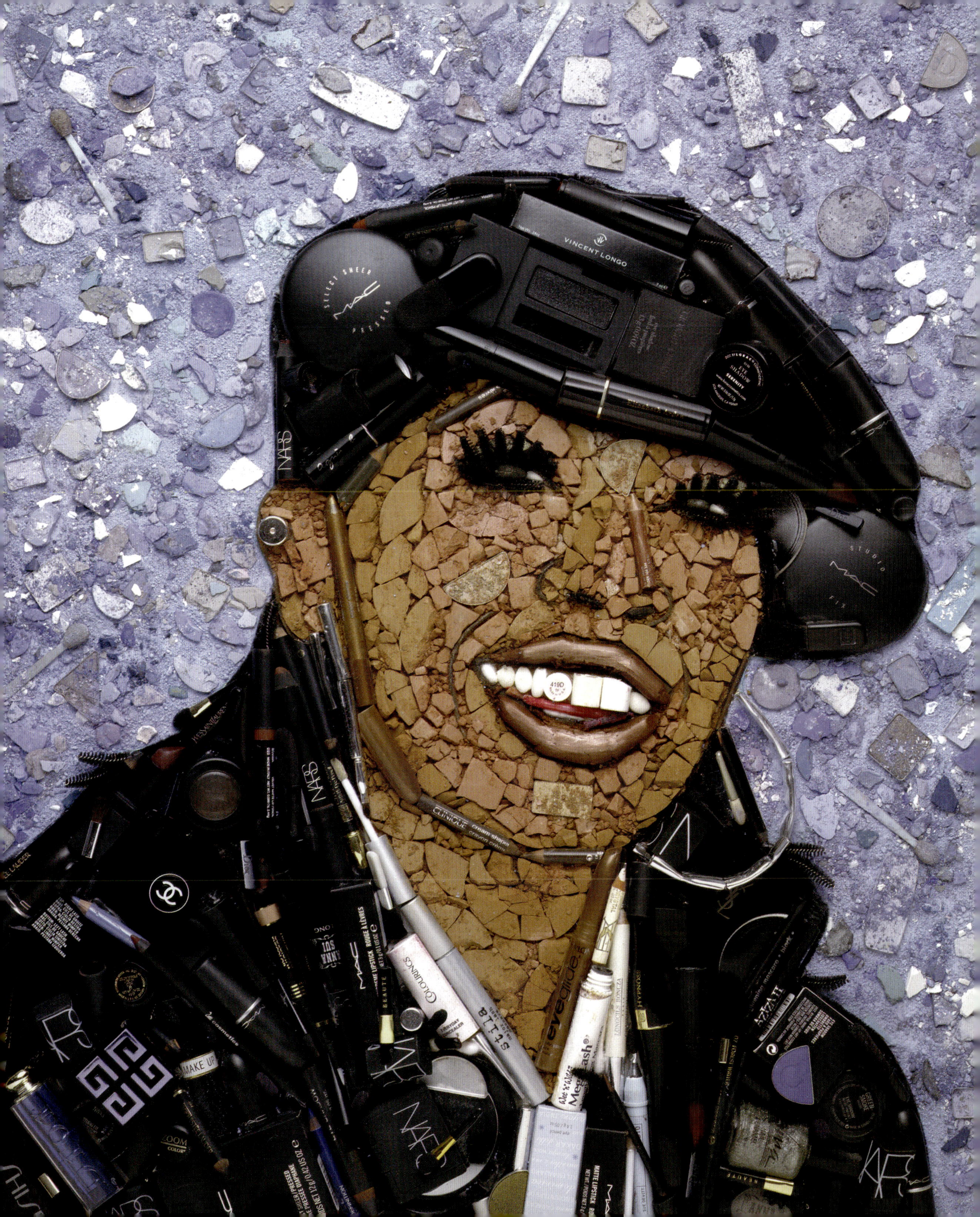
VINCENT LONGO
NARS
CLINIQUE
stila
eyeglide
MAKE UP

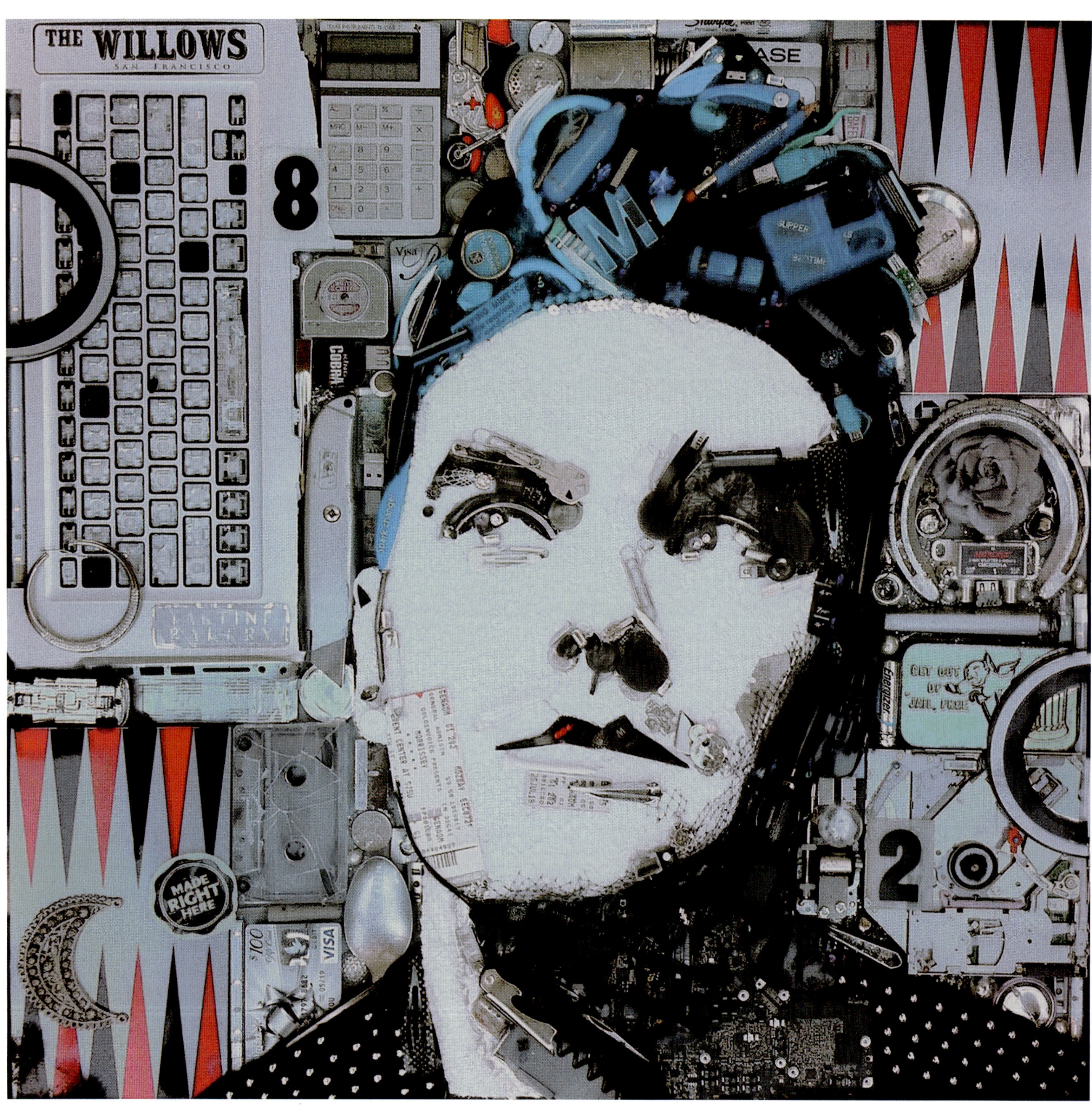

MORRISSEY • Plastic flower, horseshoe, game boards, concert ticket, electronics, pill container, fabric, 2015

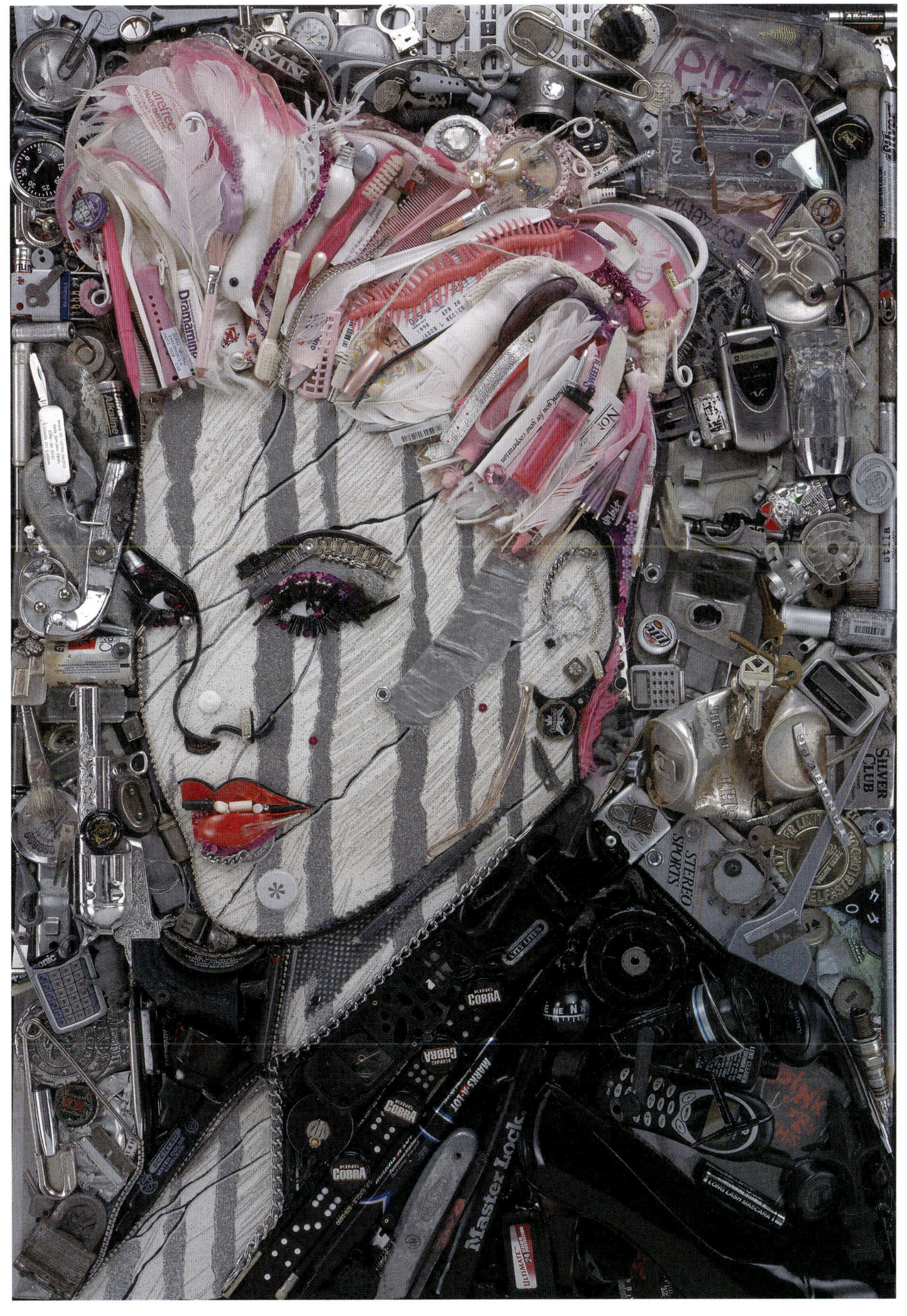

P!NK • Fabric, feathers, bottle caps, cell phones, indelible markers, keys, CDs, cassette tape, rubber centipede, 2006
Tour poster. Collection of P!nk. Also featured in her video for "Please Don't Leave Me."

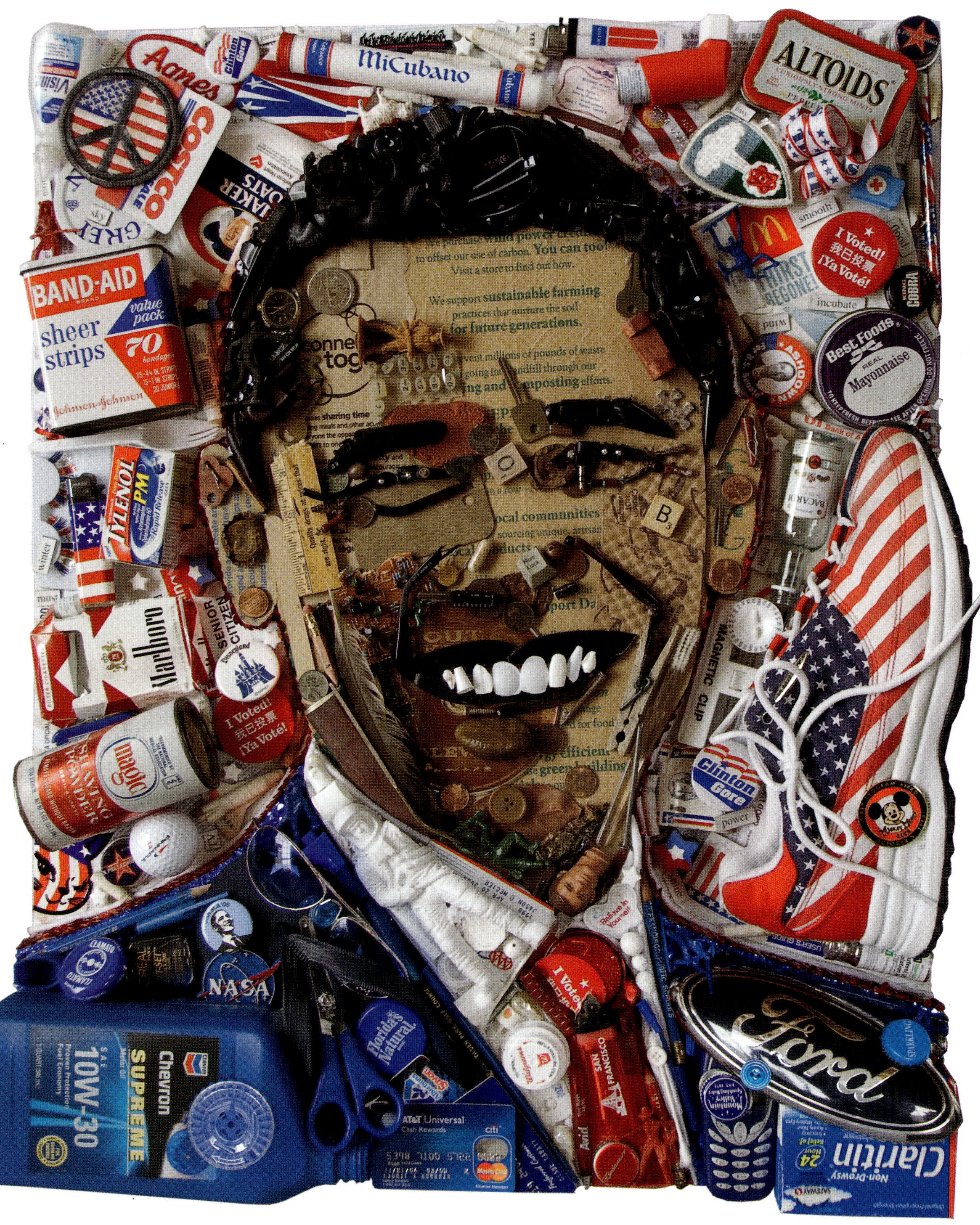

BARACK OBAMA • Political buttons, voting stickers, sneaker, cigarette packaging, liquor bottle, breath mints, golf ball, sunglasses, cardboard, automobile logo, 2009

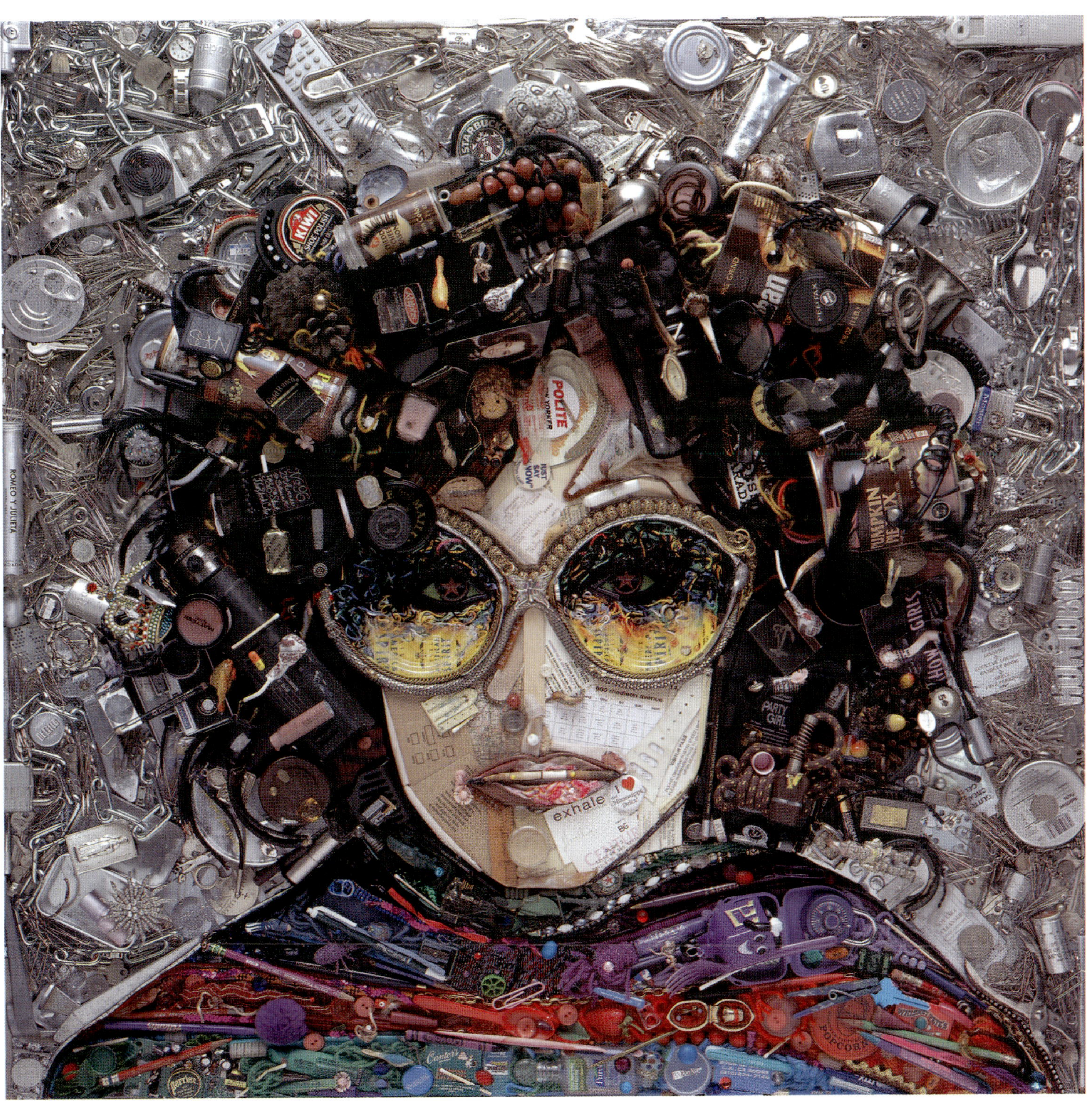

PARKER POSEY • Paper clips, chains, bottle caps and lids, sunglasses, personal photo, pinecone, jewelry, pencils, drill, yarn, night guard (Posey's own junk), 2007
Collection of Parker Posey.

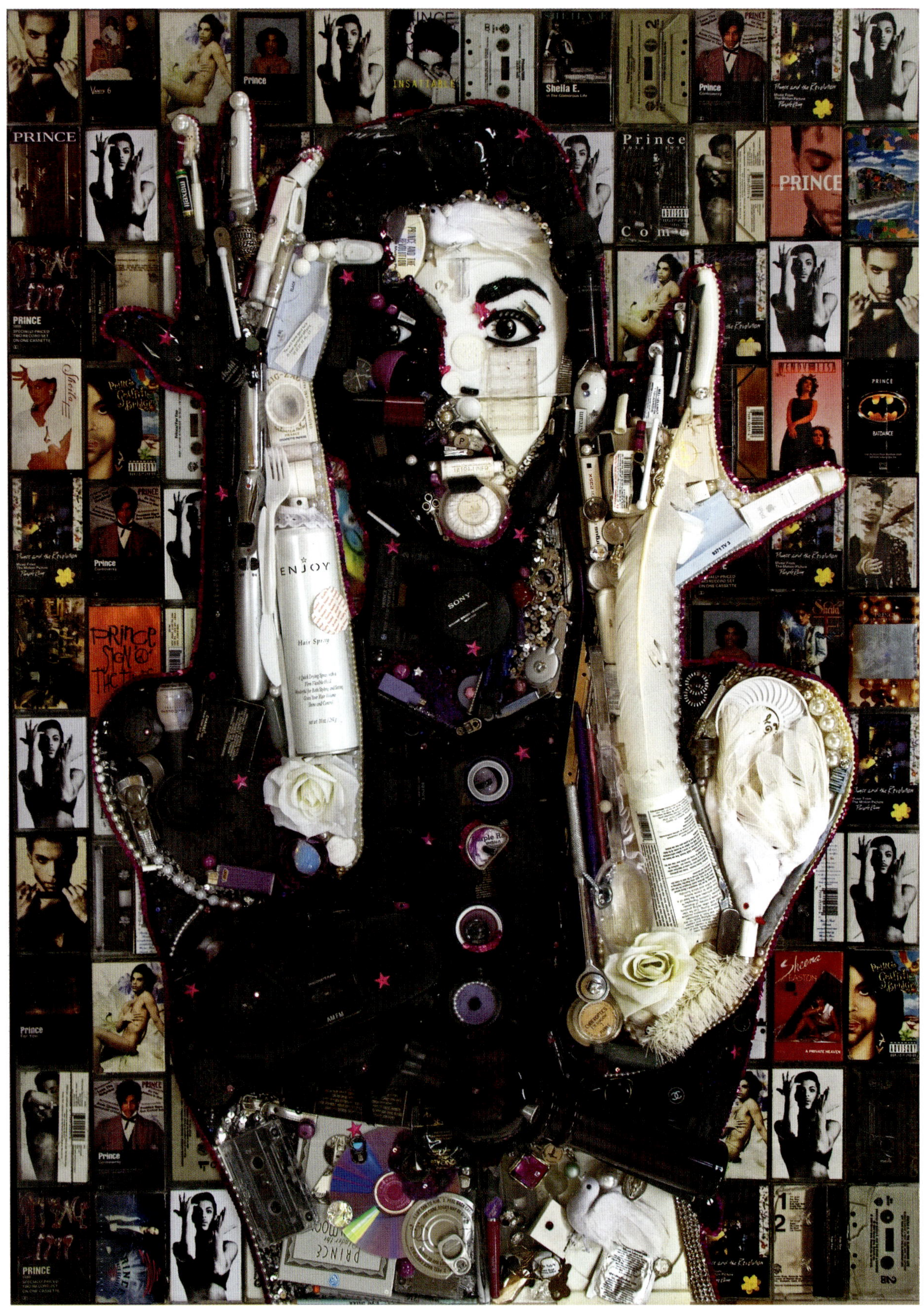

PRINCE • Cassette tapes, feathers, doves, cosmetics, CDs, hairspray, boom box, pearls, 2009

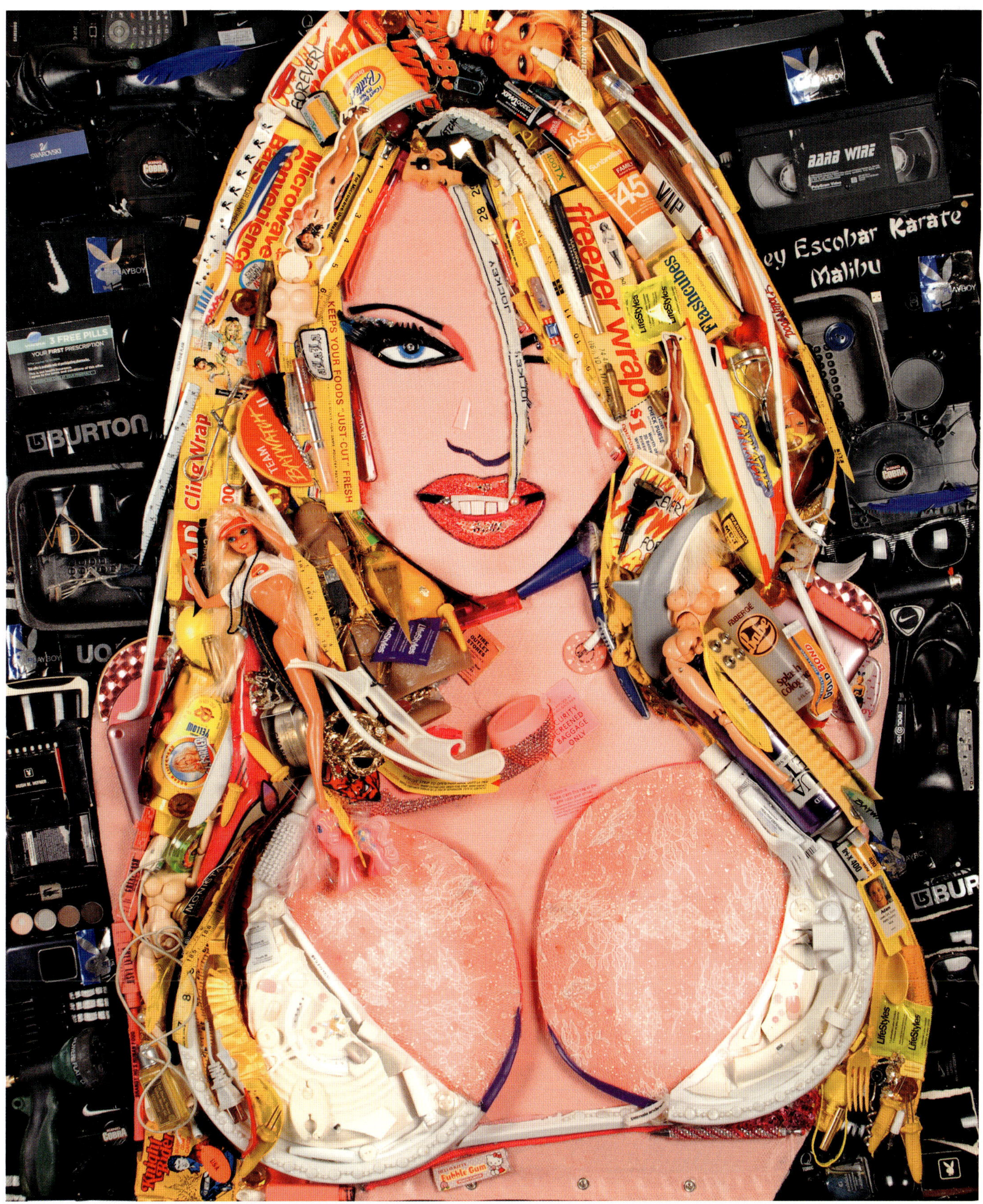

PAMELA ANDERSON • Videocassette, dolls and doll parts, measuring tape, flashbulbs (Anderson's own junk: T-shirt, shoelaces, athletic pants, lace top, belt buckle), 2016

The stuff I incorporated here from Anderson's own junk came from the aftermath of a yardsale she had for an episode of her reality show (obtained by a friend).

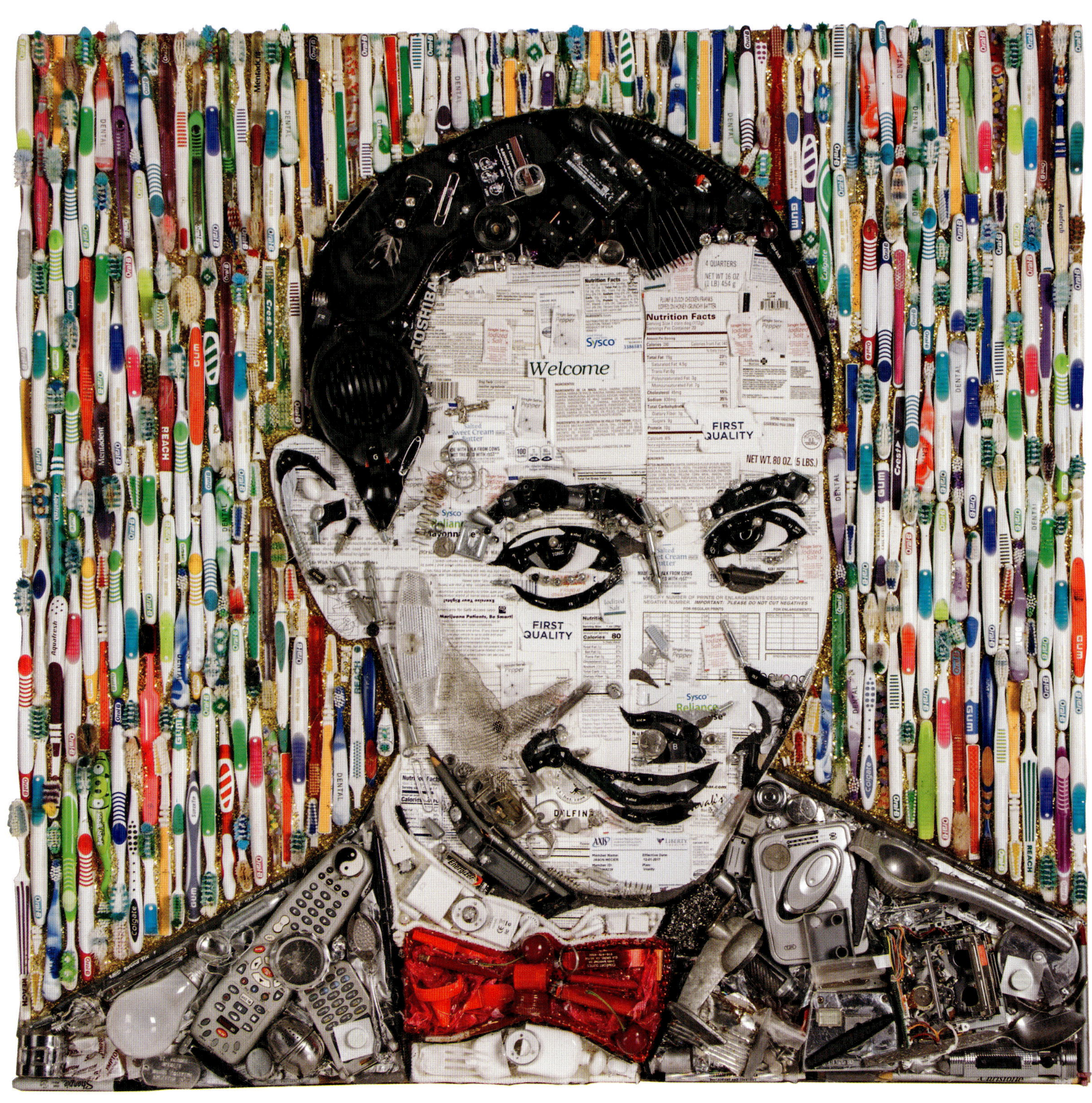

PEE-WEE HERMAN • Toothbrushes, glitter, nutritional facts, electronics, vintage beer pull tabs, lightbulbs, 2018

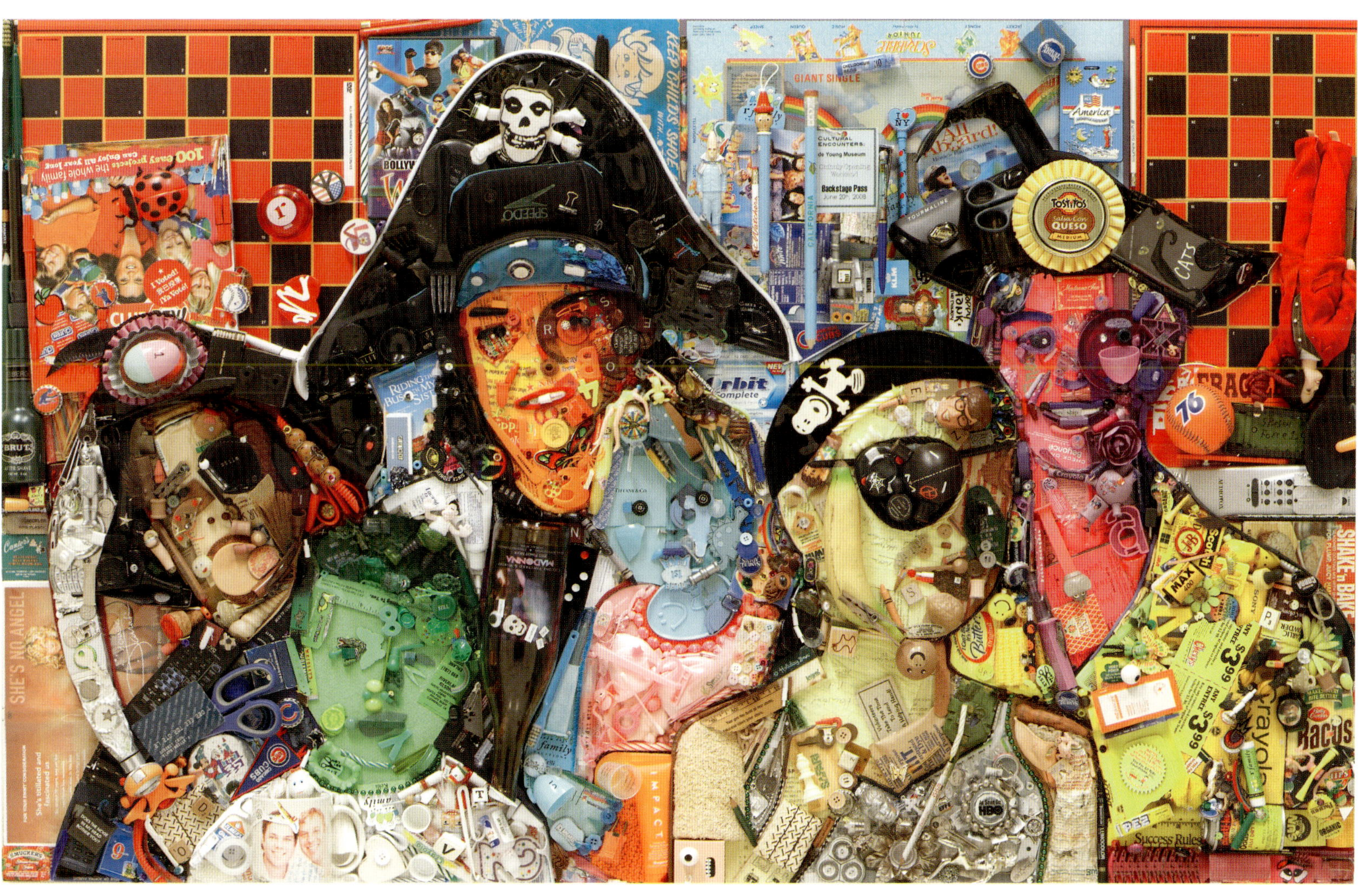

ROSIE O'DONNELL AND FAMILY • Toys, games, museum pass, wine bottle, skull patch, photo mug, cosmetics, fabric (O'Donnell family's own junk), 2008

Collection of Rosie O'Donnell.

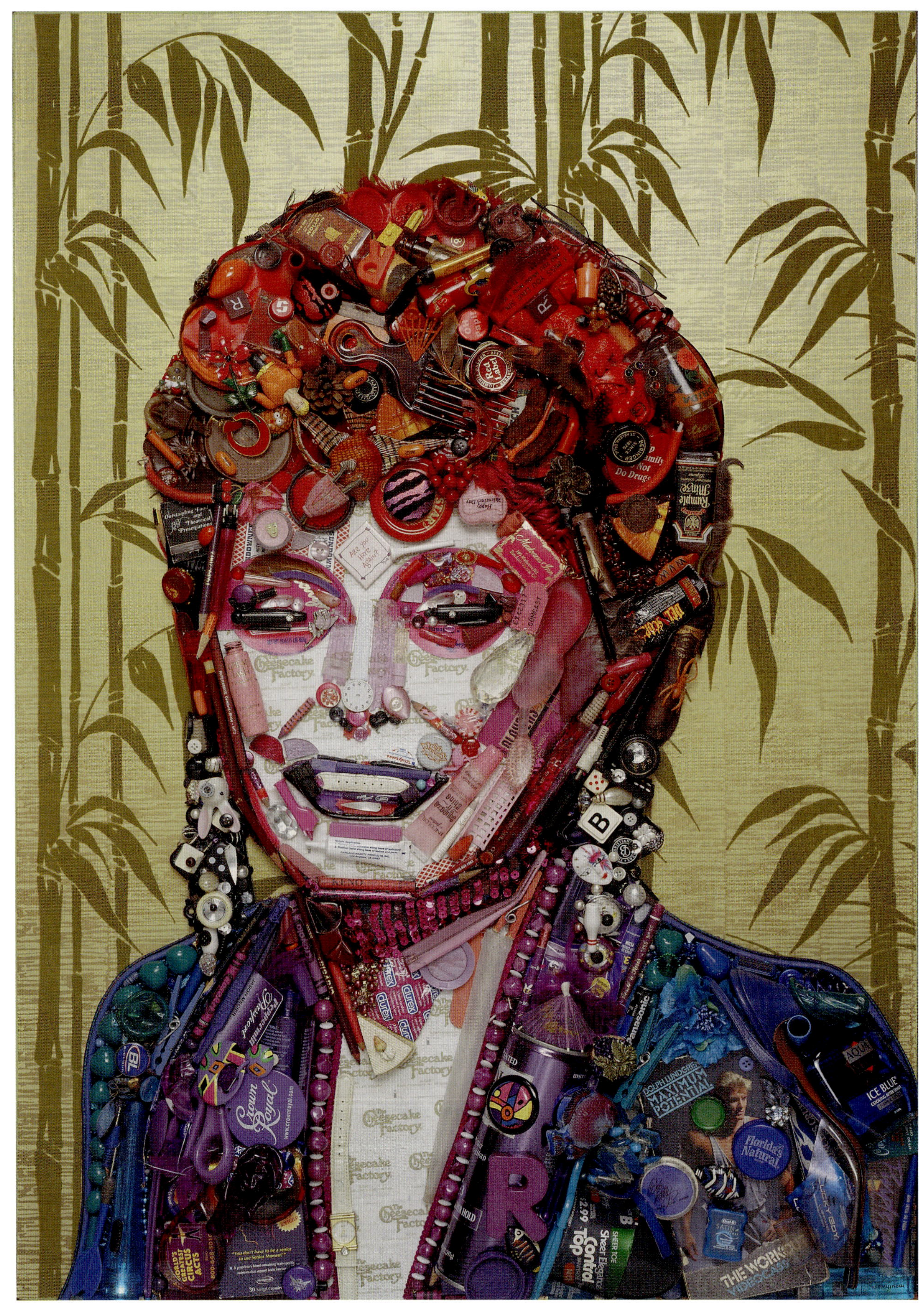

RUE McLANAHAN • Cosmetics, jewelry, plastic bric-a-brac, wallpaper, sugar packaging, sequins, 2007

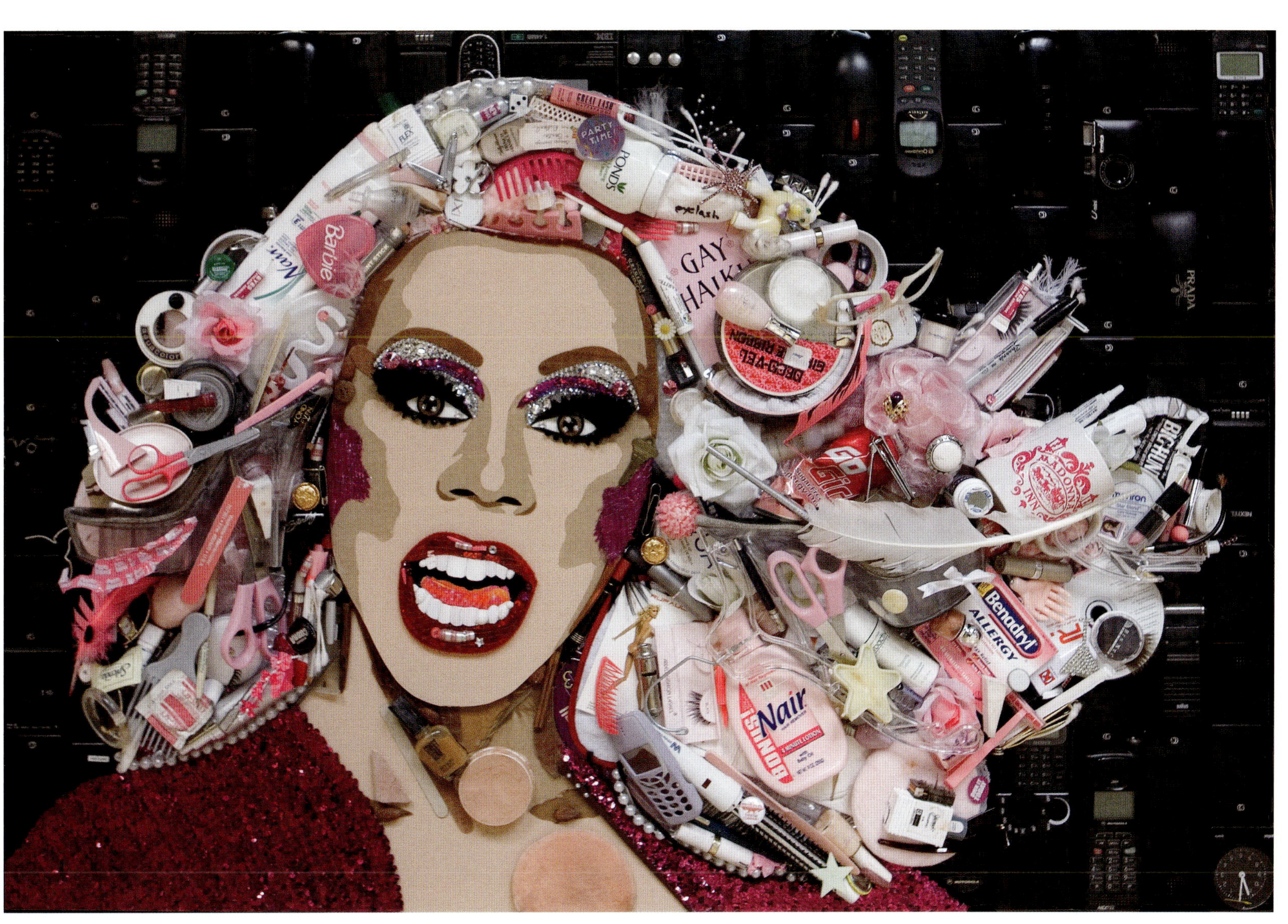

RuPAUL • Phones, cameras, cosmetics, sequins, hotel mug, plastic pony (RuPaul's own junk), 2008

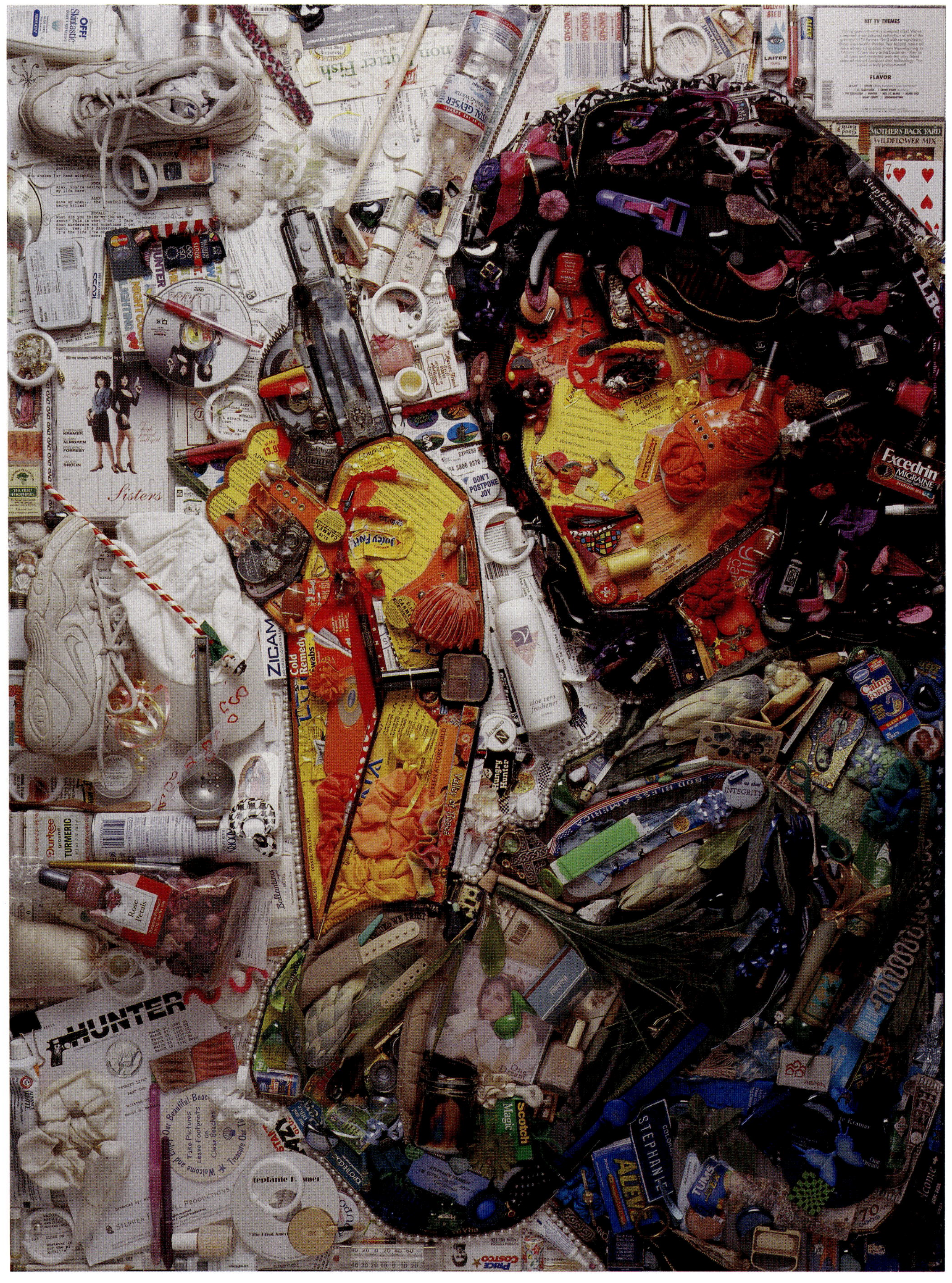

STEPFANIE KRAMER • Sneakers, script pages, DVDs, potpourri, cosmetics, membership cards, novelty license plate (Kramer's own junk), 2007

Collection of Stepfanie Kramer.

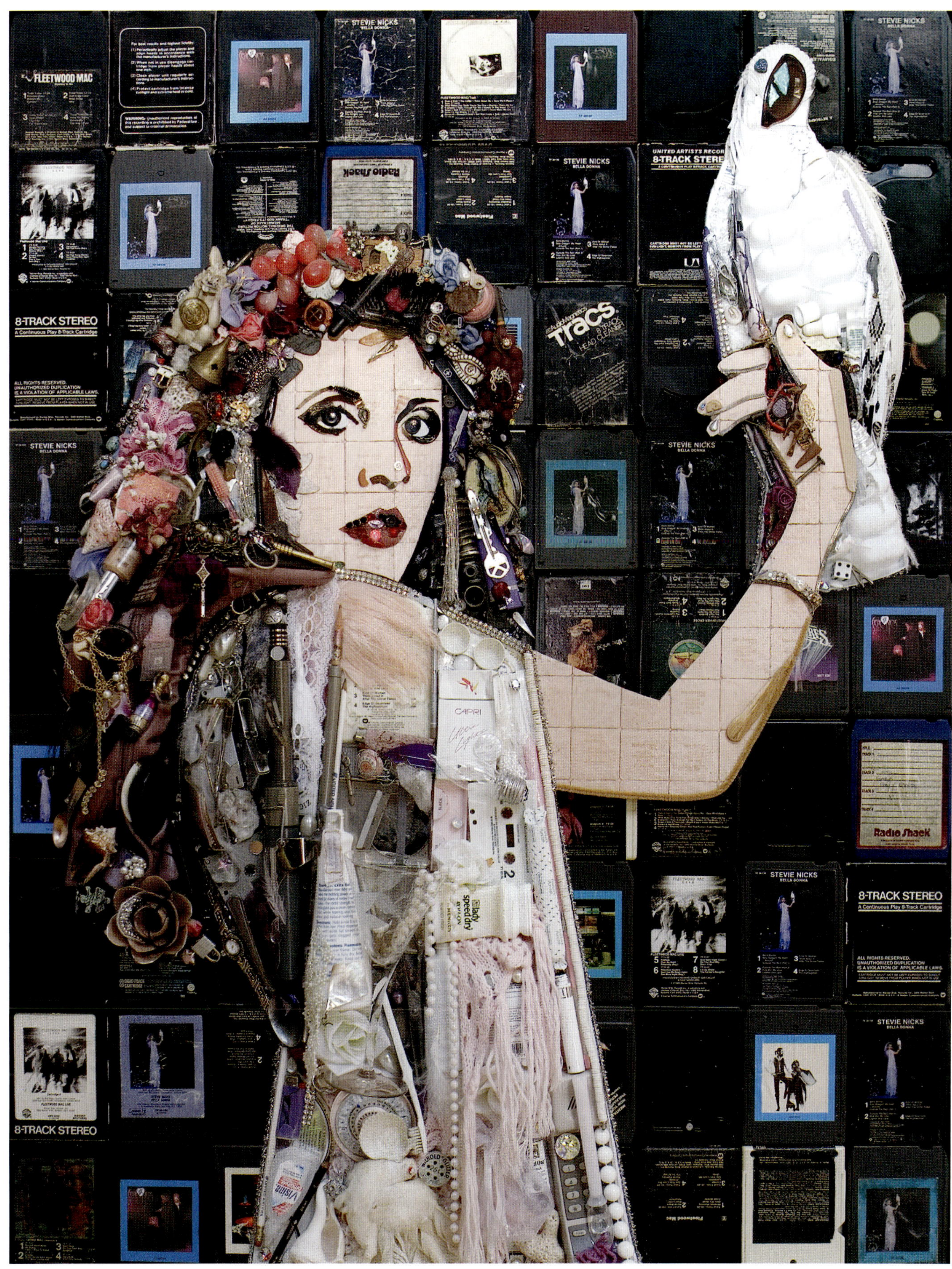

STEVIE NICKS • 8-track tapes, cotton, leather, lace, macramé, jewelry, cosmetics, cigarettes, 2008

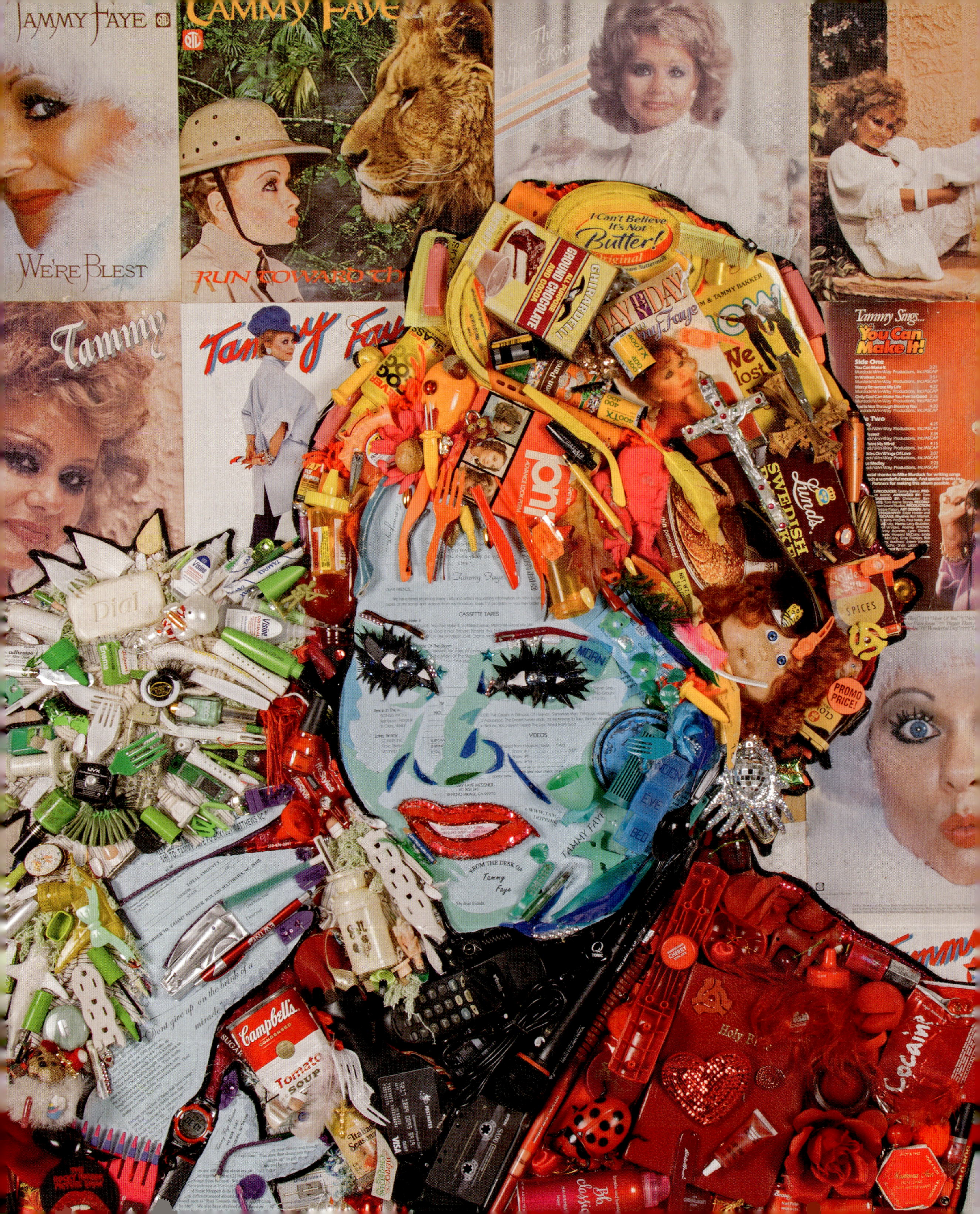

TAMMY FAYE
TAMMY FAYE
WE'RE BLEST
In The Upper Room
Tammy
Tammy Sings...
You Can Make It!
Side One
Side Two
I Can't Believe It's Not Butter!
Original
GHIRARDELLI
GROUND CHOCOLATE
Dial
SWEDISH
SPICES
PROMO PRICE!
CASSETTE TAPES
VIDEOS
FROM THE DESK OF
Tammy Faye
Campbell's
Tomato Soup
Cocaine

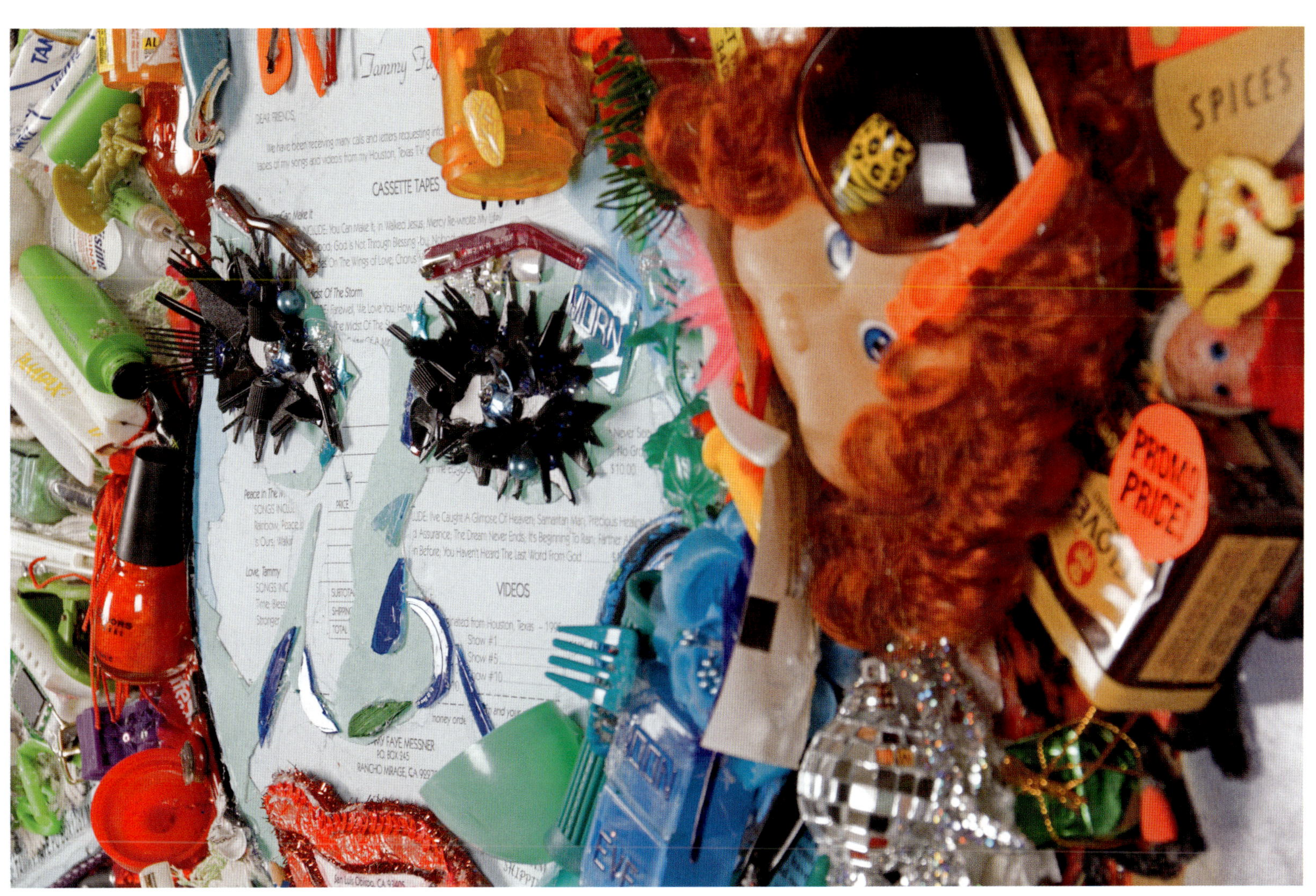

OPPOSITE: TAMMY FAYE • Record sleeves, doll head, Bible, prescription bottle, eye drops, nail polish, order form (Tammy Faye's own junk), 2017

THIS PAGE: Detail

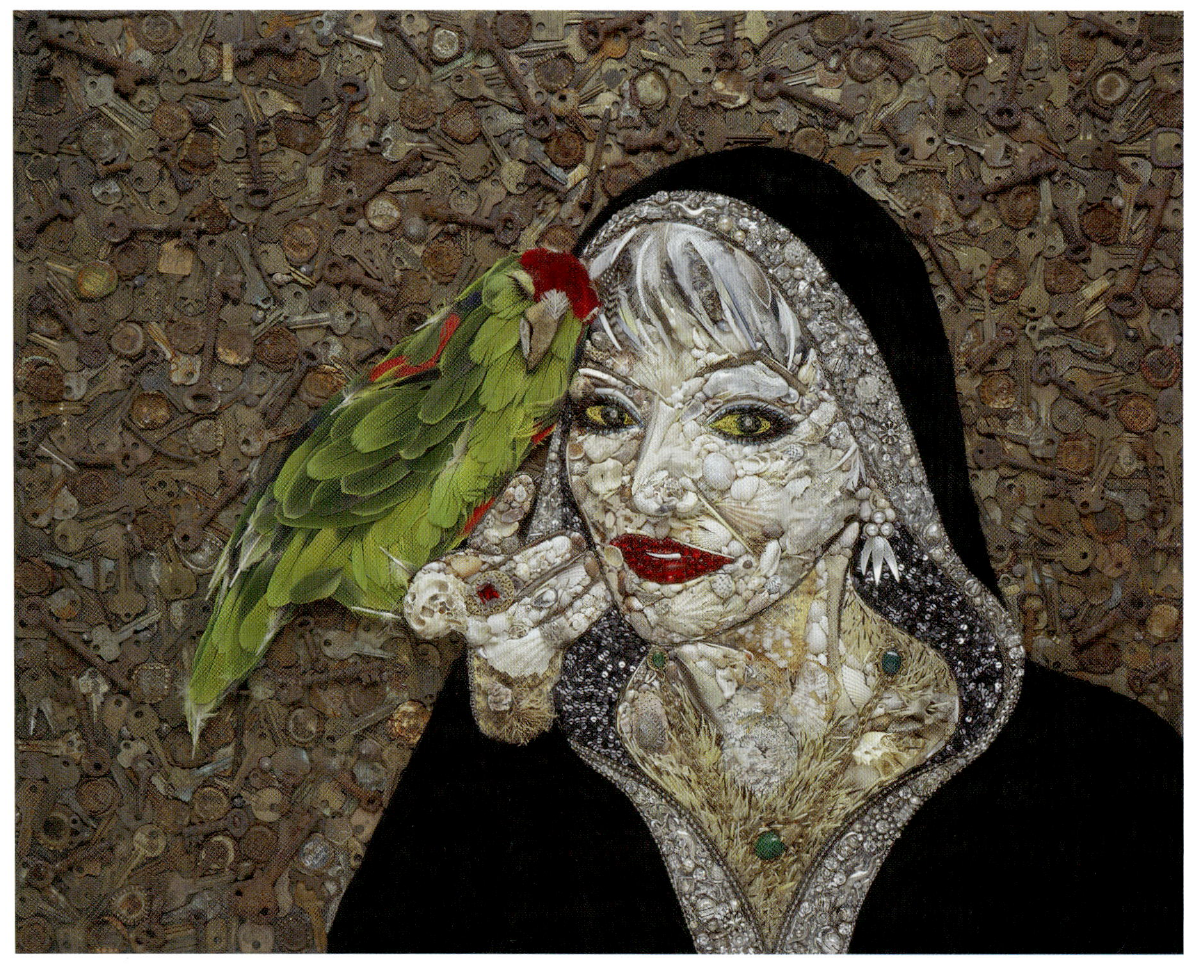

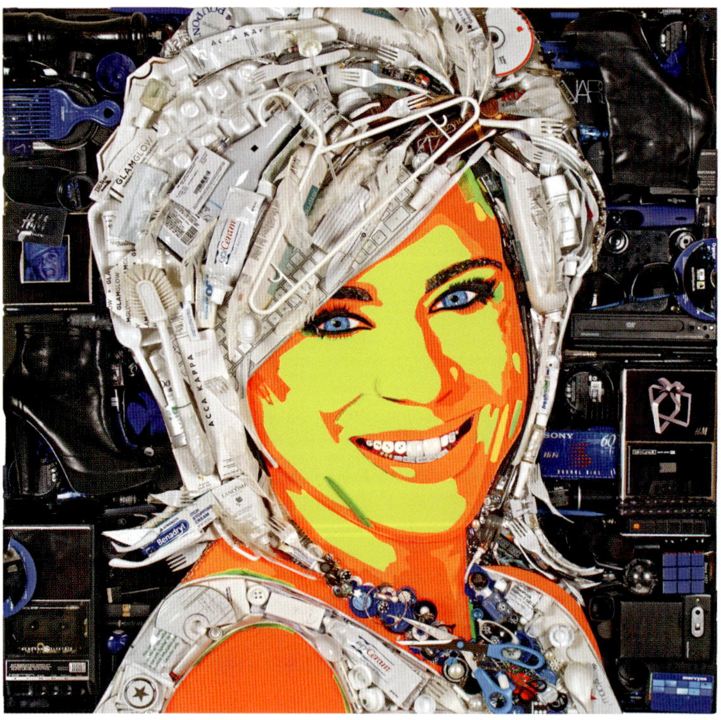

TOP: SUSAN TYRRELL • Keys, shells, jewelry, feathers, sequins, porcupine quills (Tyrrell's own junk), 2006

Collection of Susan Tyrrell

BOTTOM: THERESA CAPUTO • Plastic utensils, cassette recorders and tapes, boots, cosmetics, hairspray (Caputo's own junk), 2013

Collection of TLC.

OPPOSITE: TINA FEY • TV listings, doll, jar lids, game tiles, glasses frames, light bulbs, credit cards, 2010

Commissioned by the *Washington Post*.

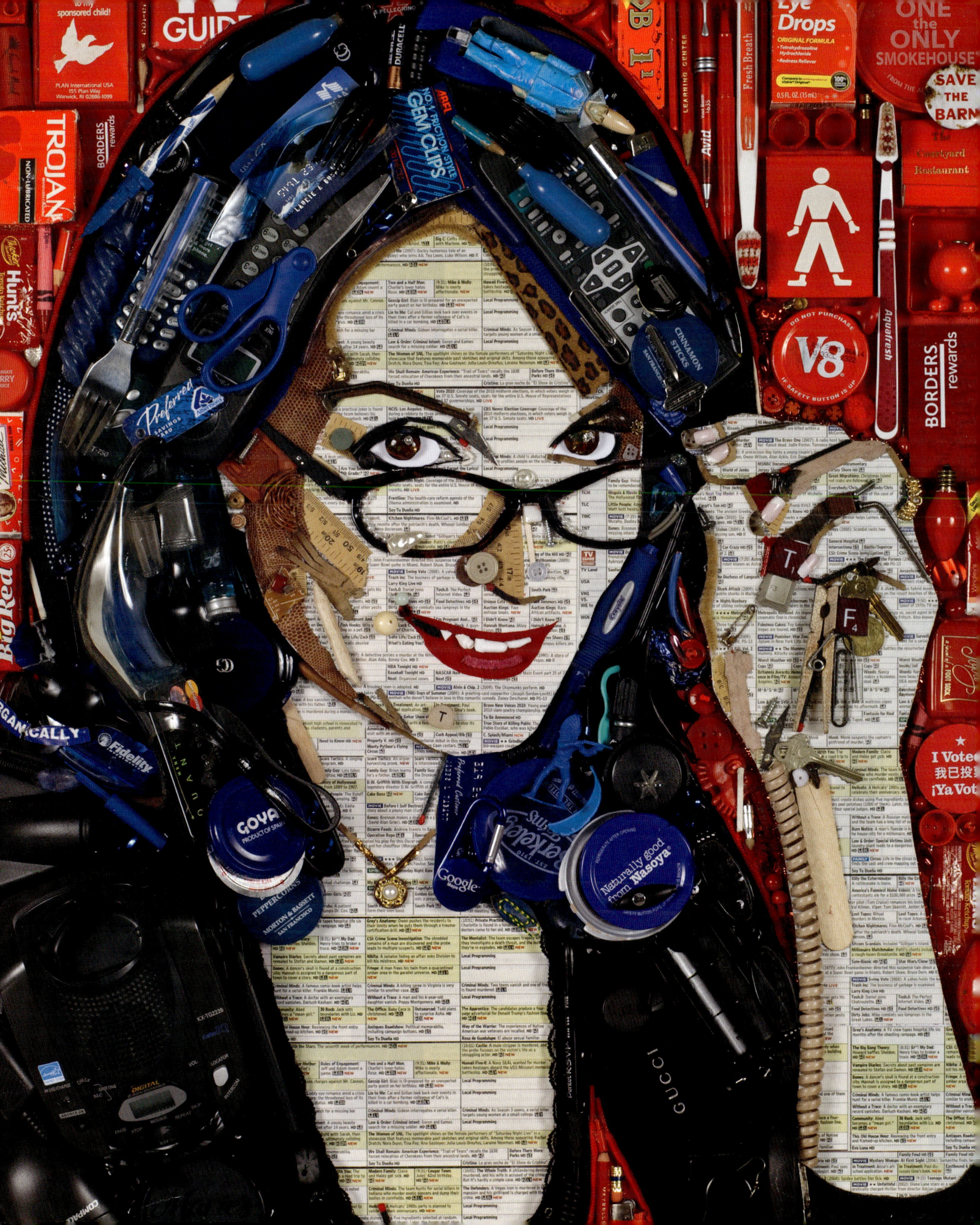

sponsored child!
GUID
TROJAN
BORDERS rewards
Eye Drops
ORIGINAL FORMULA
ONE the ONLY SMOKEHOUSE
SAVE THE BARN
Fresh Breath
DURACELL
GEM CLIPS
CINNAMON STICKS
V8
Aquafresh
BORDERS rewards
Hunt's
Big Red
Preferred
Fidelity
GOYA
Google
Naturally good from Nasoya
I Voted
我已投
¡Ya Vot
GUCCI

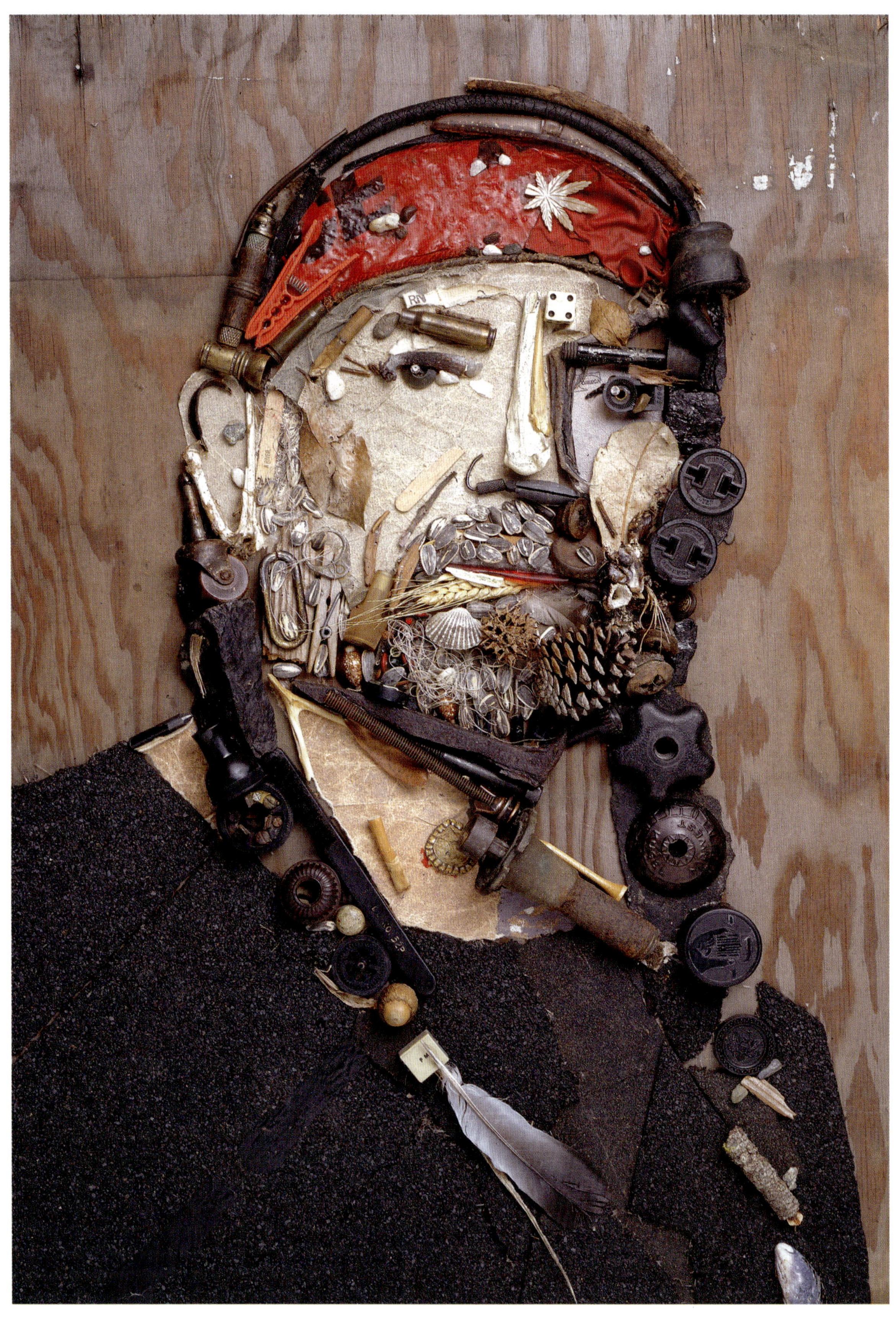

WILLIE NELSON • Wood, electrical items, pinecone, pipe, railroad tie, poker chip, tar paper, sunflower seeds, shell casings, 2002
Tour poster. Collection of The Fillmore.

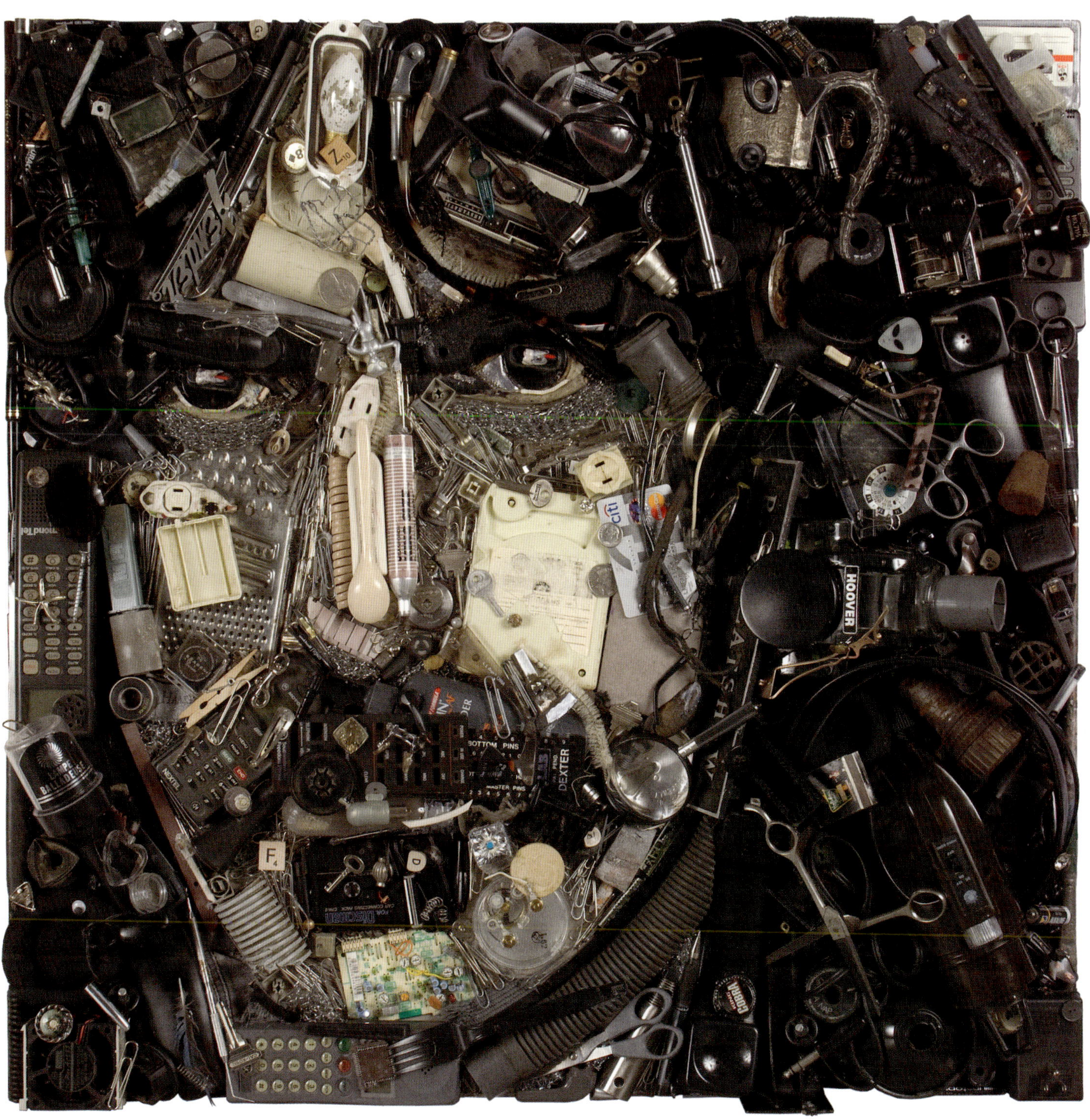

FRANK ZAPPA • Vacuum cleaner parts, phones, cords and cables, cheese grater, credit card, guitar pick, 2010

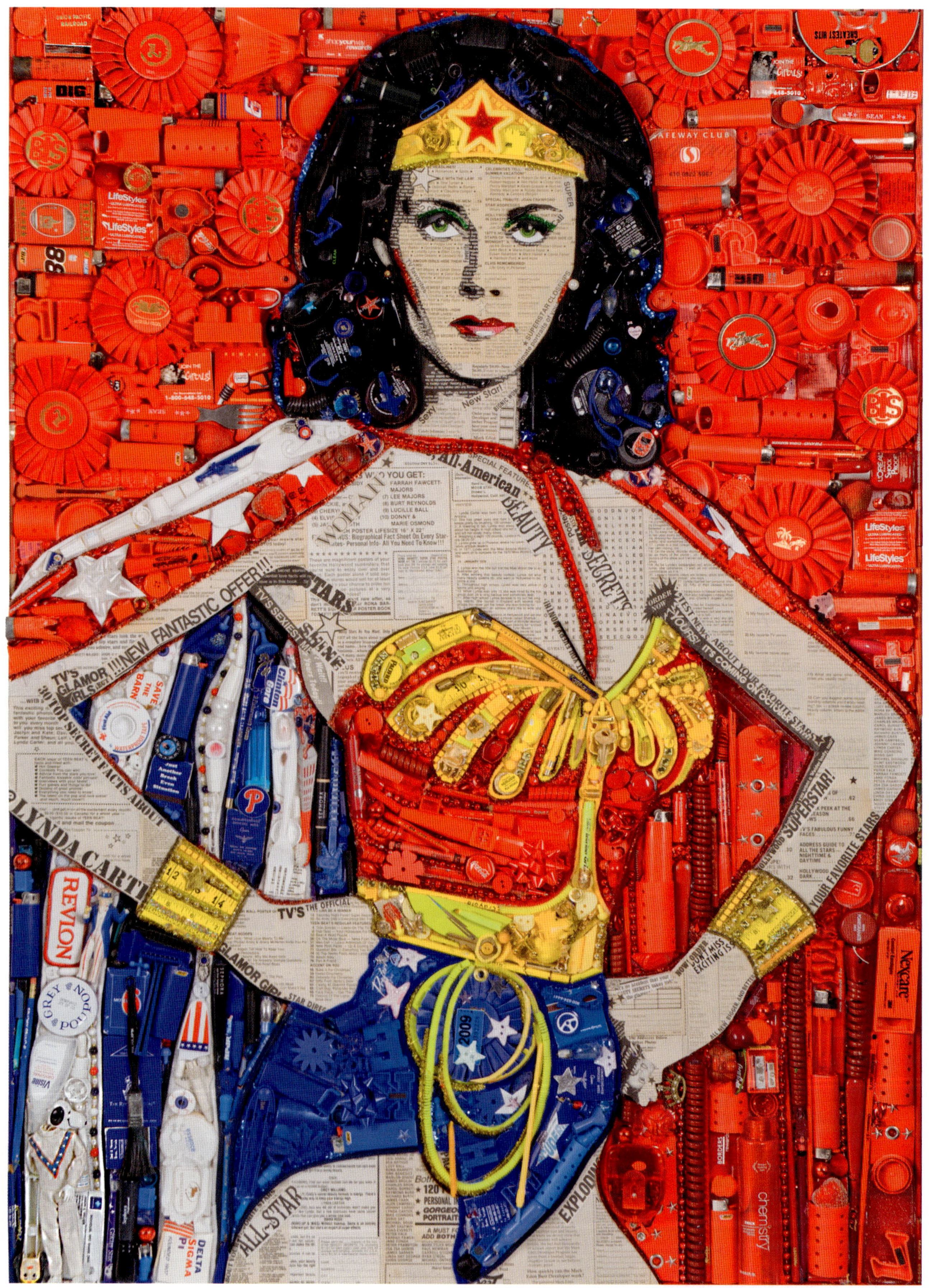

WONDER WOMAN • Prize ribbons, cosmetics, telephone cords, vintage magazine pages, plastic lighters, doll, 2012

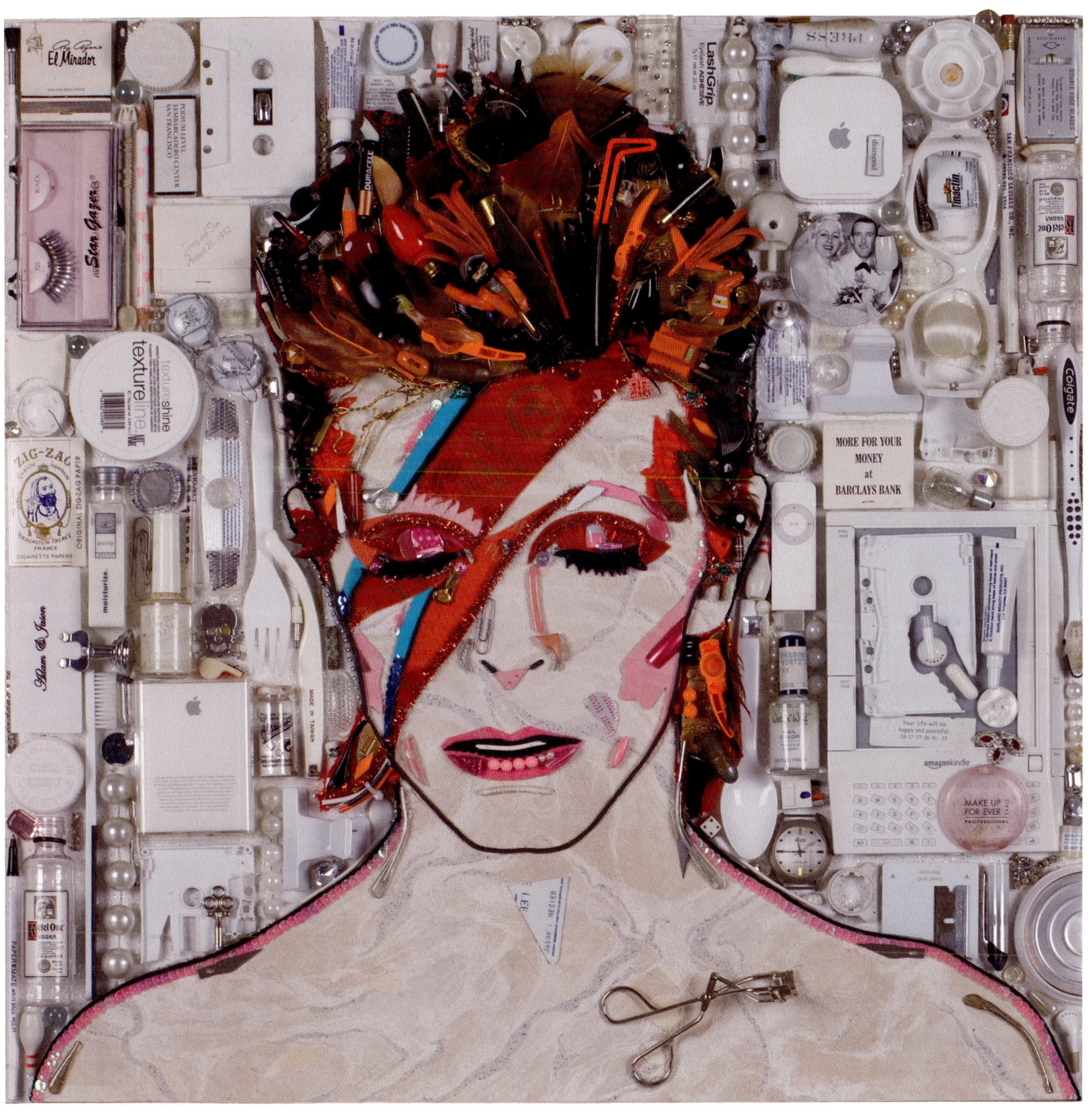

DAVID BOWIE • Cosmetics, cassette tapes, feathers, electronics, liquor bottles, glitter, sequins, 2011

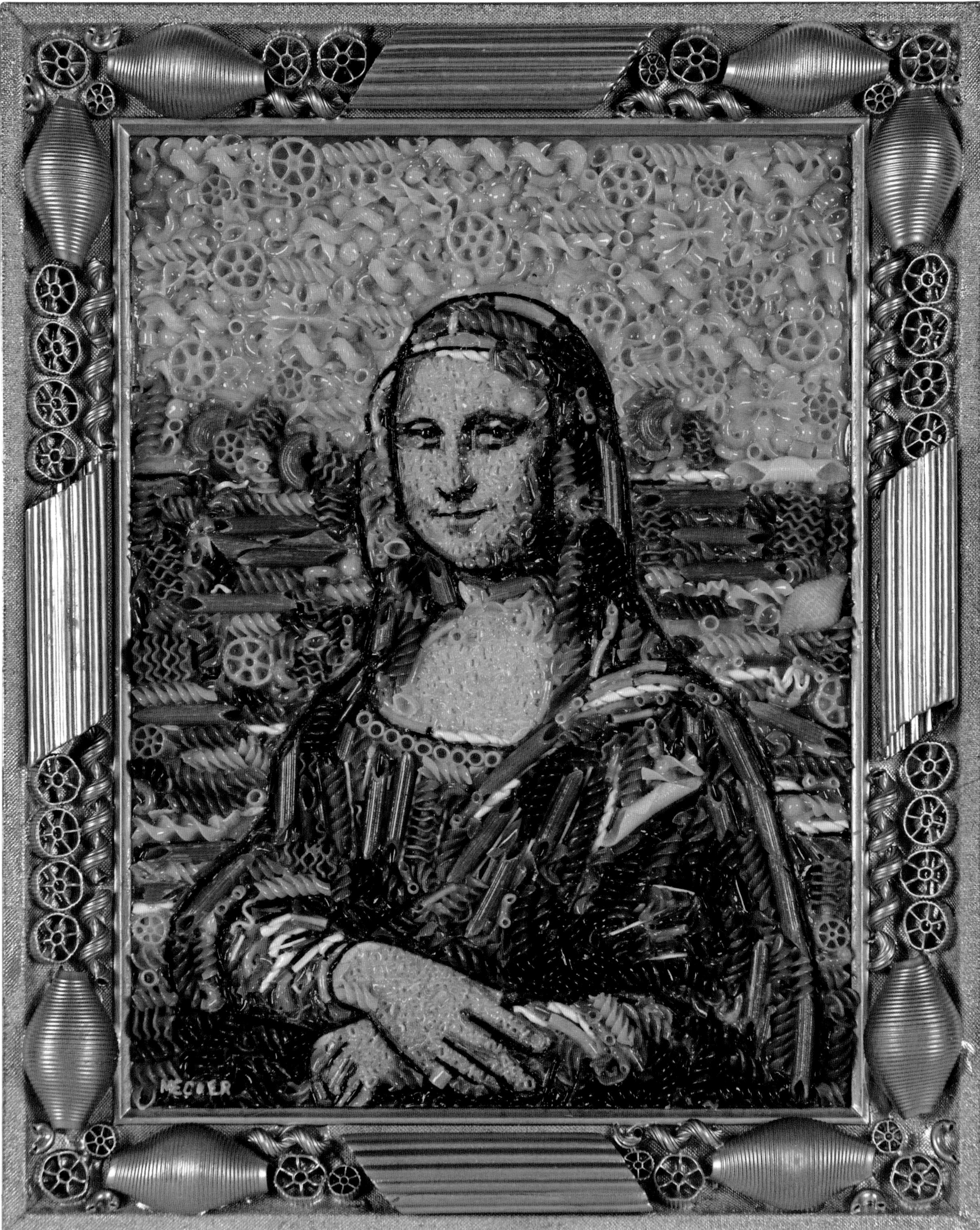

Food

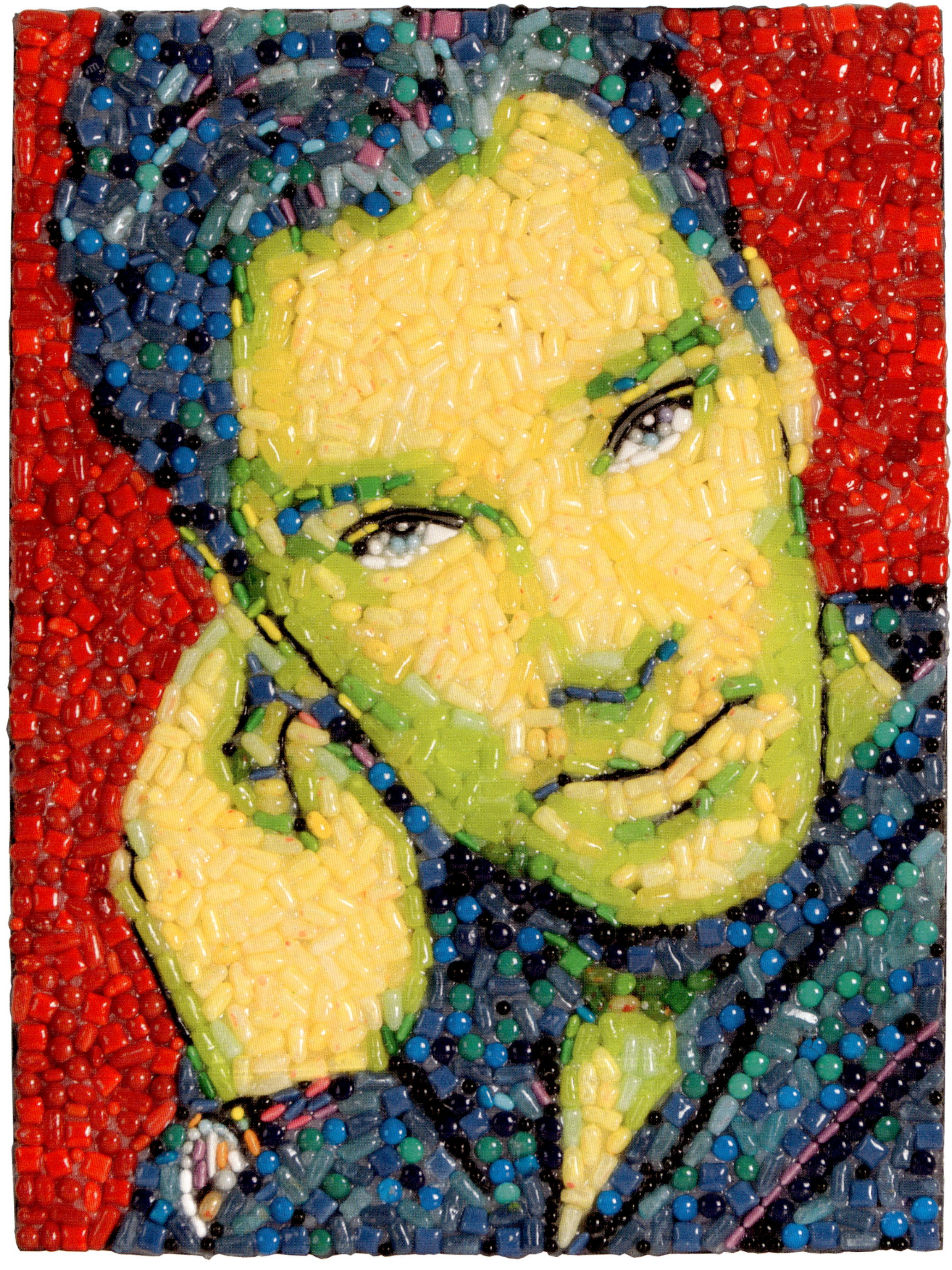

PREVIOUS SPREAD: MONA LISA • Noodles, 2017

BENEDICT CUMBERBATCH • Various candies, 2017

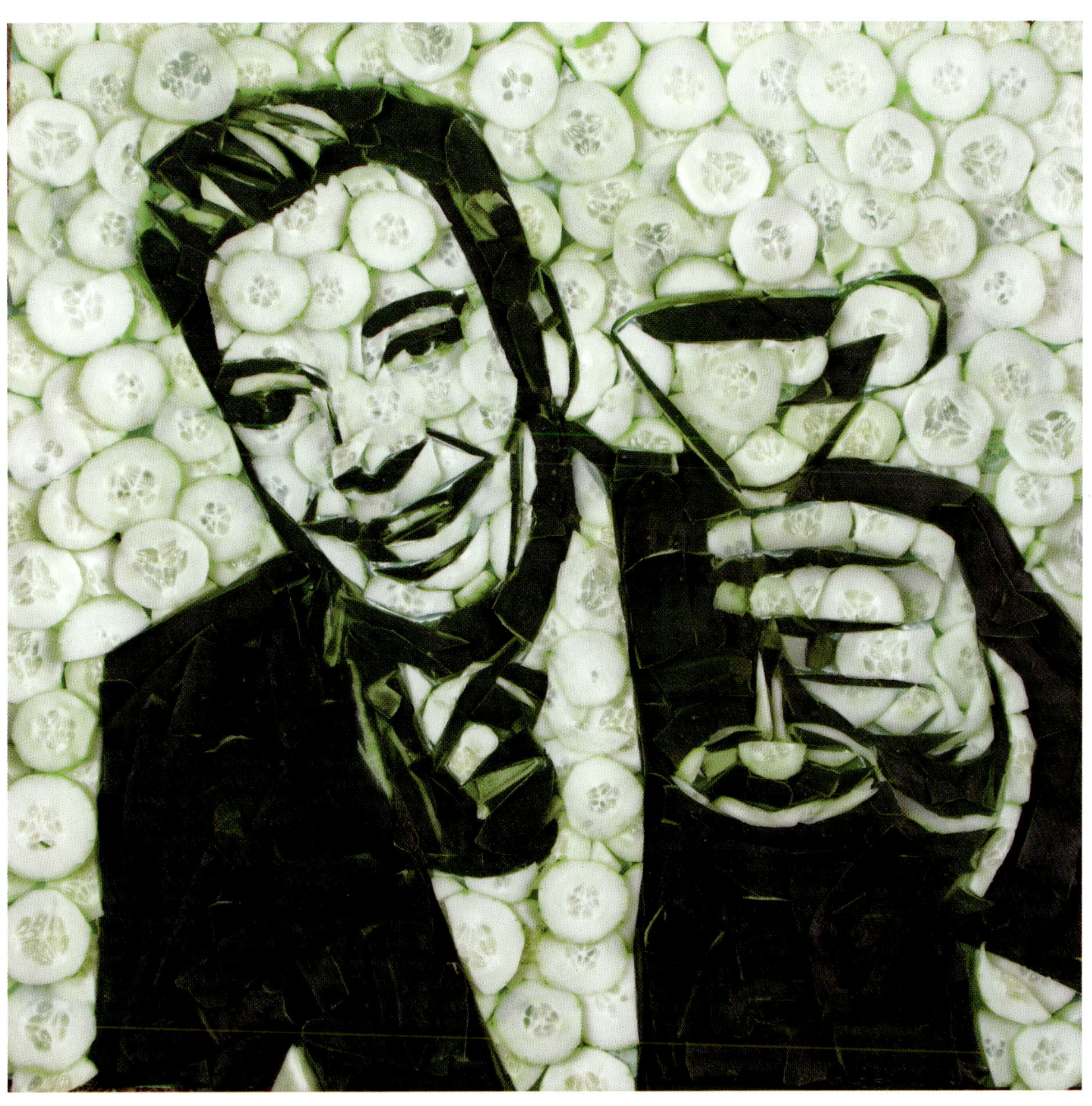

JIMMY FALLON • More than fifty cucumbers, 2016
Commissioned by Hendrick's Gin.

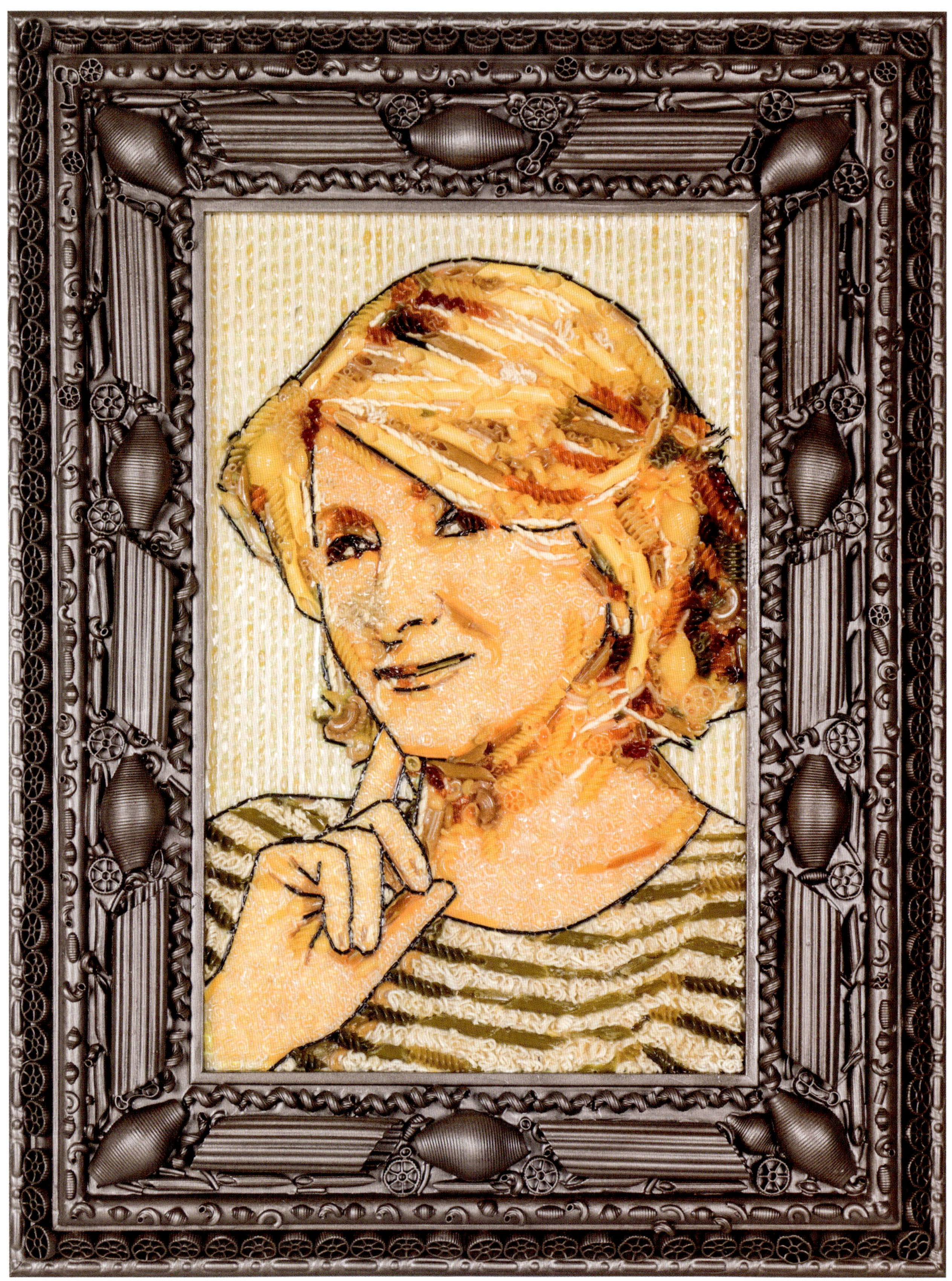

MARTHA STEWART • Pasta, 2017
In 2011 I made a portrait of Snoop Dogg out of weed that he liked so much he commissioned me to do a portrait of Martha that he could give to her on their show *Martha & Snoop's Potluck Dinner Party*.

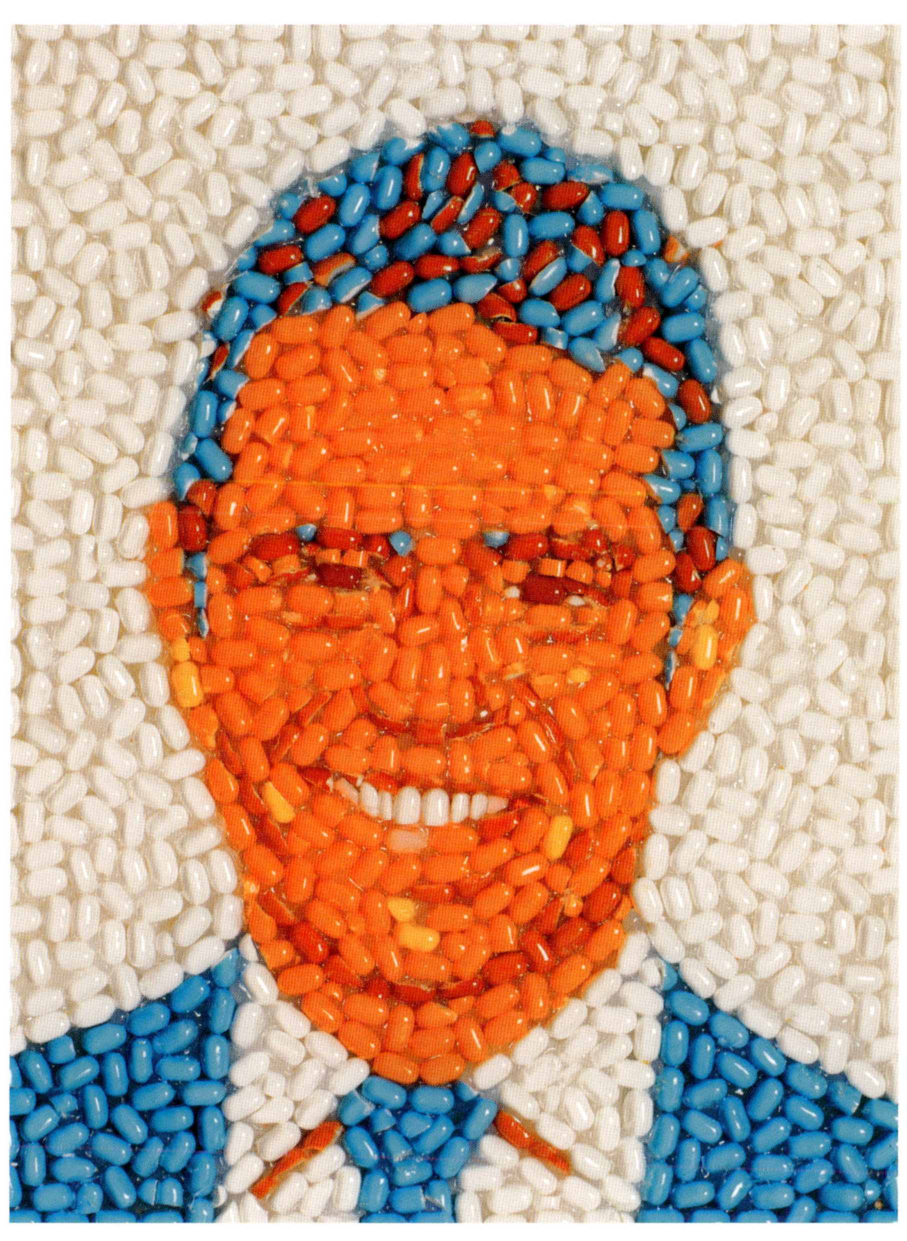

ANDY COHEN • Five hundred Tic Tacs, 2015
I gave Andy this portrait, which he keeps in his *Watch What Happens Live* TV show dressing room. He is obsessed with people's breath.

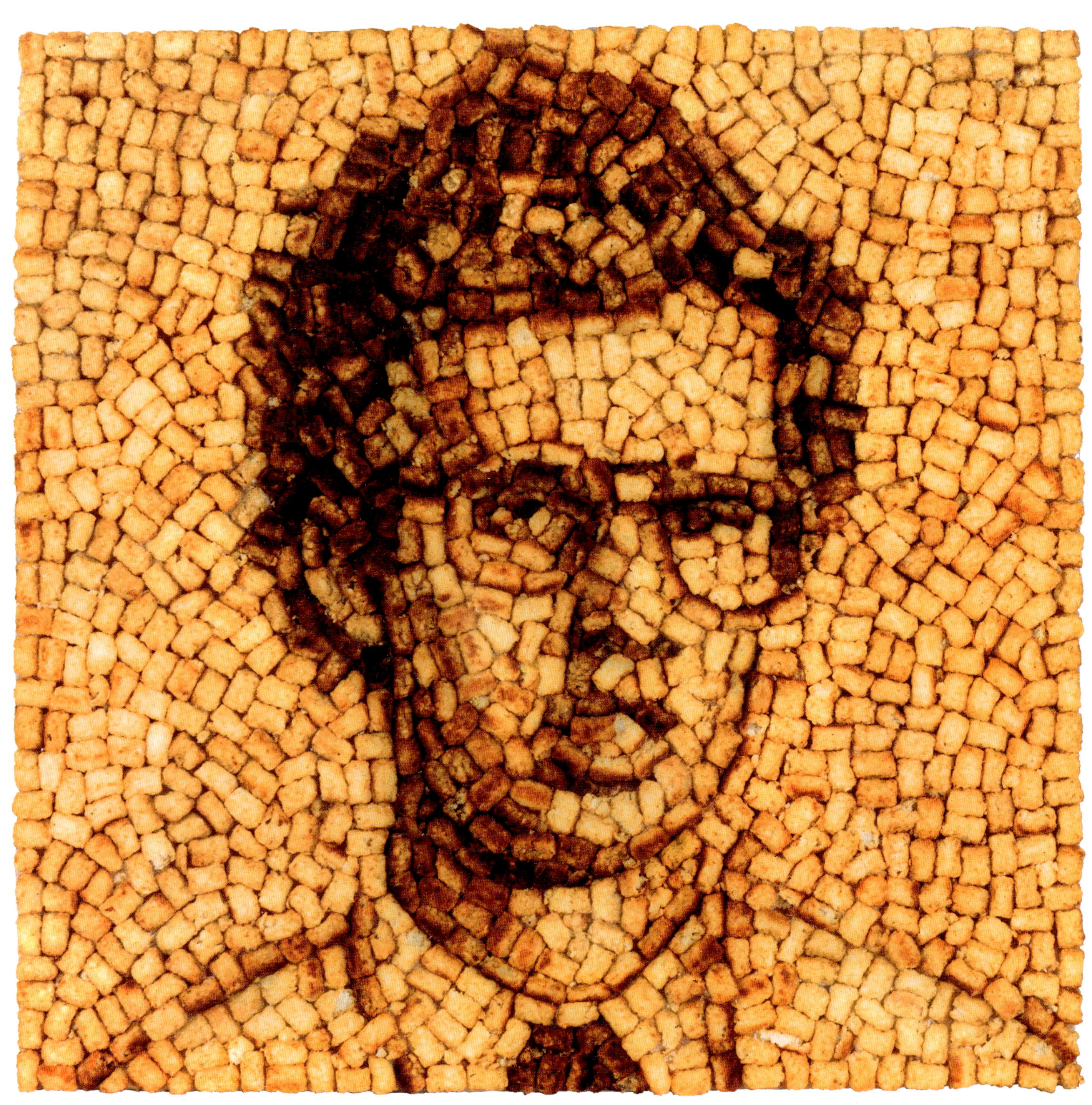

NAPOLEON DYNAMITE • Twenty-five pounds of Tater Tots, 2018

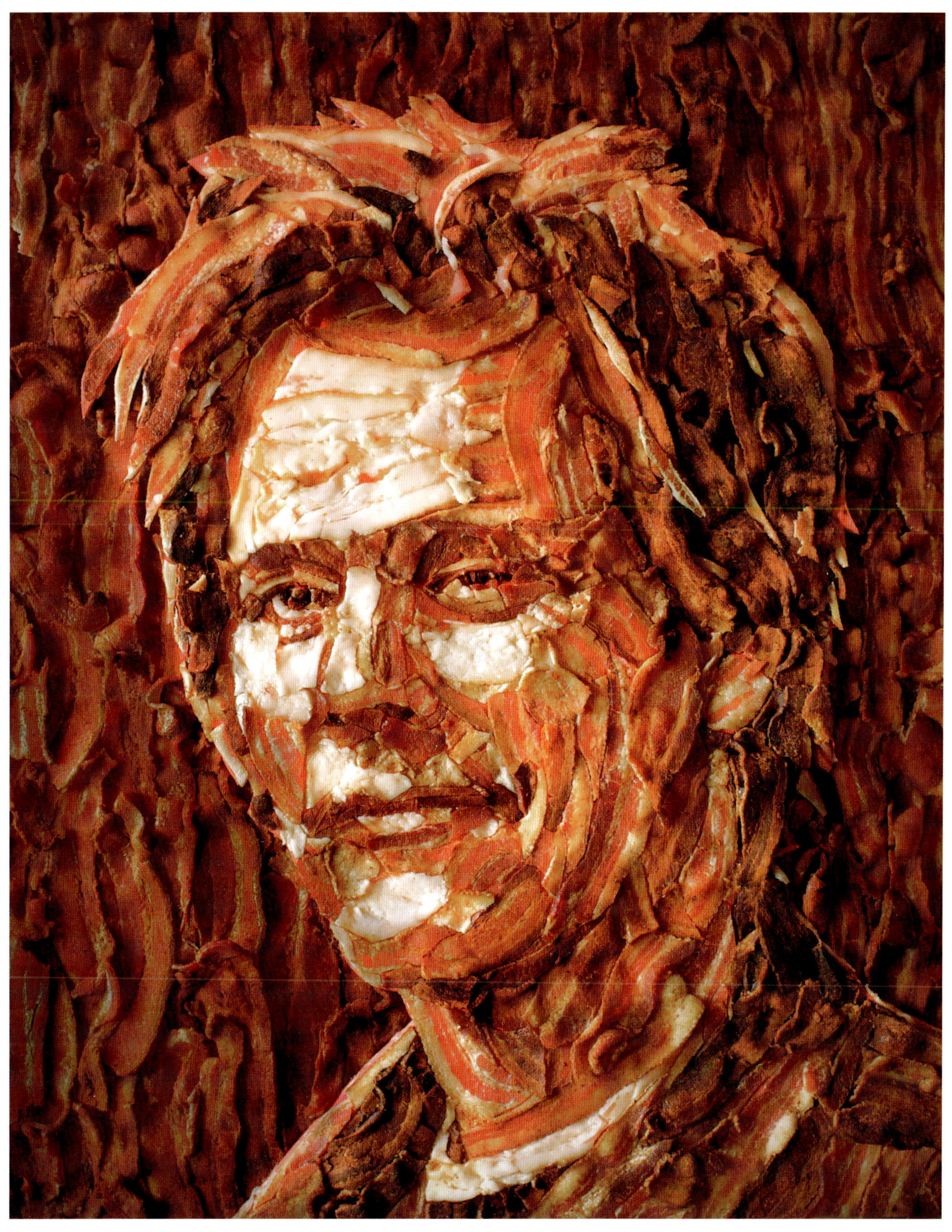

KEVIN BACON • Fifteen pounds of bacon, 2012

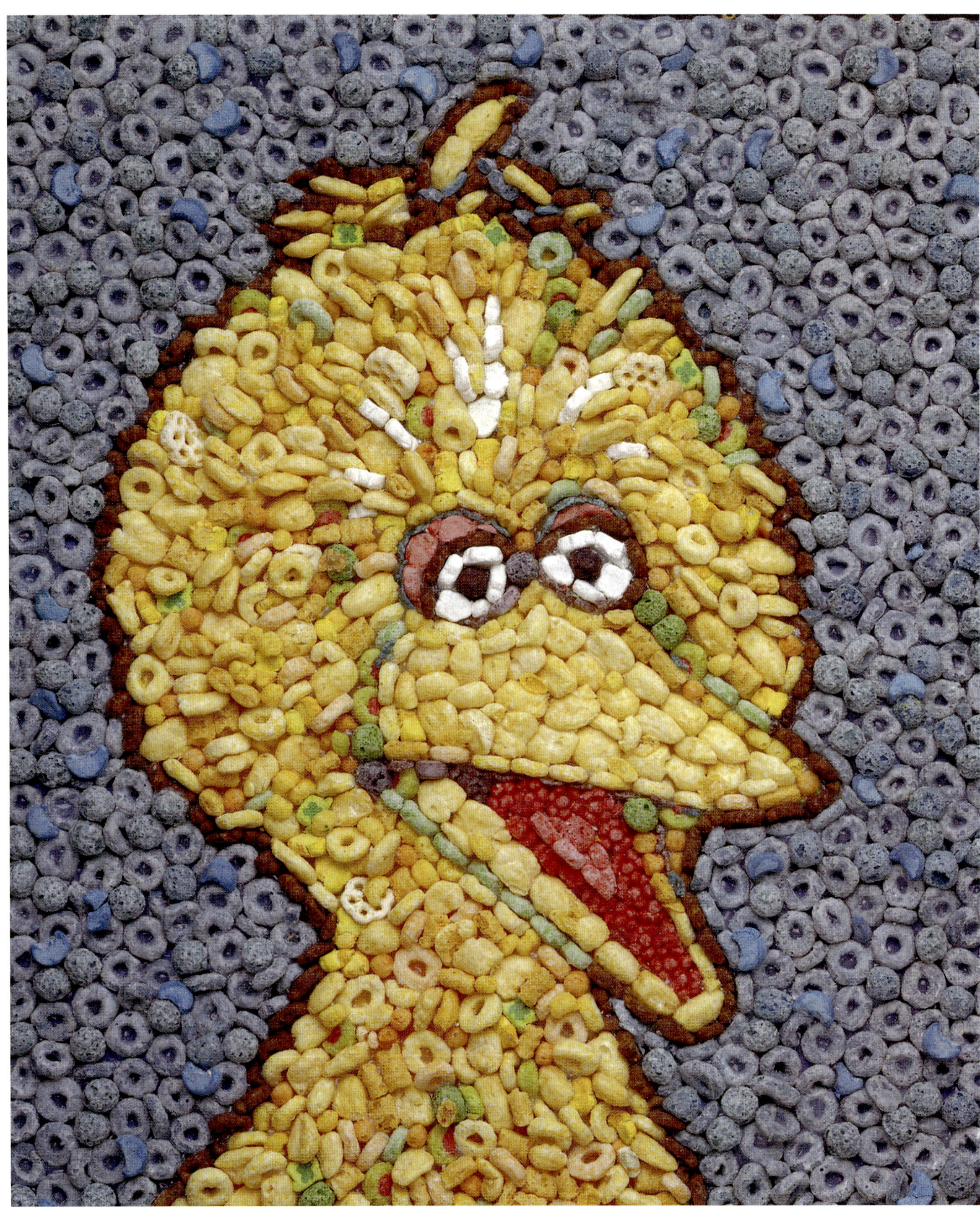

BIG BIRD • Various breakfast cereals, 2009

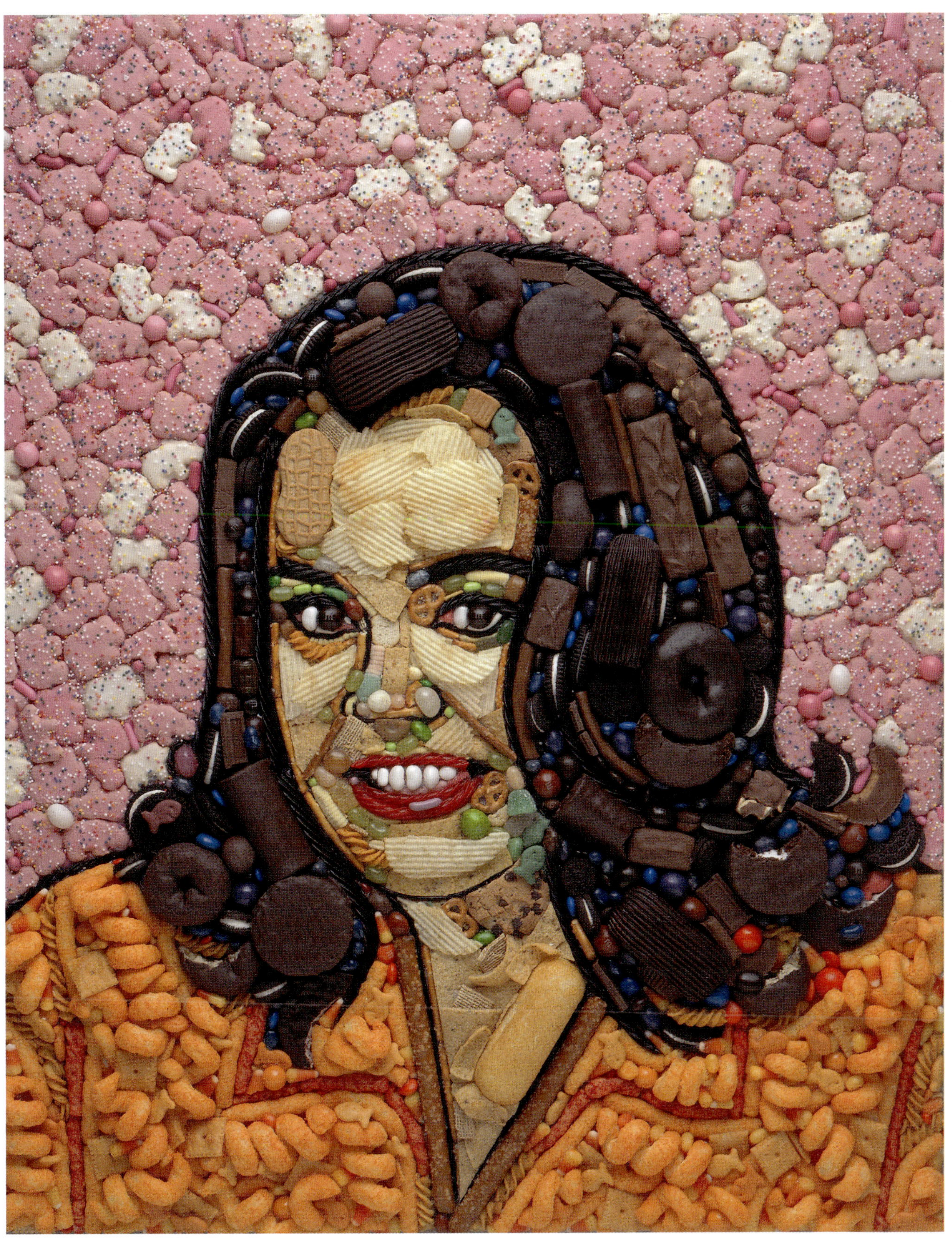

ROSIE O'DONNELL • Fifteen pounds of junk food, 2007
I sent Rosie a framed print of this piece, which her daughter hung in her room.

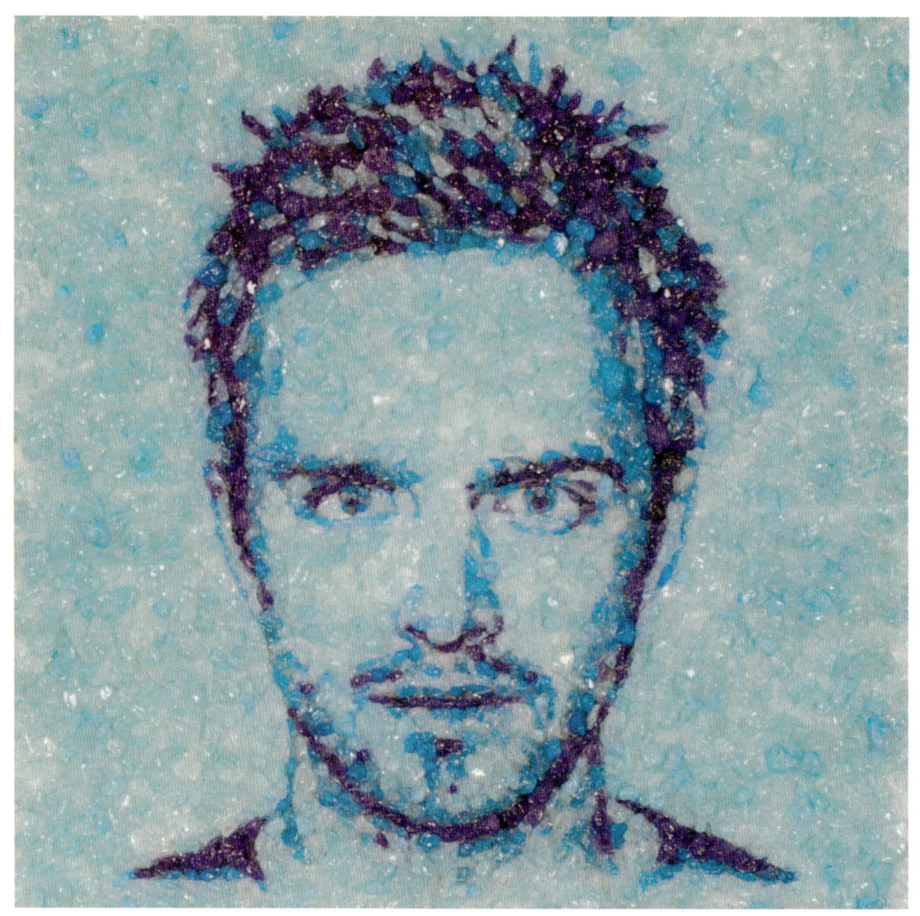

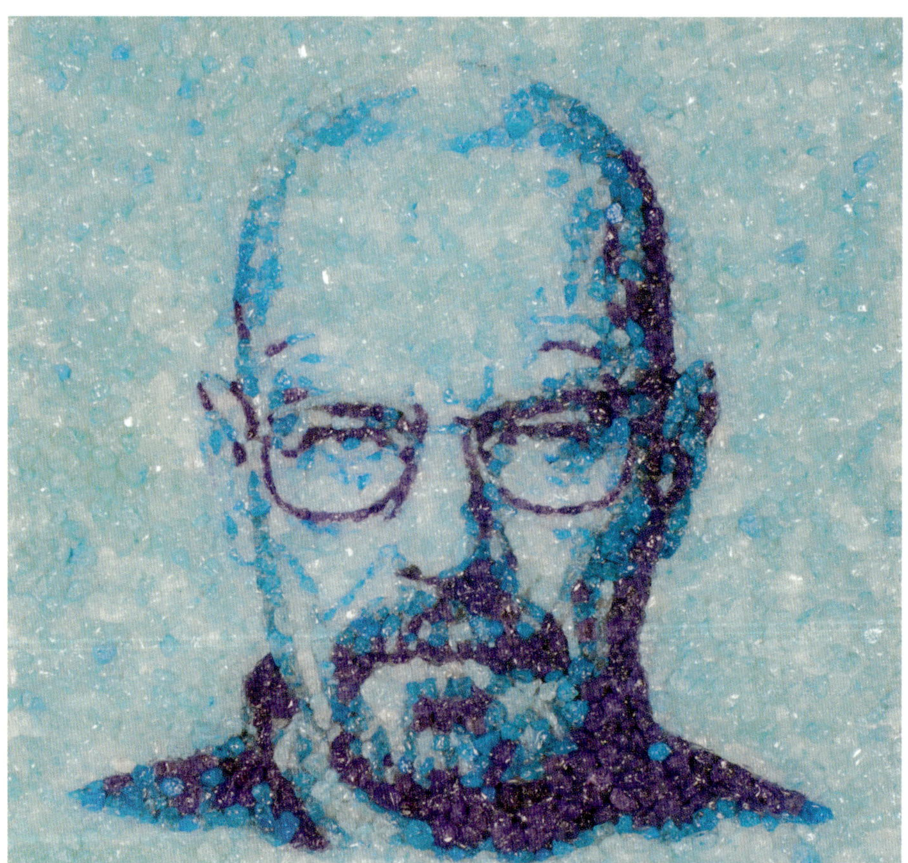

TOP: BREAKING BAD (AARON) • One half kilo of hard rock candy, 2014

BOTTOM: BREAKING BAD (BRYAN) • One half kilo of hard rock candy, 2014
The blue meth on the TV show was simulated using blue rock candy.

OPPOSITE: BACON BAD • Twenty pounds of bacon, 2014

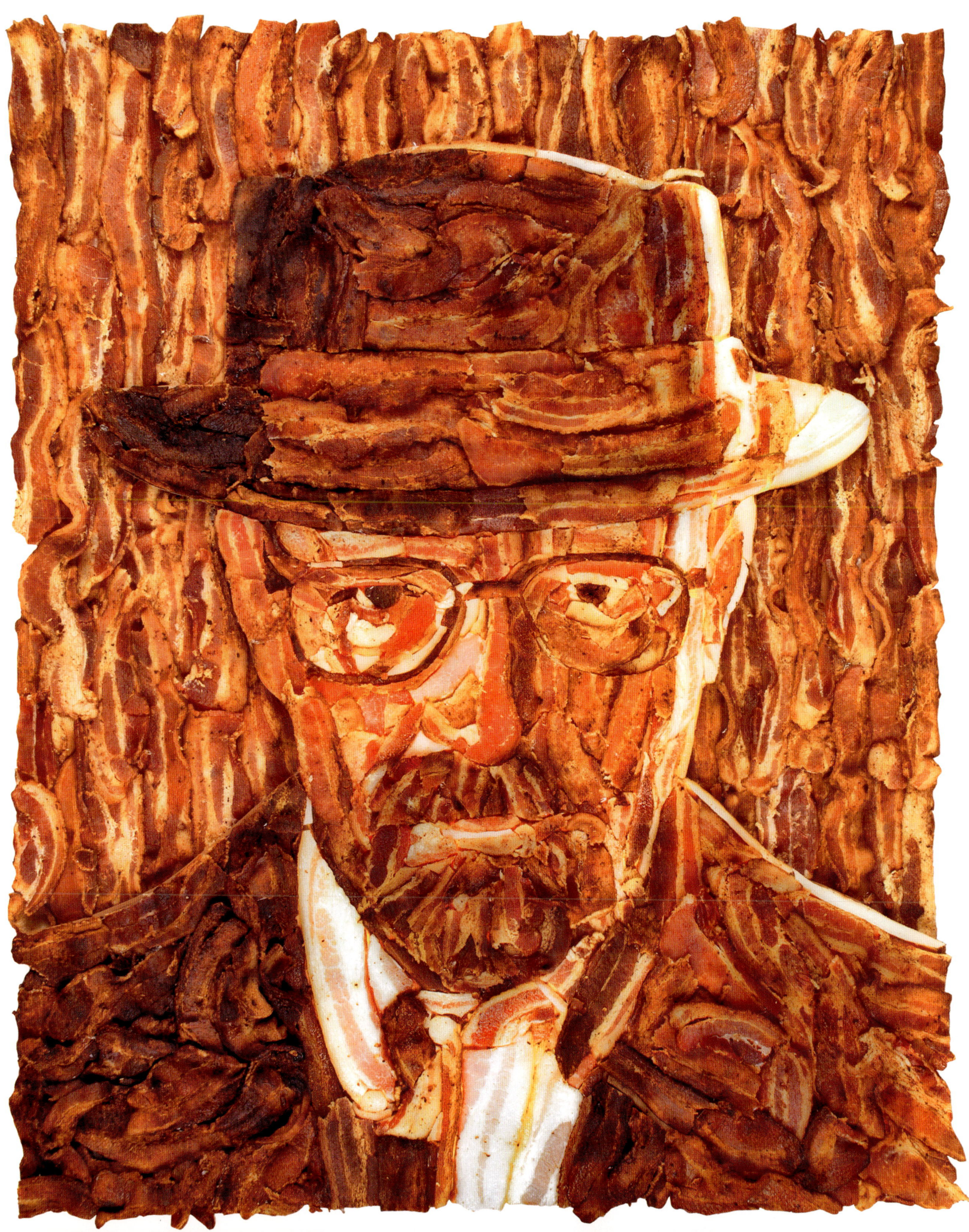

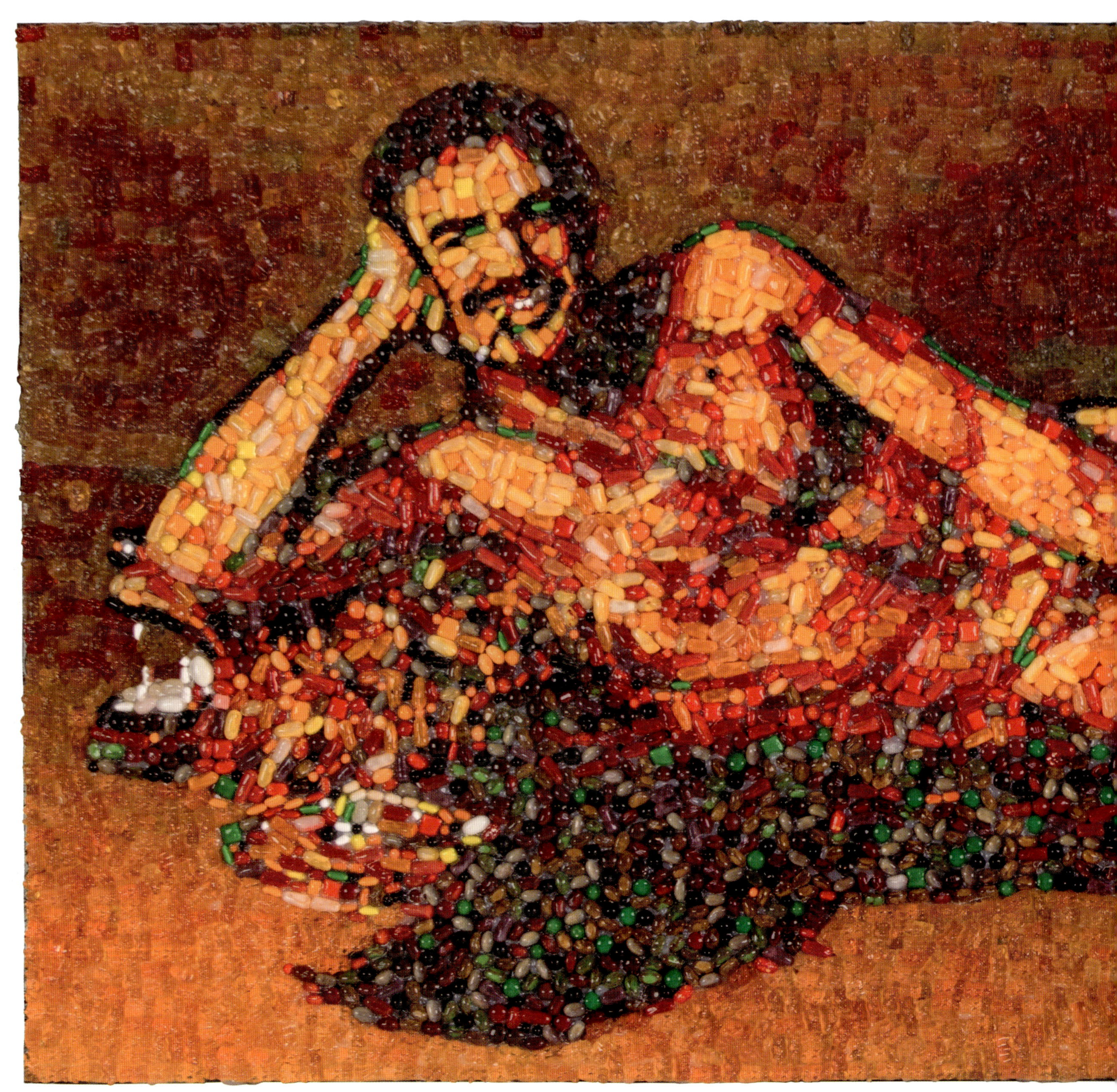

BURT REYNOLDS • Various candies, 2015

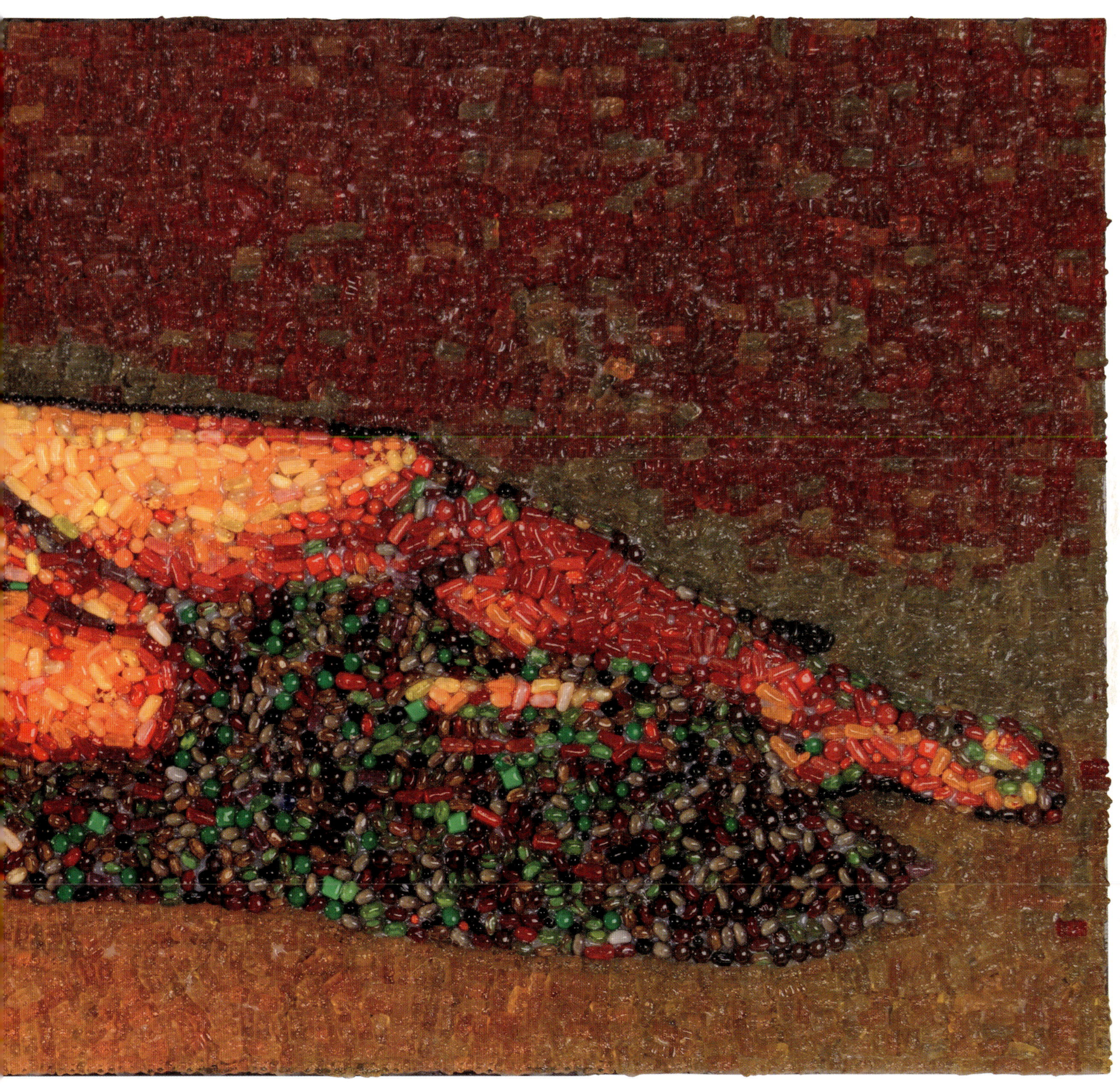

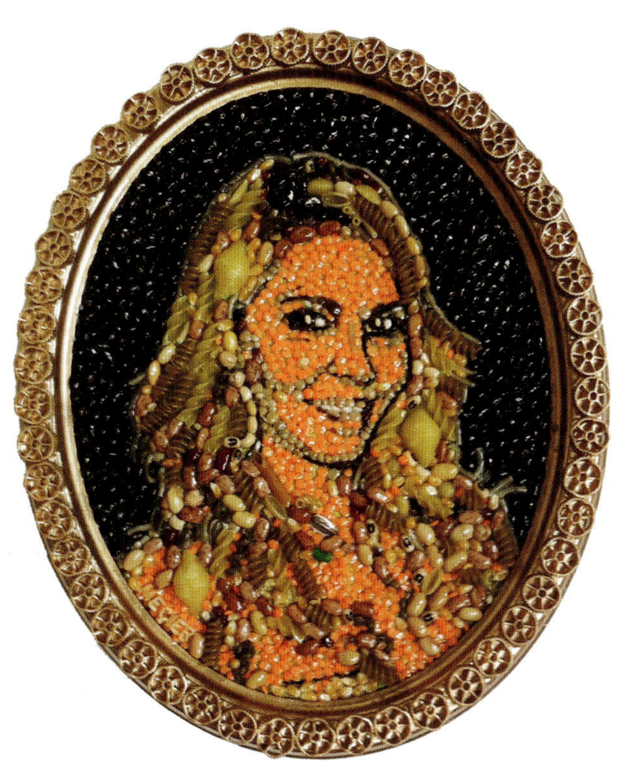

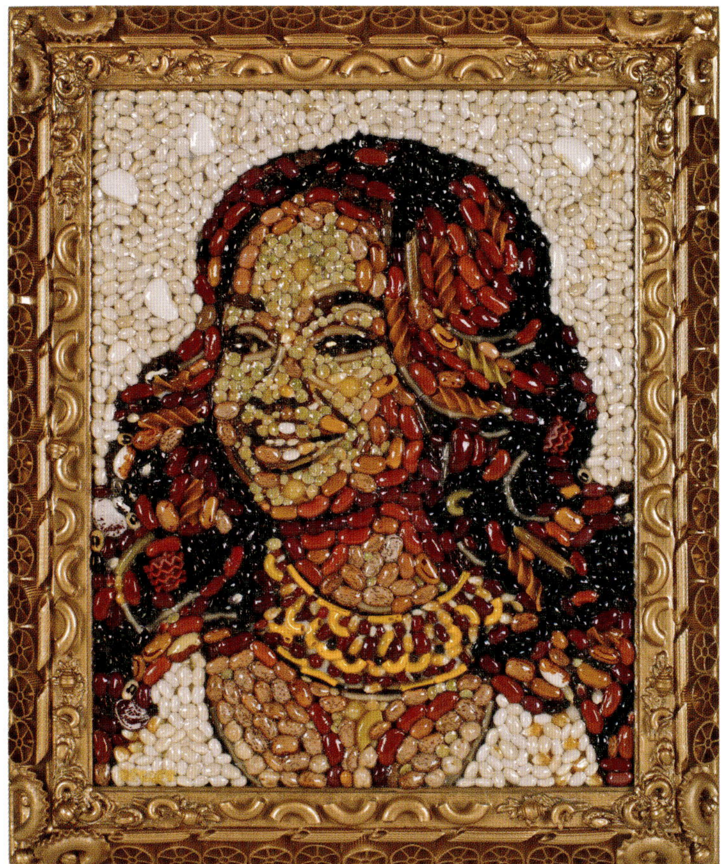

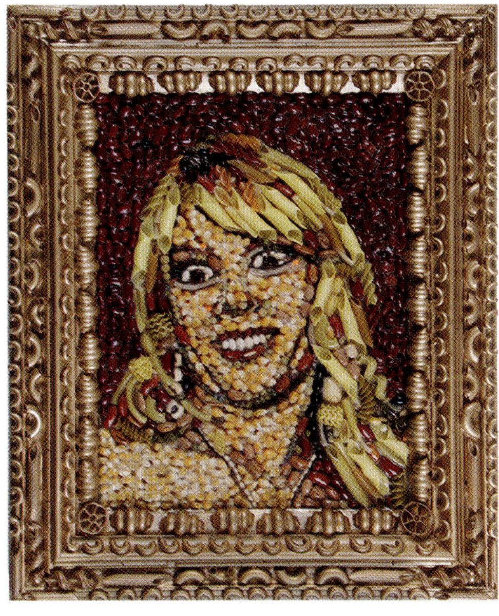

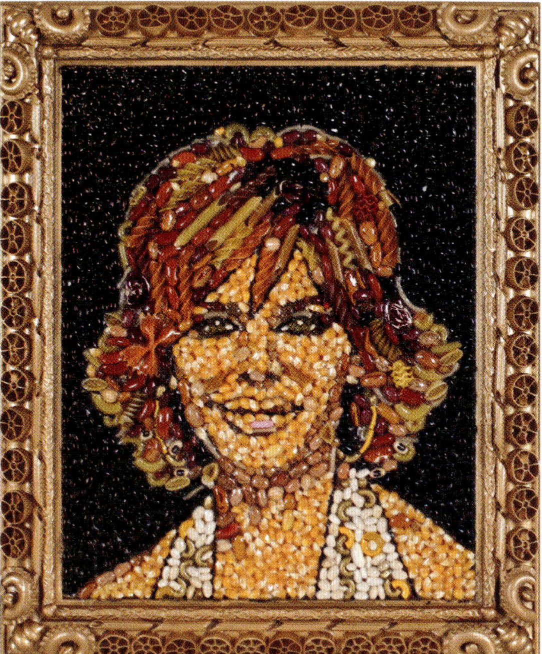

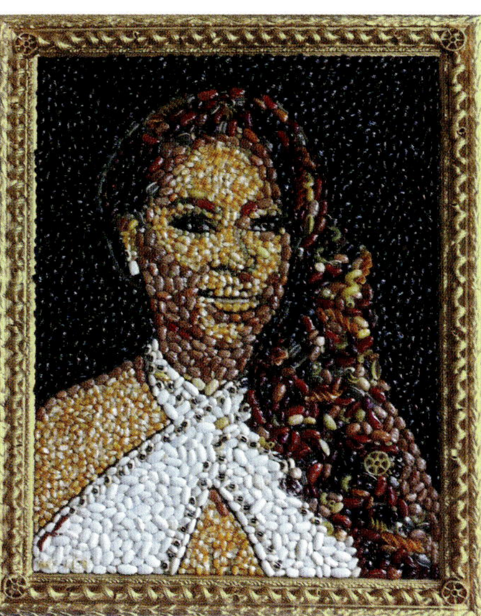

The Real Housewives of Macaroni Series

TOP LEFT: BRANDI GLANVILLE • Beans and noodles, 2017

TOP RIGHT: PHAEDRA PARKS • Beans and noodles, 2017

BOTTOM LEFT: RAMONA SINGER • Beans and noodles, 2017

BOTTOM MIDDLE: LISA RINNA • Beans and noodles, 2017

BOTTOM RIGHT: KENYA MOORE • Beans and noodles, 2017

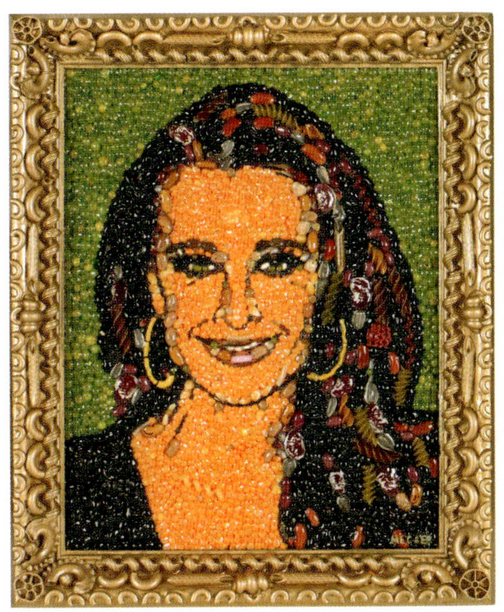

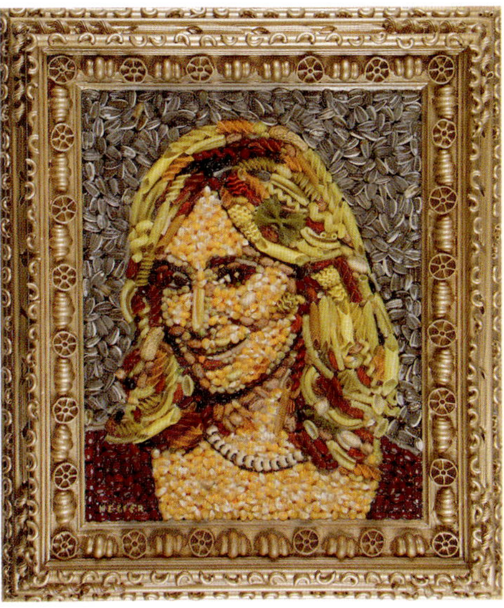

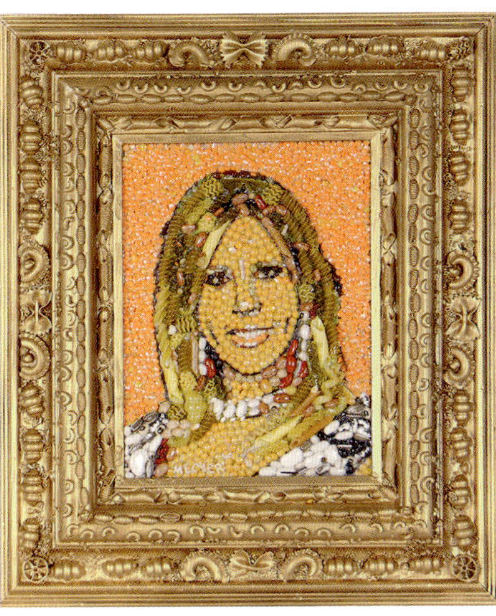

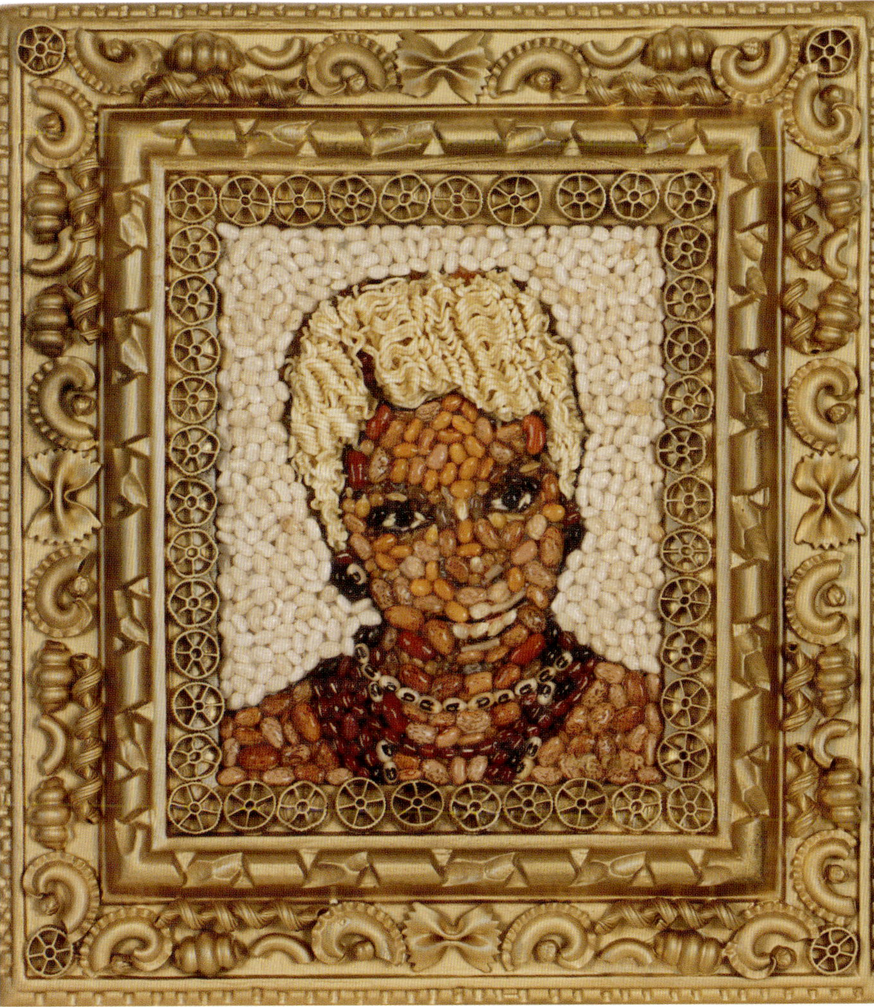

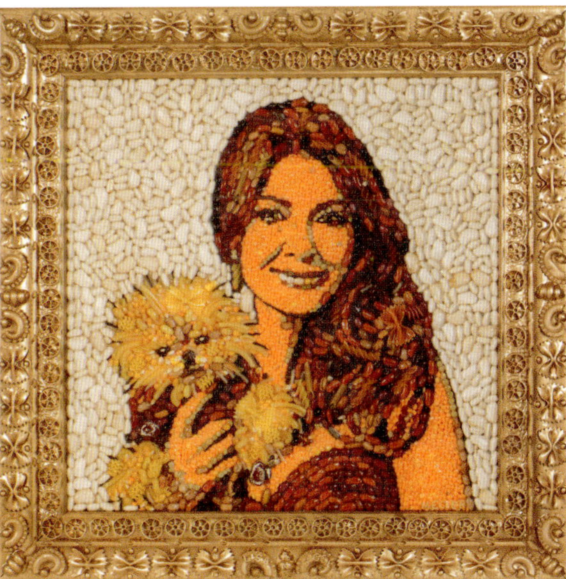

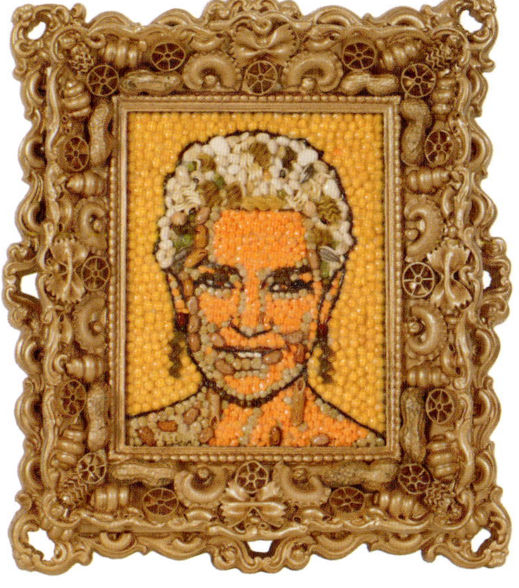

TOP LEFT: KYLE RICHARDS • Beans and noodles, 2017

TOP MIDDLE: SONJA MORGAN • Beans and noodles, 2017

TOP RIGHT: VICKI GUNVALSON • Beans and noodles, 2017

BOTTOM LEFT: NENE LEAKES • Beans and noodles, 2017

MIDDLE RIGHT: LISA VANDERPUMP AND GIGGY • Beans and noodles, 2017

BOTTOM RIGHT: YOLANDA HADID • Beans and noodles, 2017

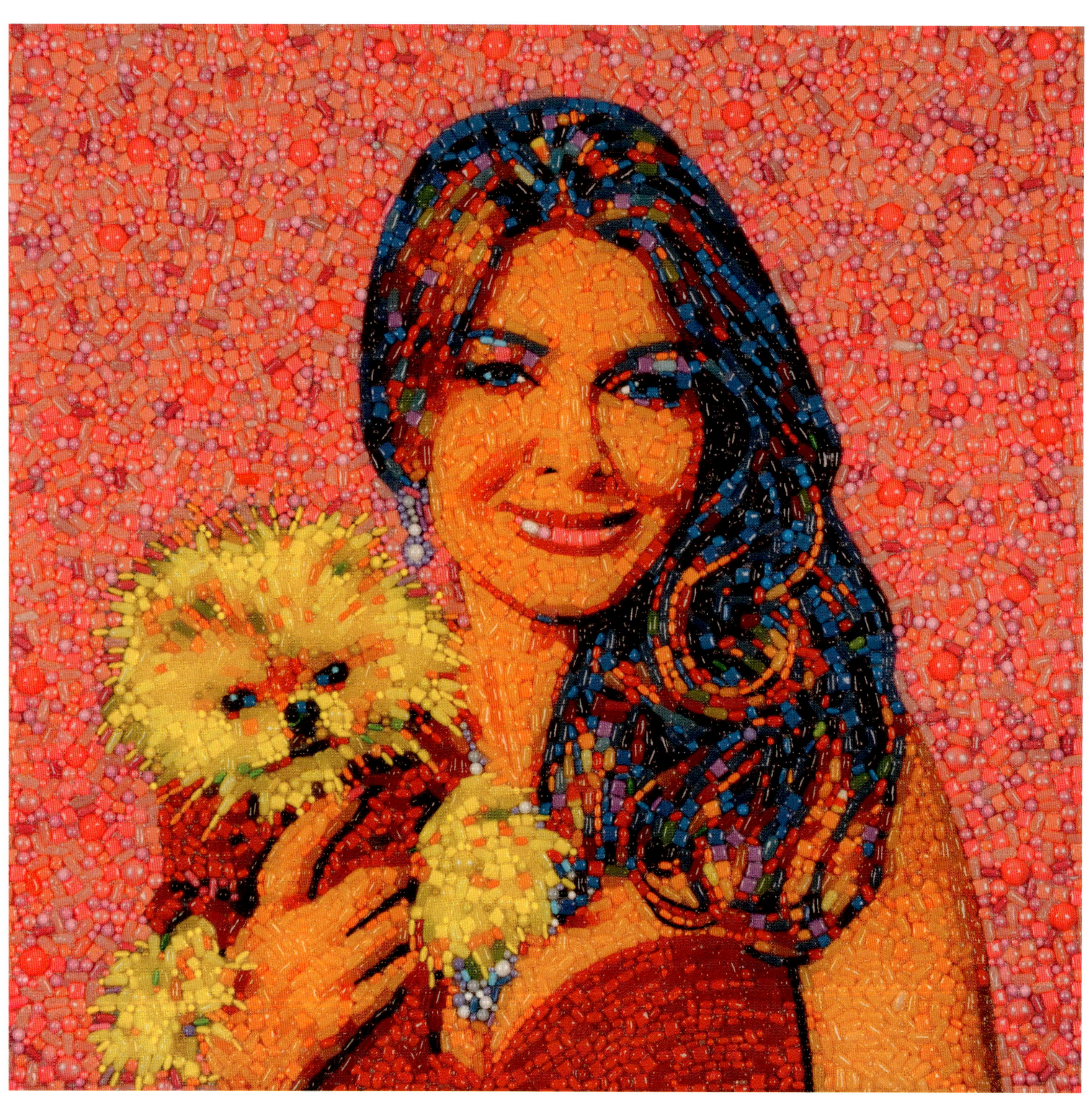

LISA VANDERPUMP AND GIGGY • Various candies, 2014

OPPOSITE: BIG ANG • Various candies, 2014

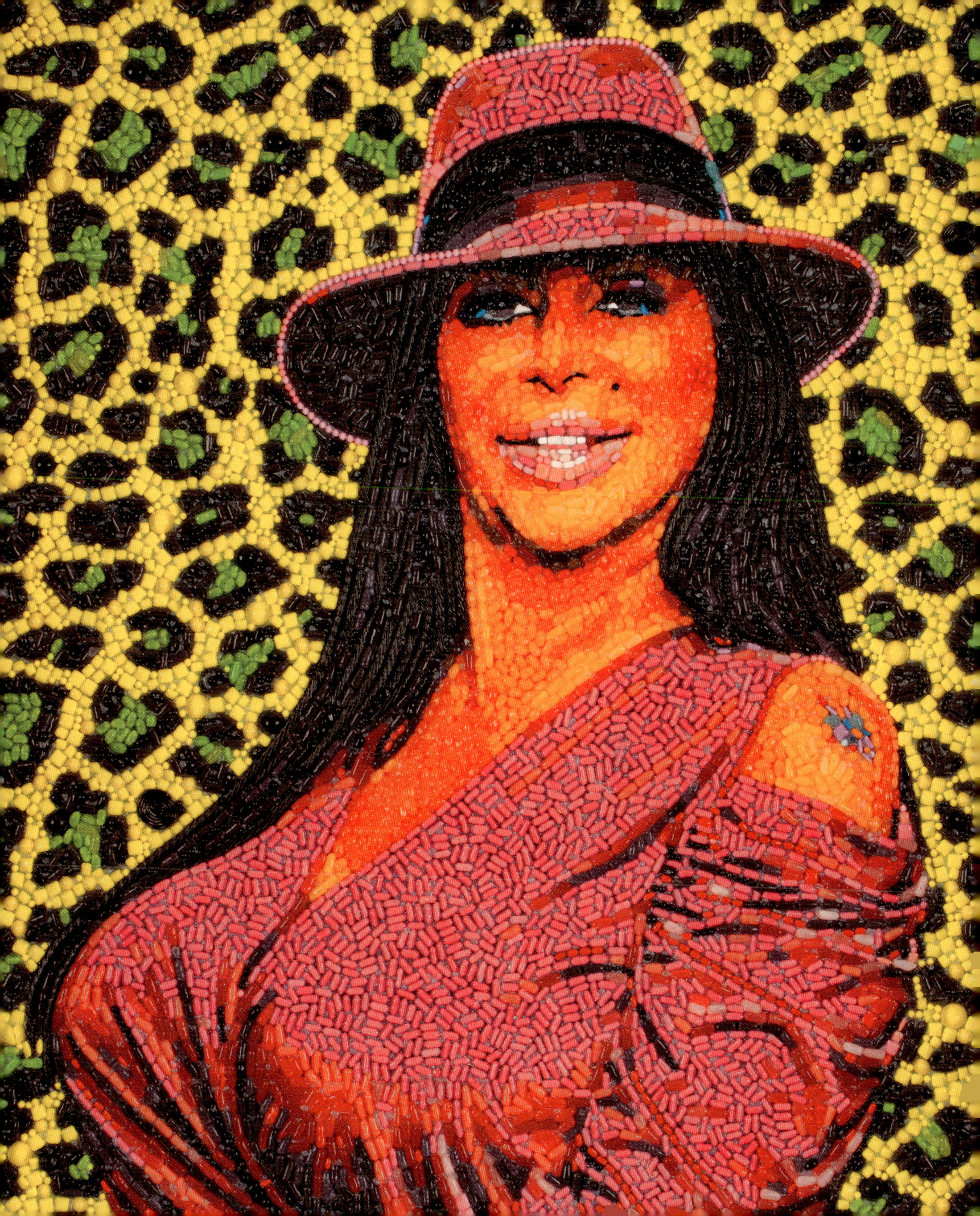

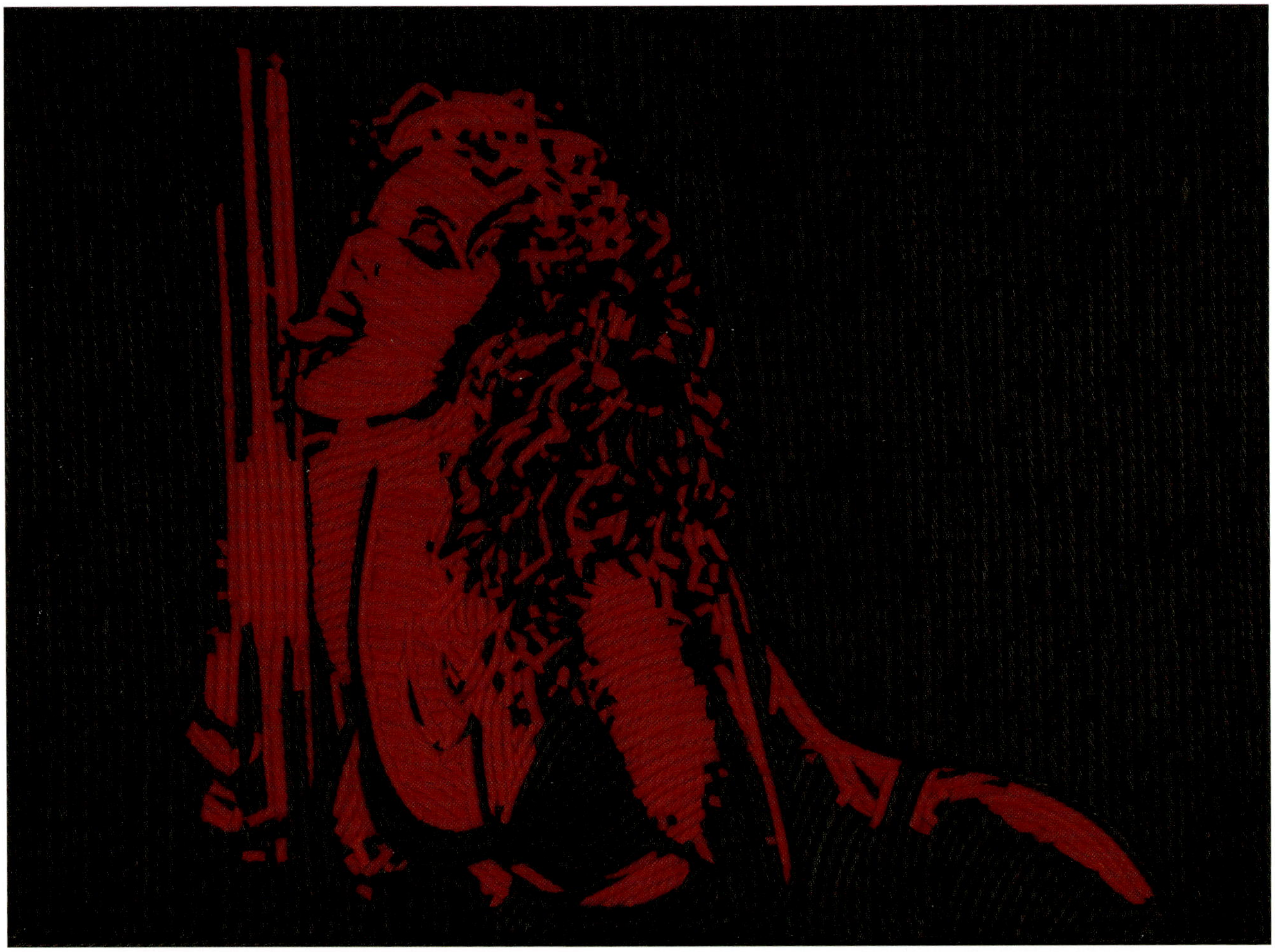

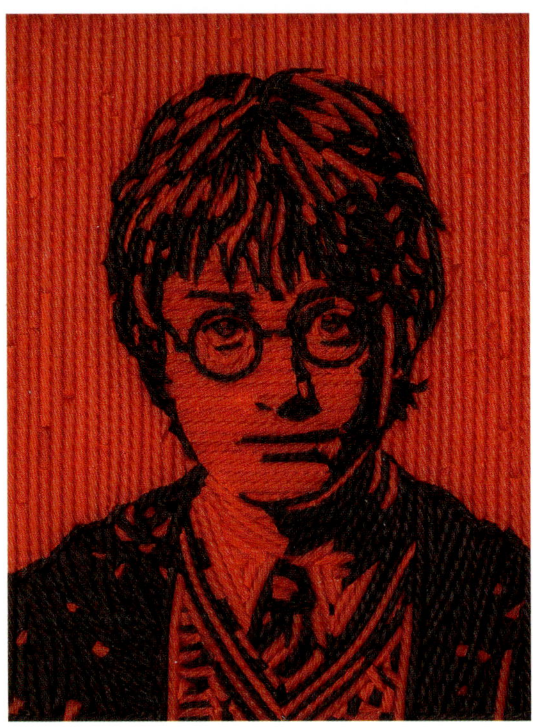

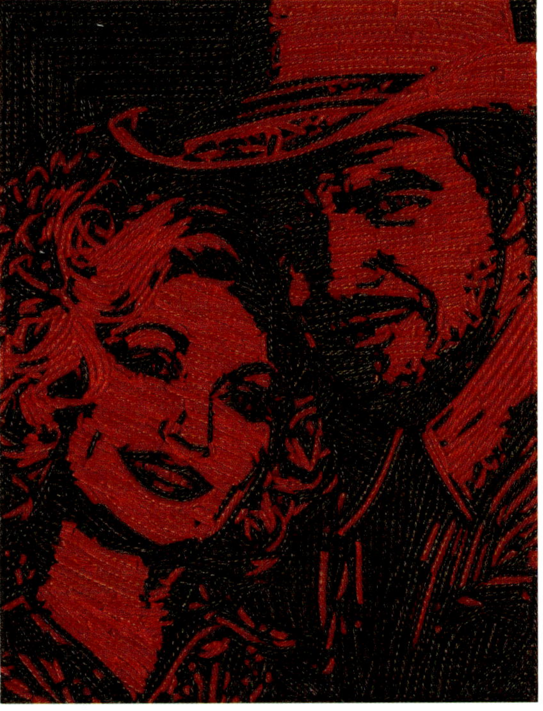

TOP: NOMI • Thirty pounds of Red Vines licorice, 2010

BOTTOM LEFT: HARRY POTTER • Fifteen pounds of Red Vines licorice, 2011

BOTTOM RIGHT: DOLLY AND BURT • Thirty pounds of Red Vines licorice, 2013

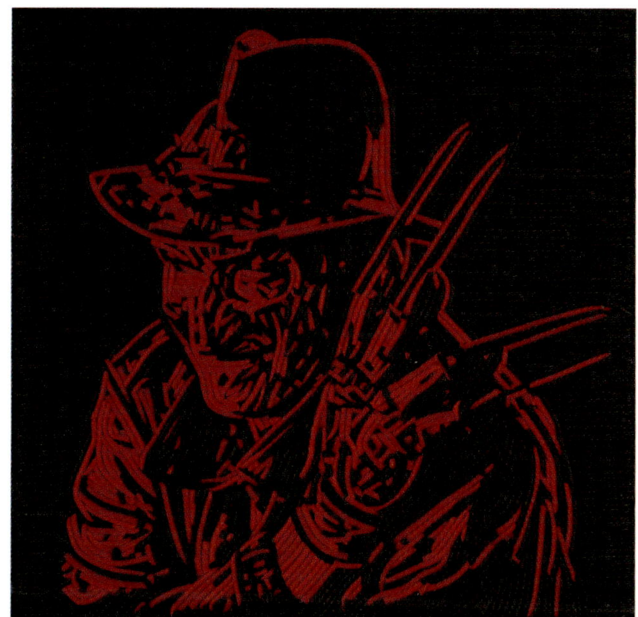

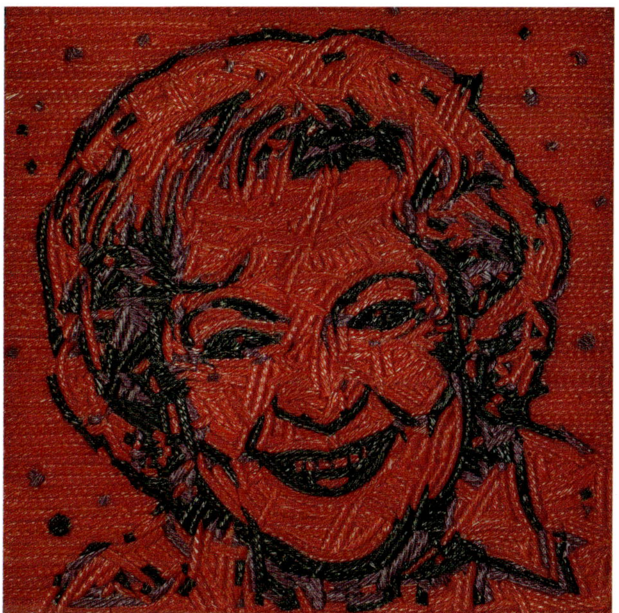

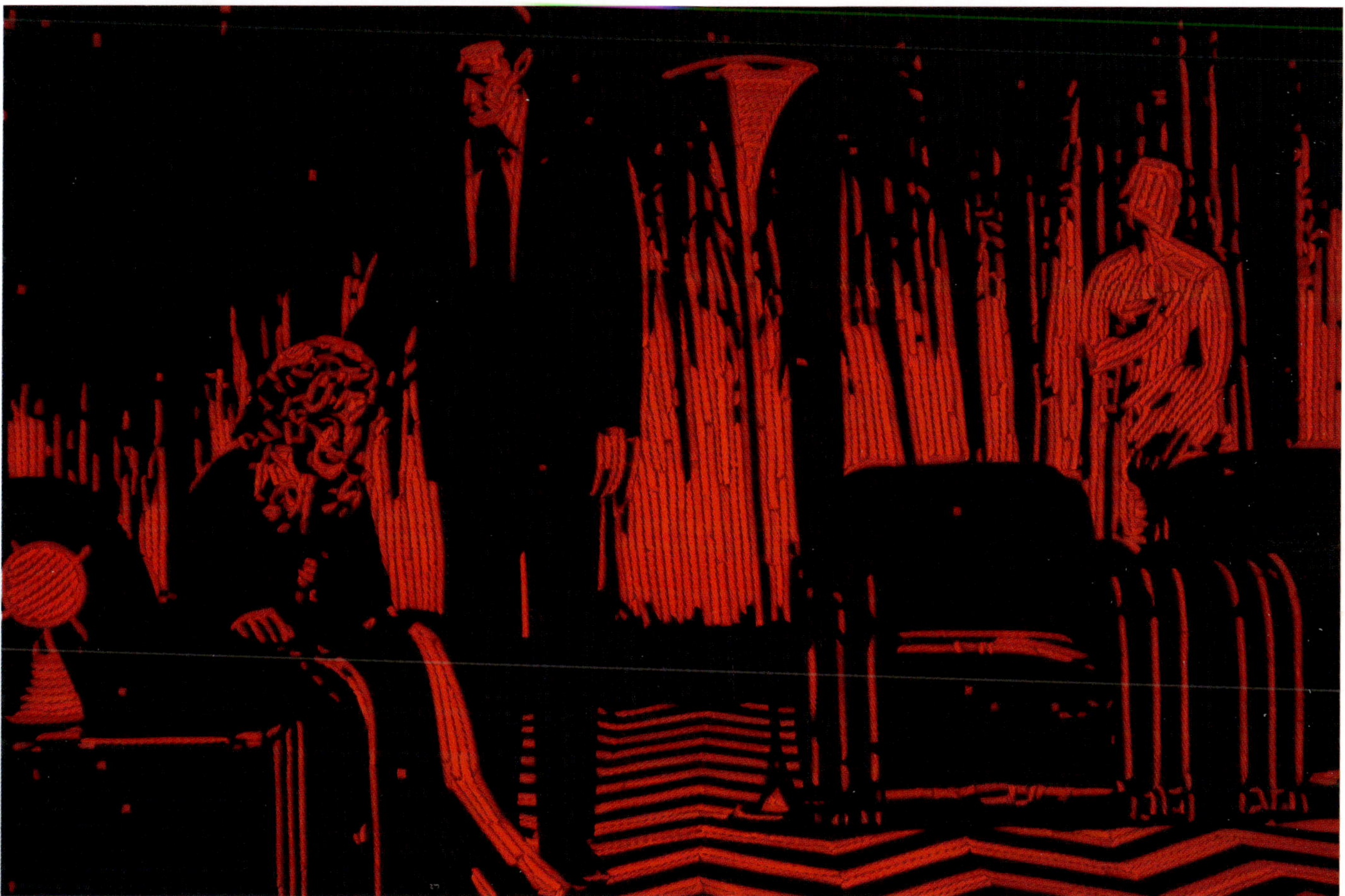

TOP LEFT: FREDDY KRUGER • Thirty pounds of Red Vines licorice, 2010

TOP RIGHT: BETTY WHITE • Thirty pounds of Red Vines licorice, 2016
Red Vines commissioned me to do this portrait of Betty for her 90th birthday. Rumor has it that on the sets of TV shows she only eats Red Vines and hot dogs.

BOTTOM: TWIN PEAKS • Fifty pounds of Red Vines licorice, 2011

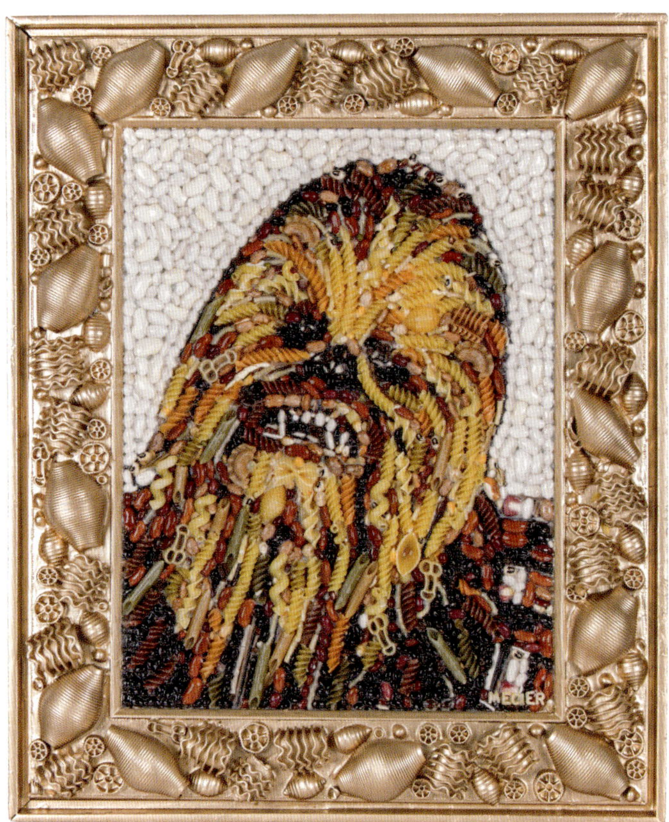

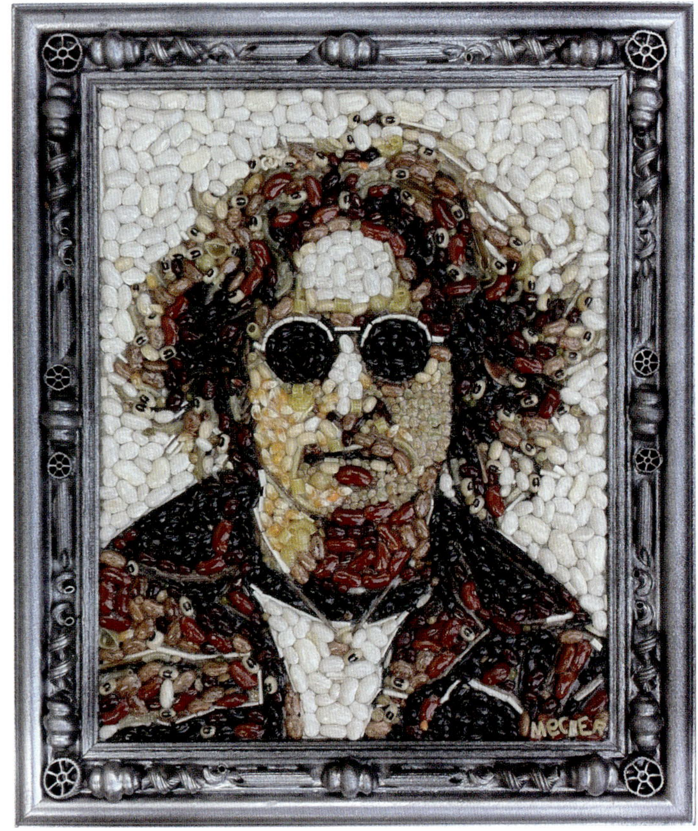

LEFT: CHEWBACCA • Beans and noodles, 2017

RIGHT: JOHN LENNON • Beans and noodles, 2018

OPPOSITE: JAMES BROWN • Beans and noodles, 2017

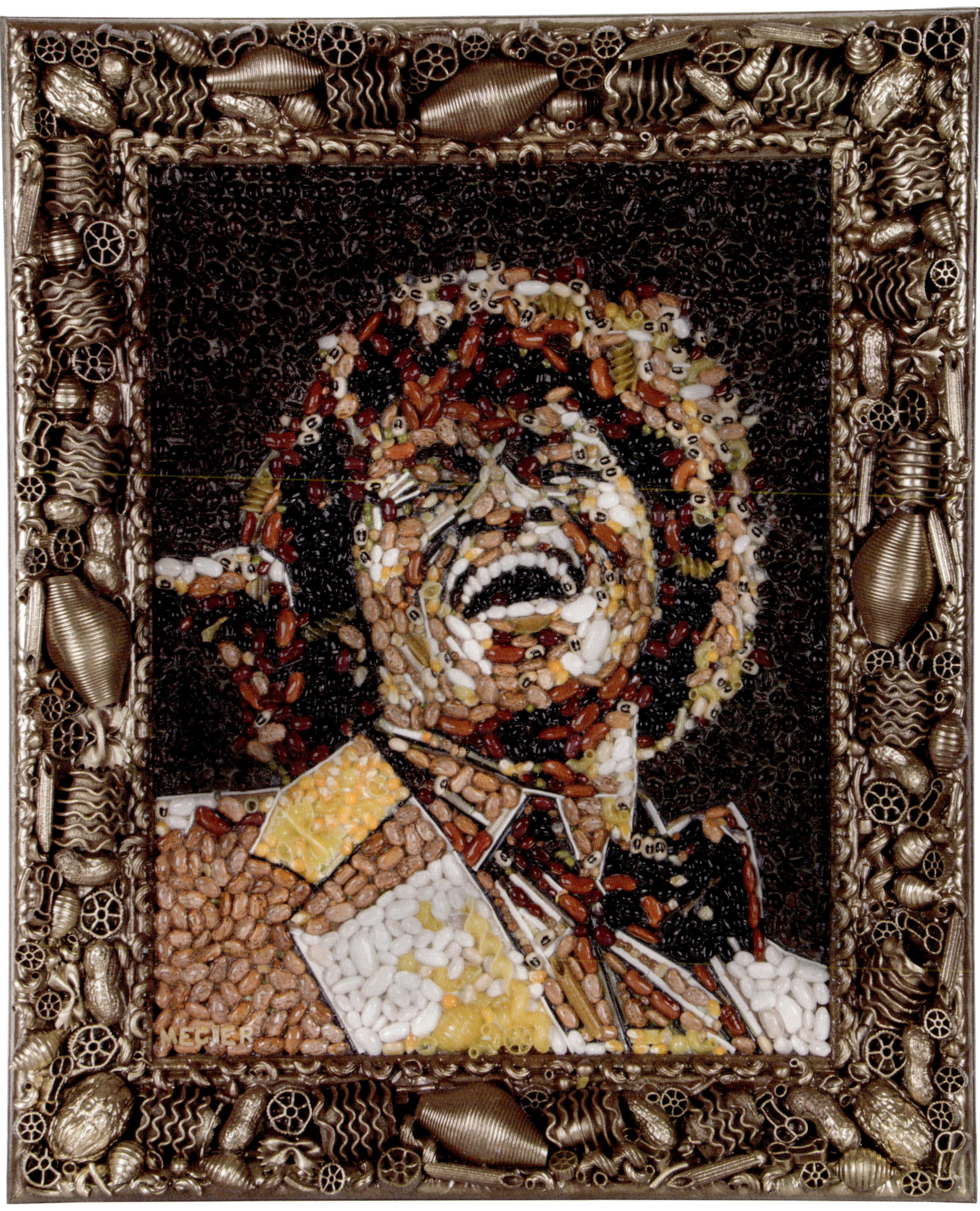
MECIER

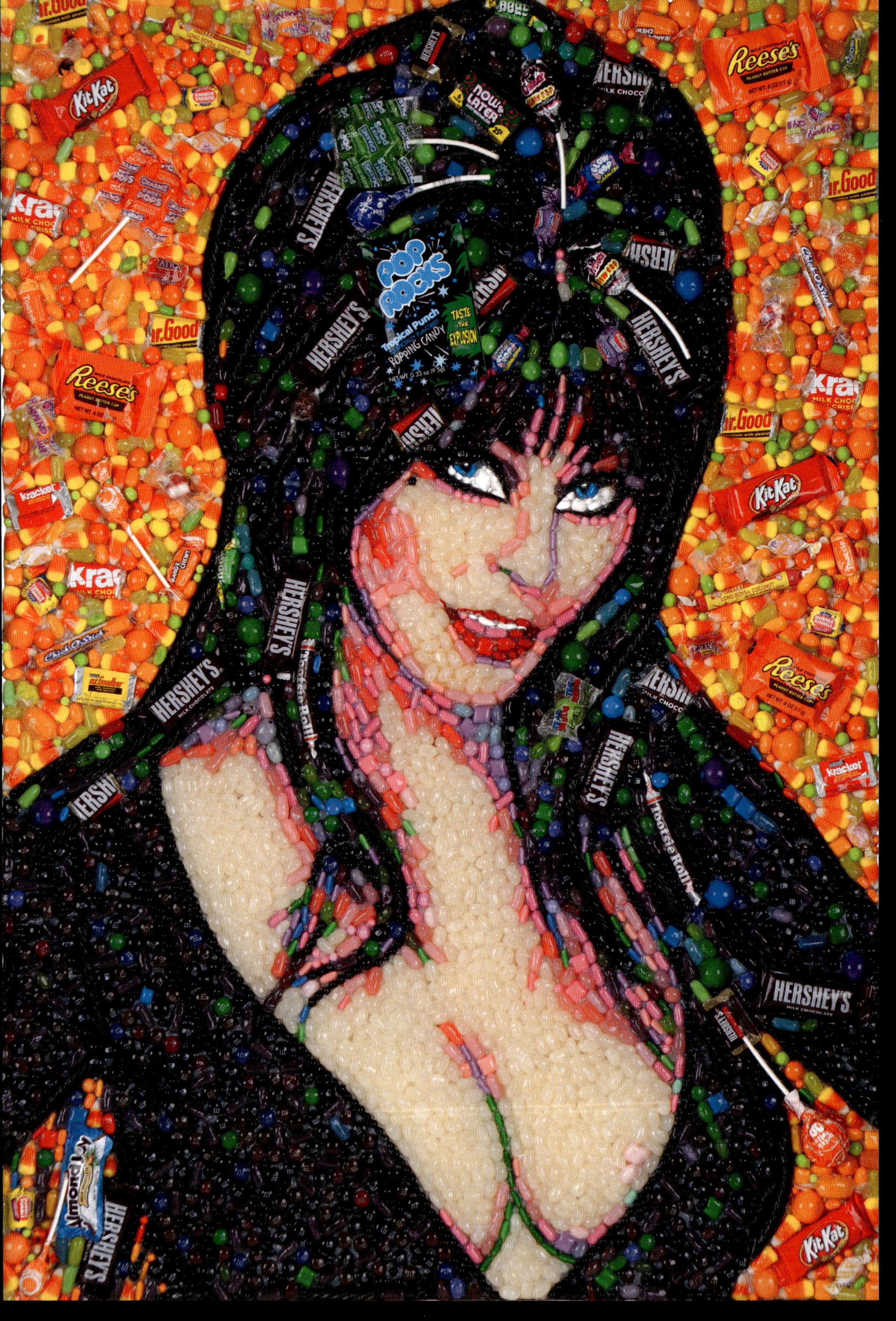

QUEEN OF HALLOWEEN (ELVIRA) • Halloween candy, 2015

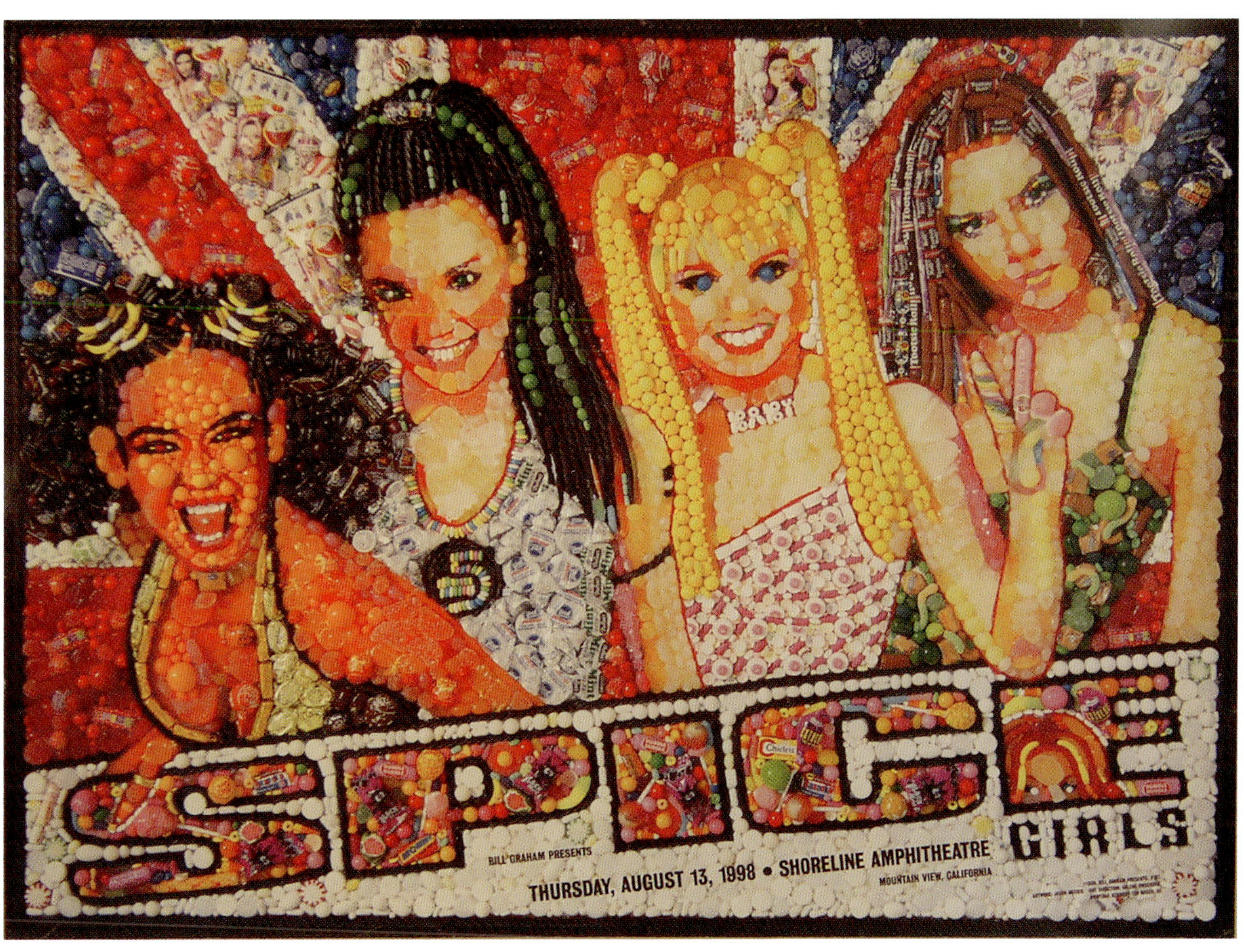

THE SPICE GIRLS • Various candies, 1998
Tour Poster. This was one of my first candy pieces, and my first poster for the Shoreline Amphitheatre. Ginger Spice quit just as I was commissioned to do the work, so I cut her out and snuck her face into the lettering. Collection of Scary Spice.

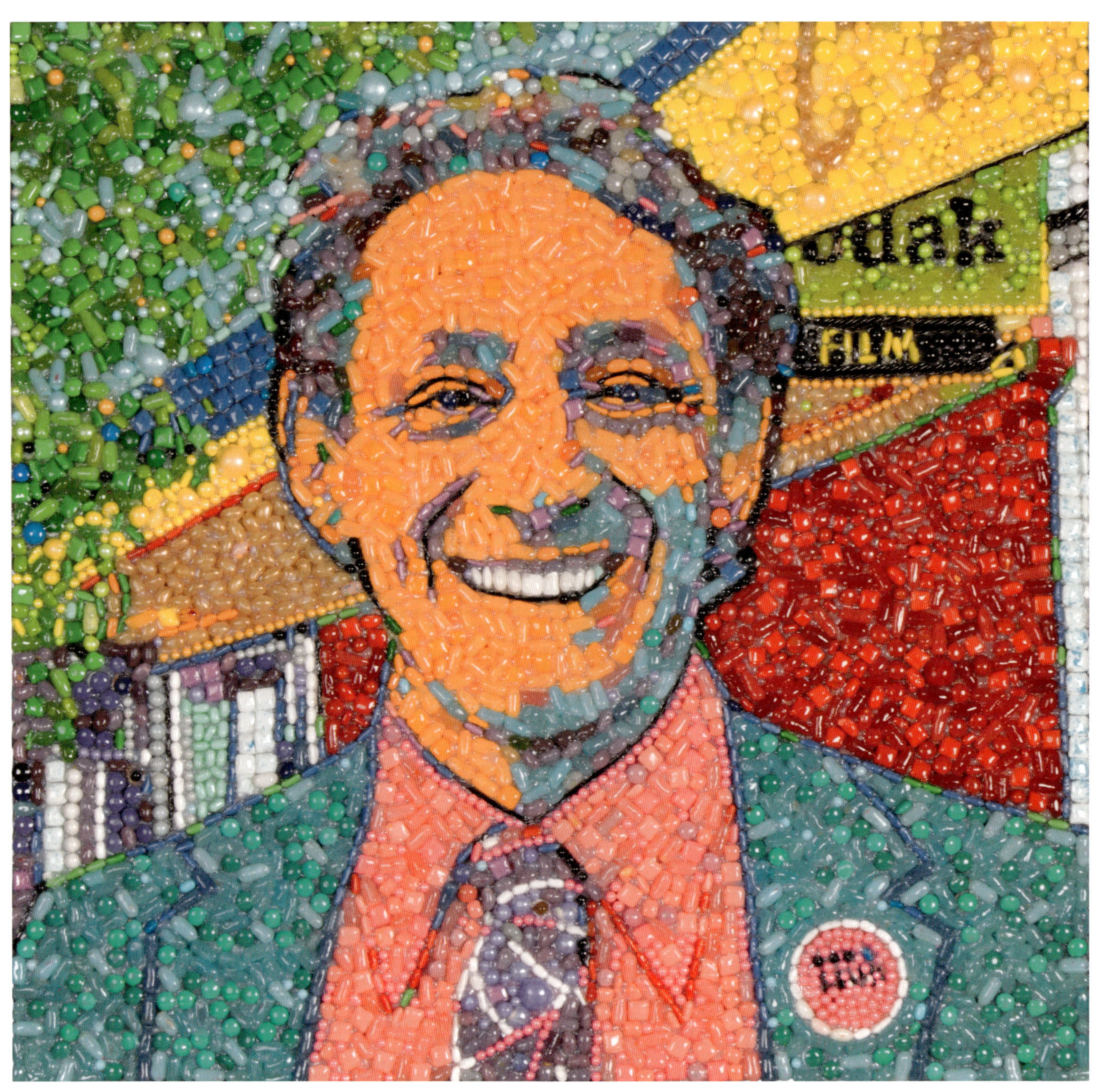

HARVEY MILK • Various candies, 2017

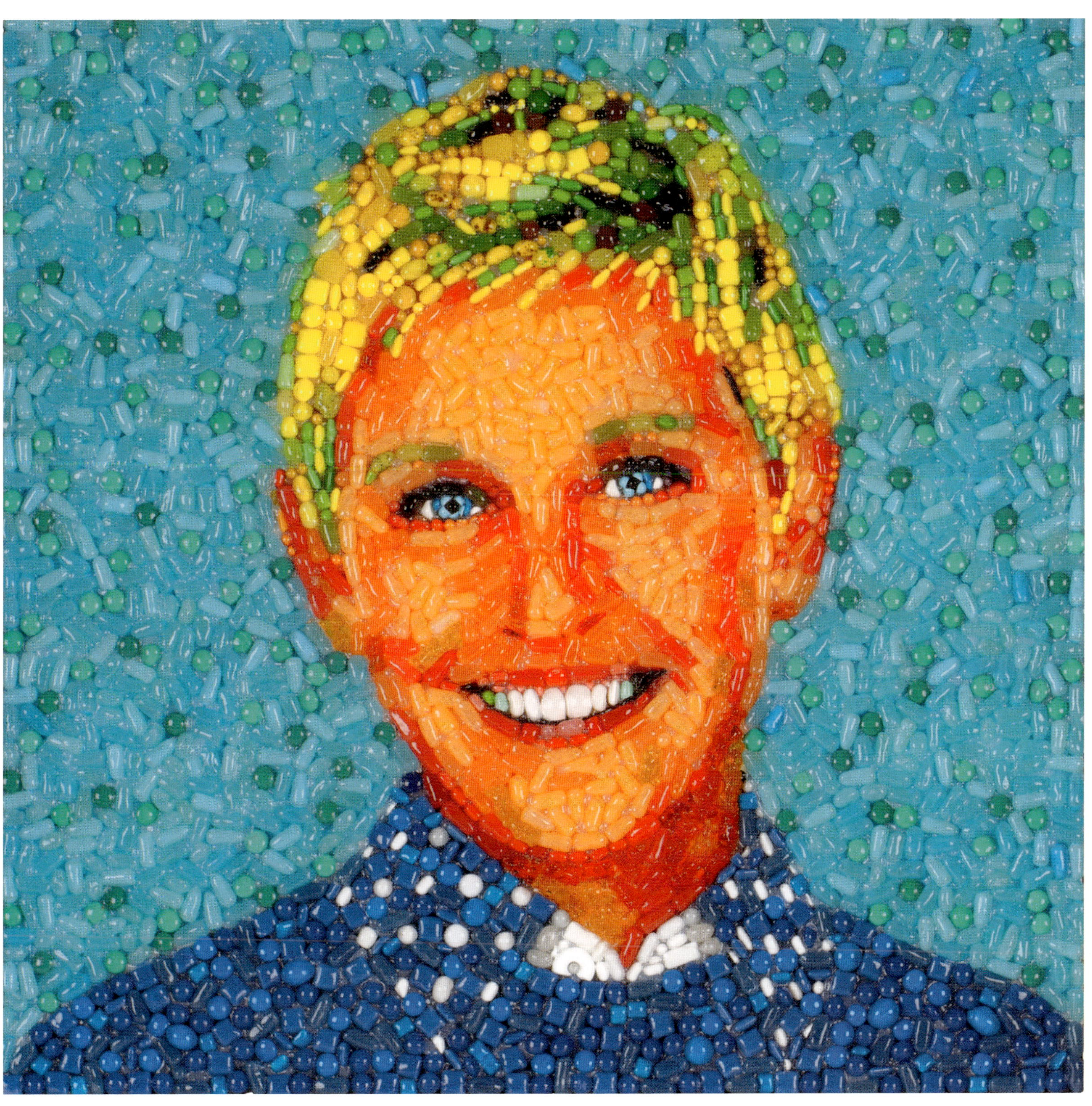

ELLEN DEGENERES • Various candies, 2015
Commissioned by Target for Ellen's birthday.

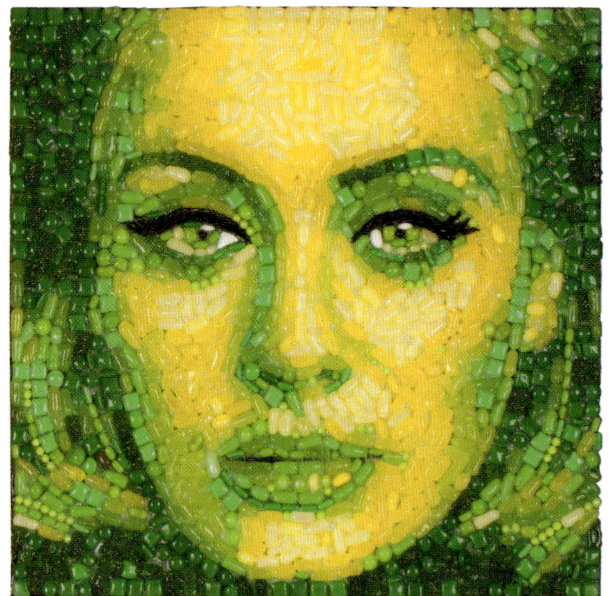

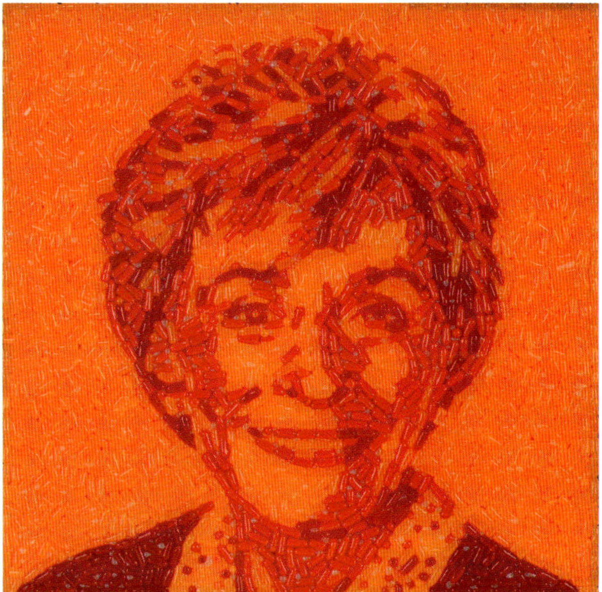

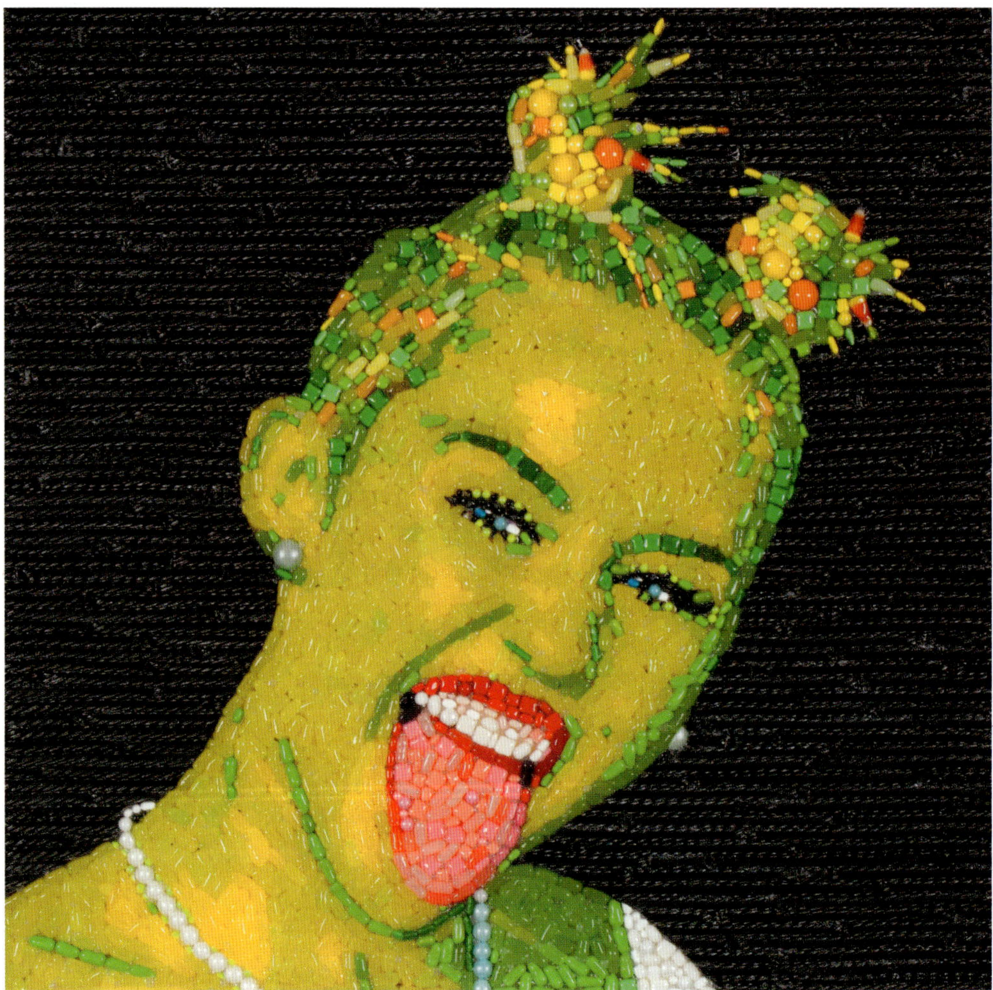

TOP LEFT: ADELE • Various candies, 2016
Adele's favorite color is green.

TOP RIGHT: JUDGE JUDY • Twenty-five hundred Hot Tamales candies, 2014

BOTTOM: MILEY CYRUS • Various candies, 2014
The background is made of ten pounds of black licorice.

OPPOSITE: KELLY OSBOURNE • Various candies, 2014

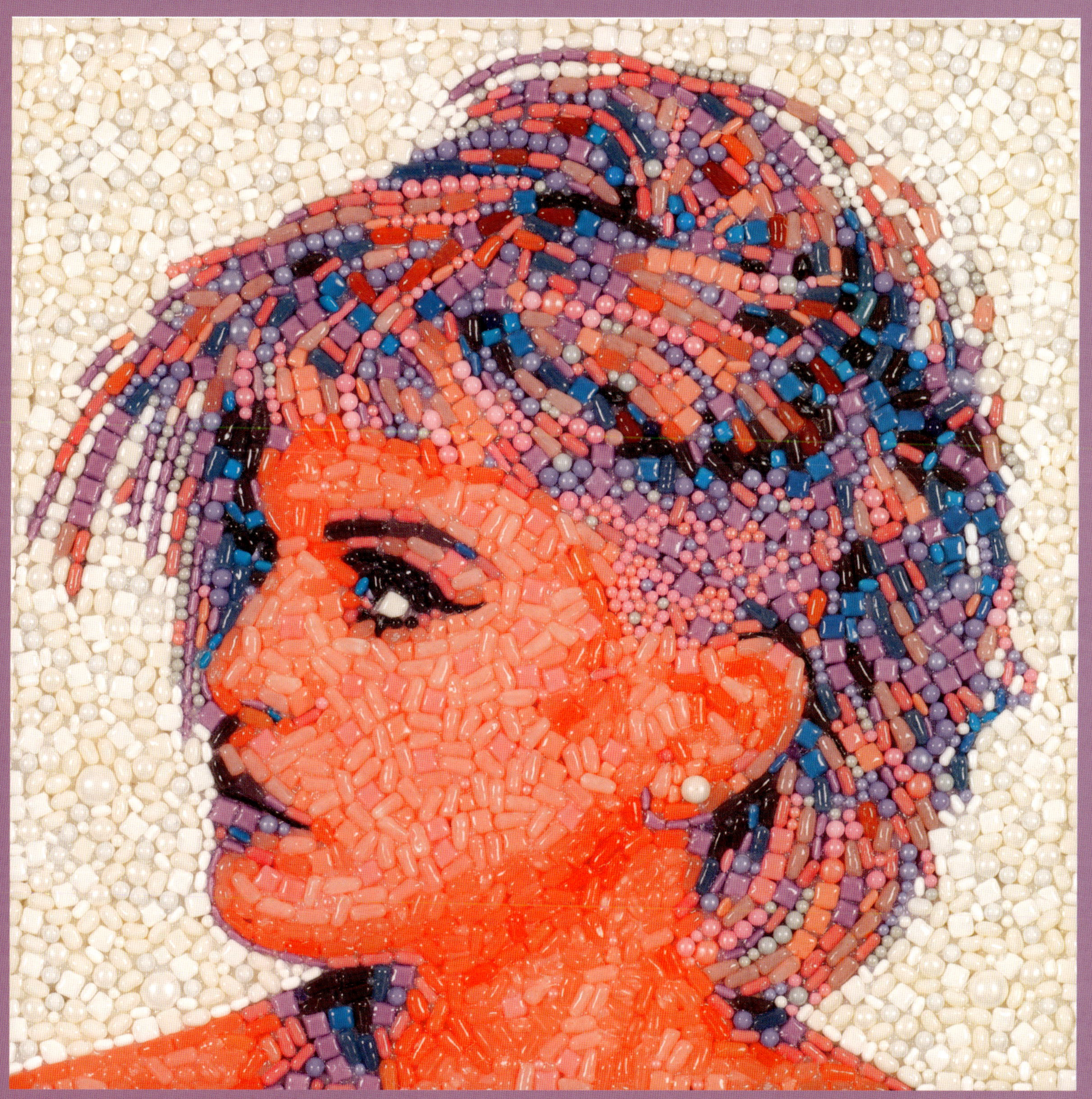

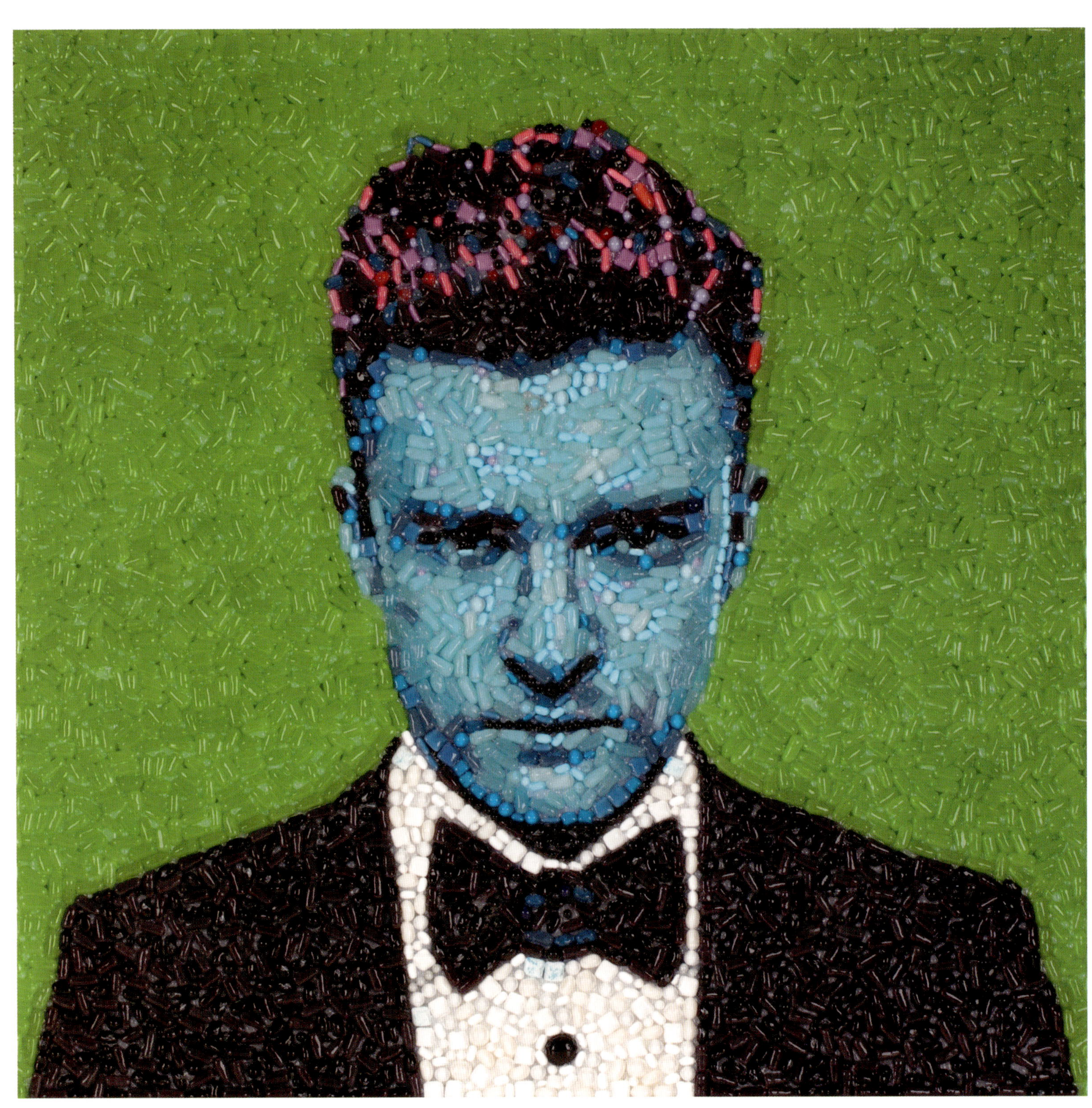

JUSTIN TIMBERLAKE • Various candies, 2014

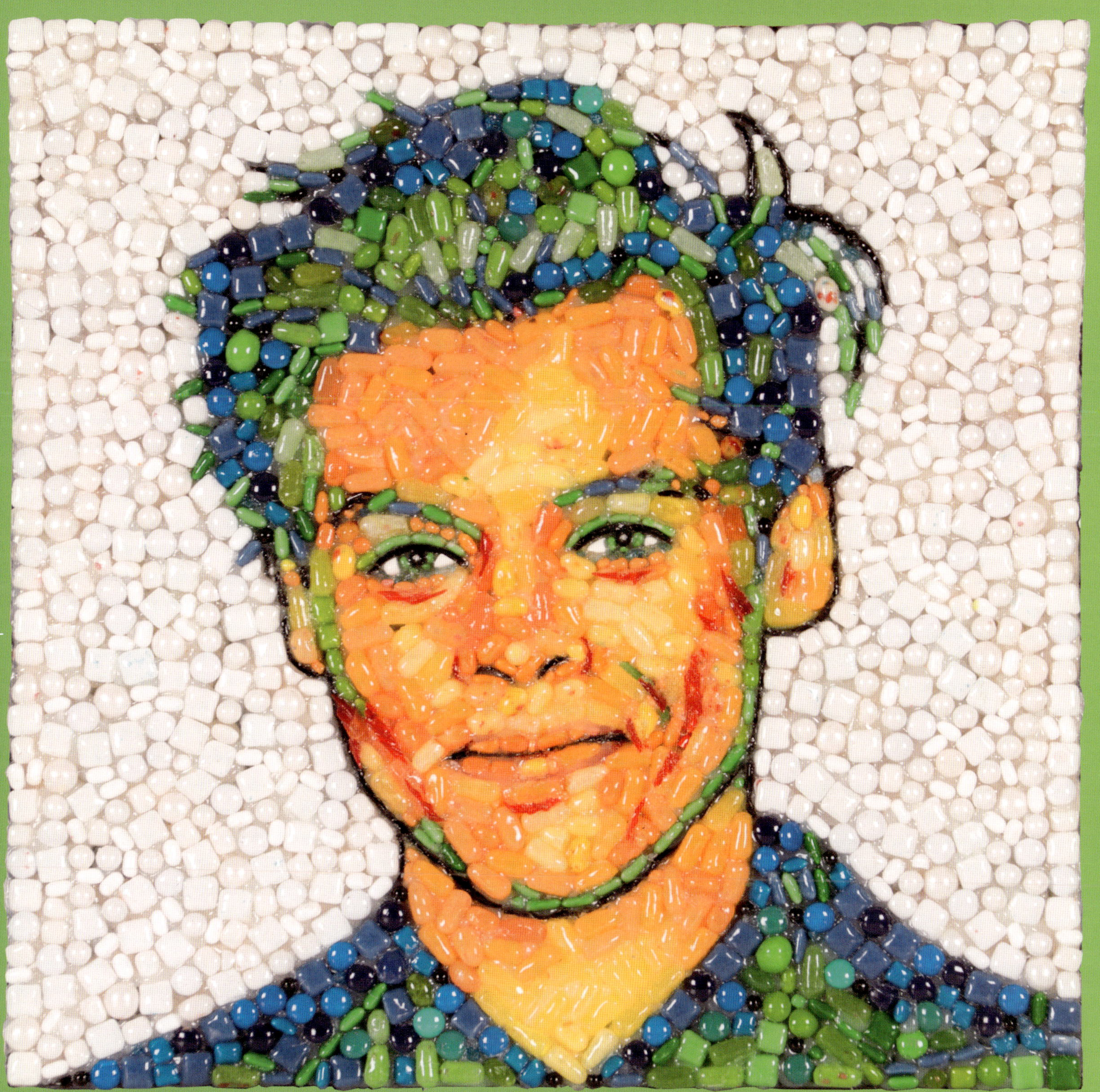

HARRY STYLES • Various candies, 2018

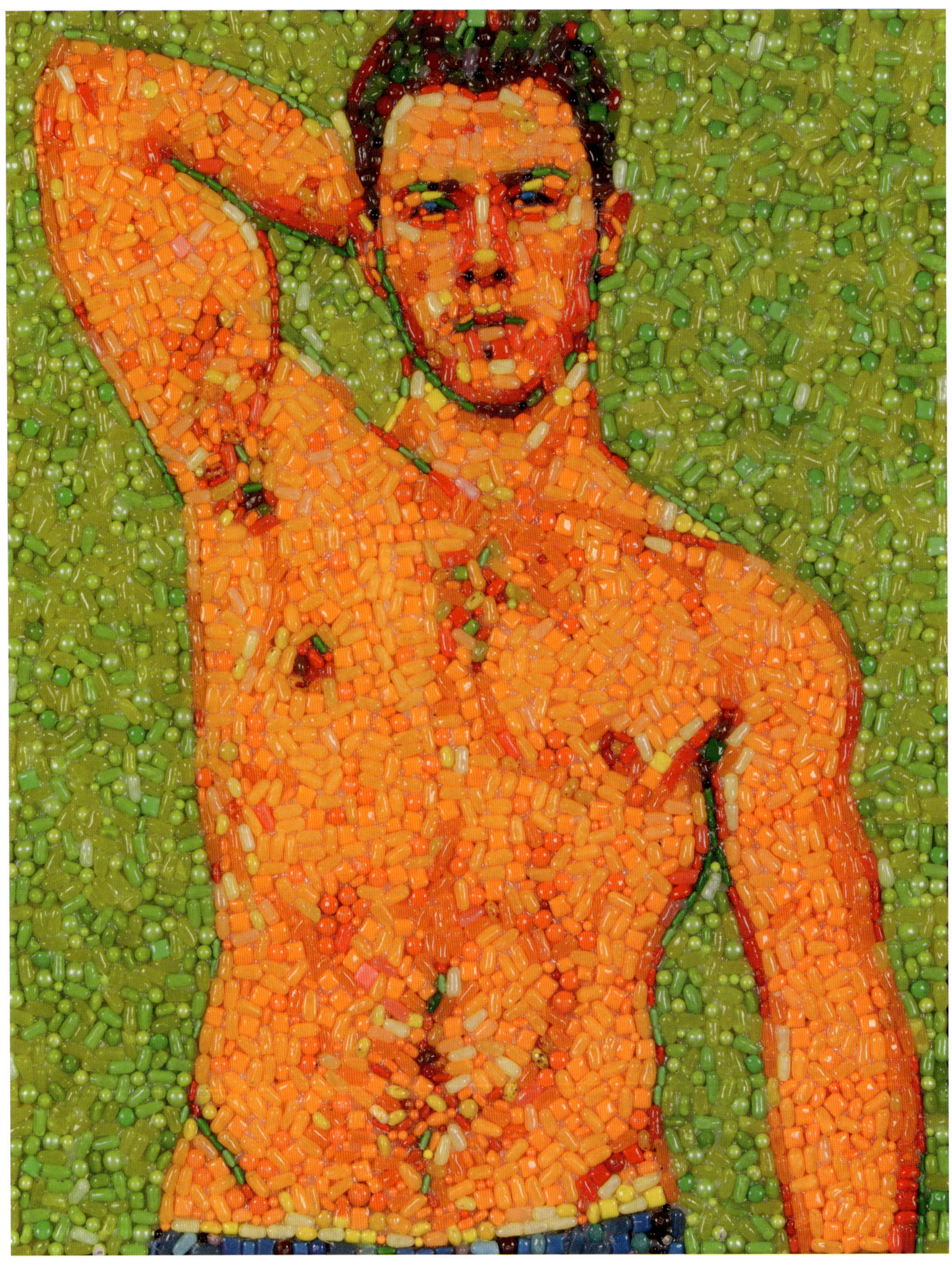

NICK JONAS • Various candies, 2016

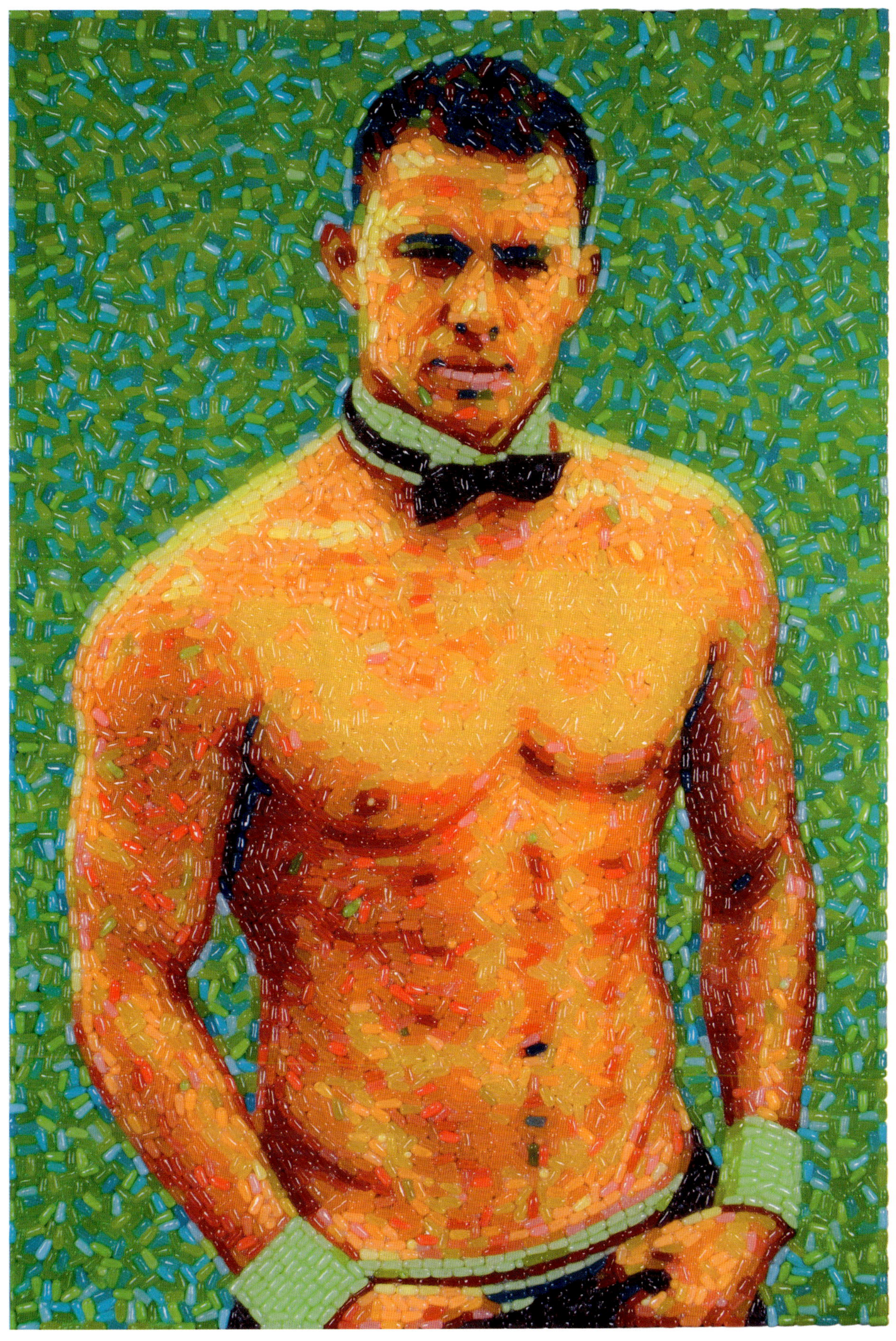

MAGIC MIKE • Five thousand Mike and Ike candies, 2013

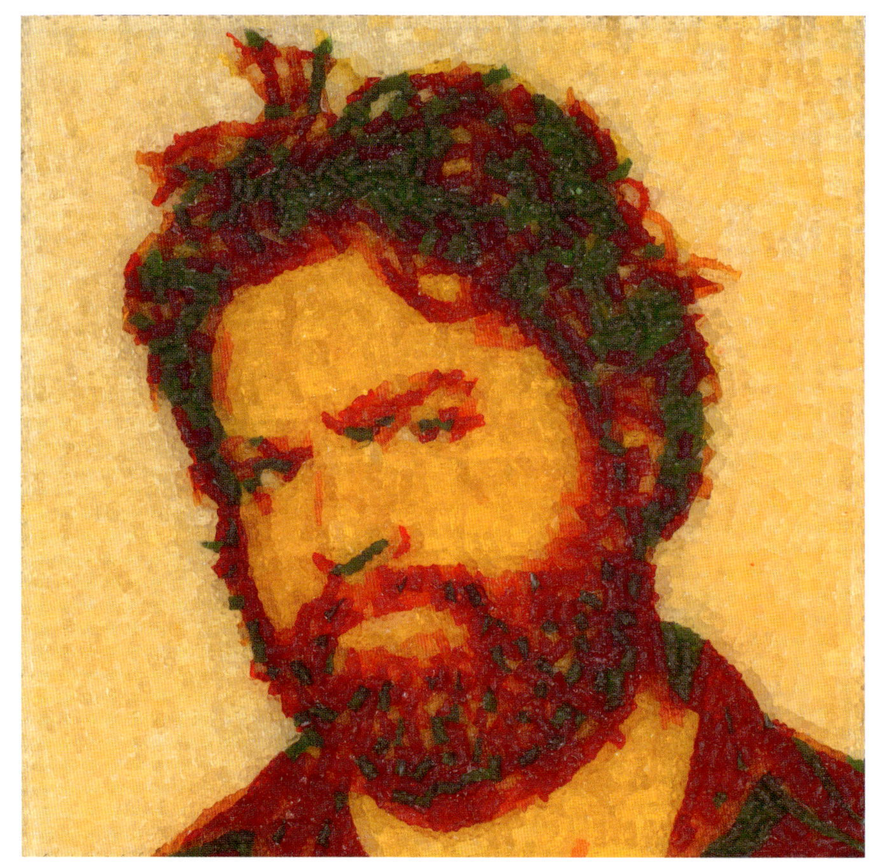

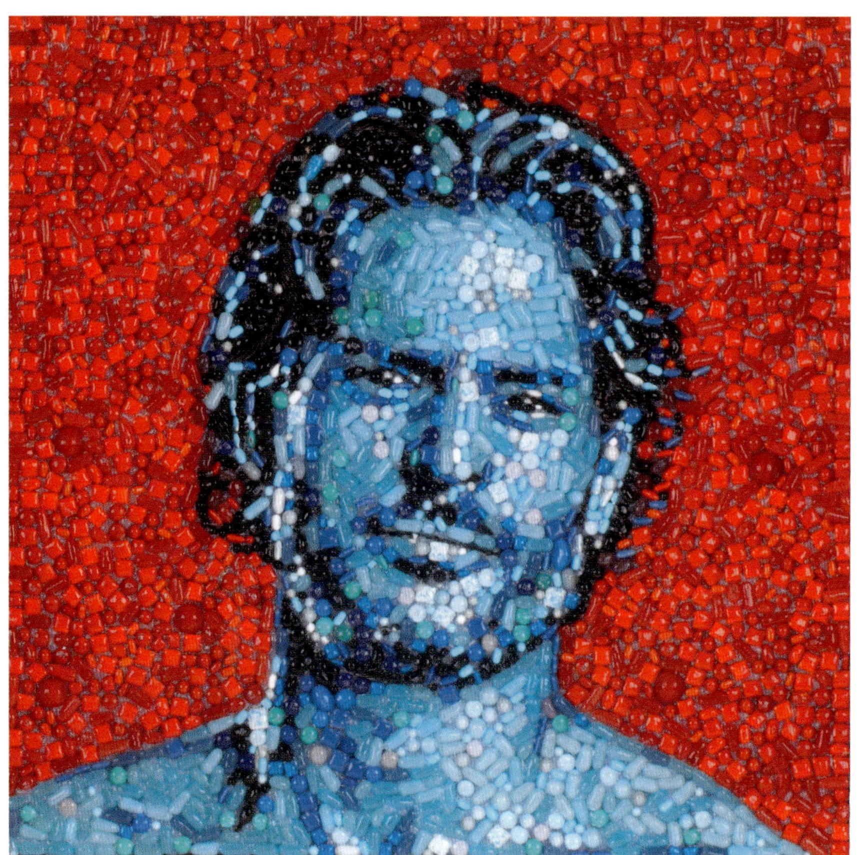

TOP: ZACH GALIFIANAKIS • Three thousand gummy bears, 2014

BOTTOM: JOE MANGANIELLO • Various candies, 2015

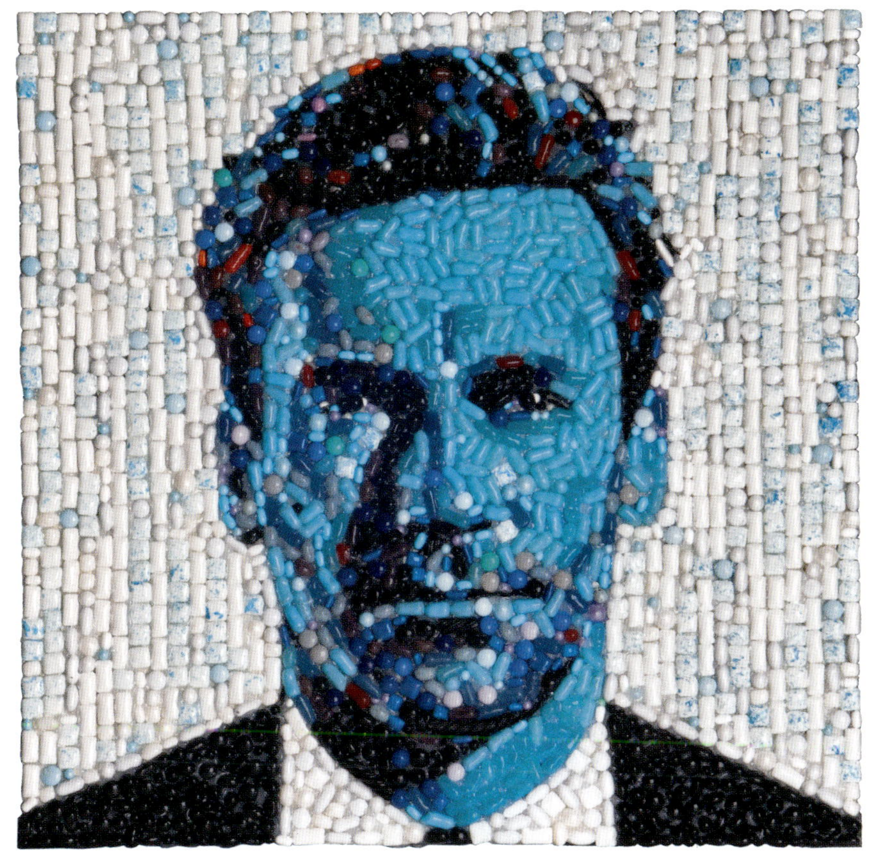

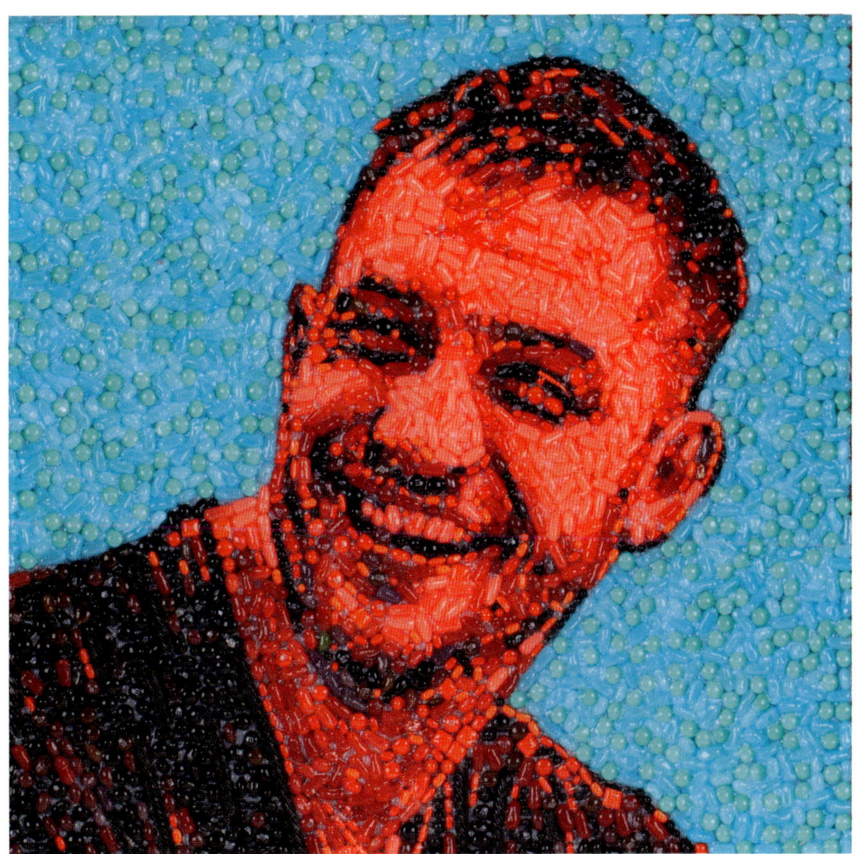

TOP: JON HAMM • Various candies, 2015

BOTTOM: TOM HARDY • Various candies, 2015

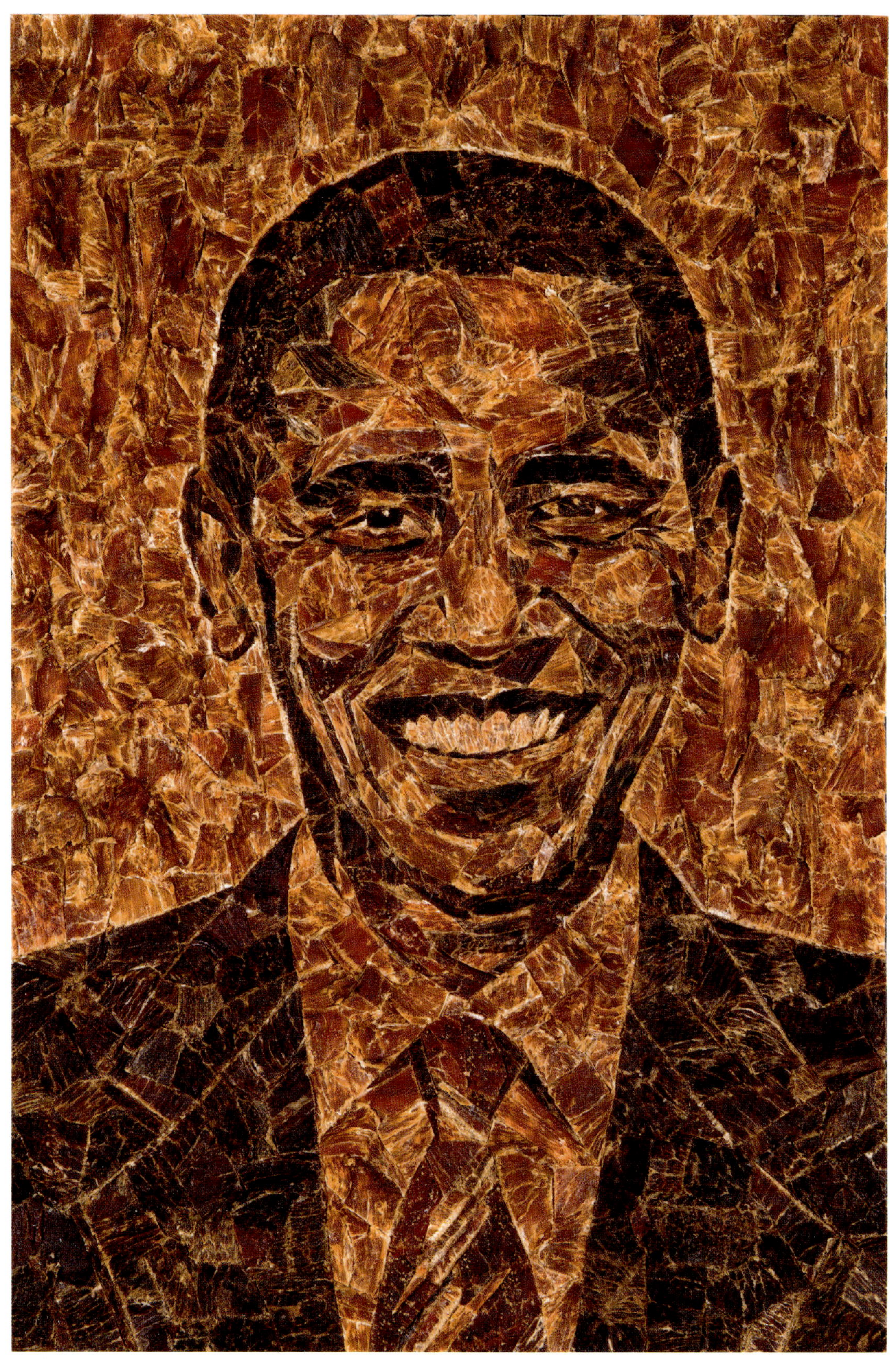

BARACK OBAMEAT • Twenty-five pounds of beef jerky, 2012
Jack Links Beef Jerky hired me to make Barack ObaMEAT and MEAT Romney during the 2012 U.S. presidential election cycle.

OPPOSITE: UDONATELLA VERSACE • Noodles, 2017

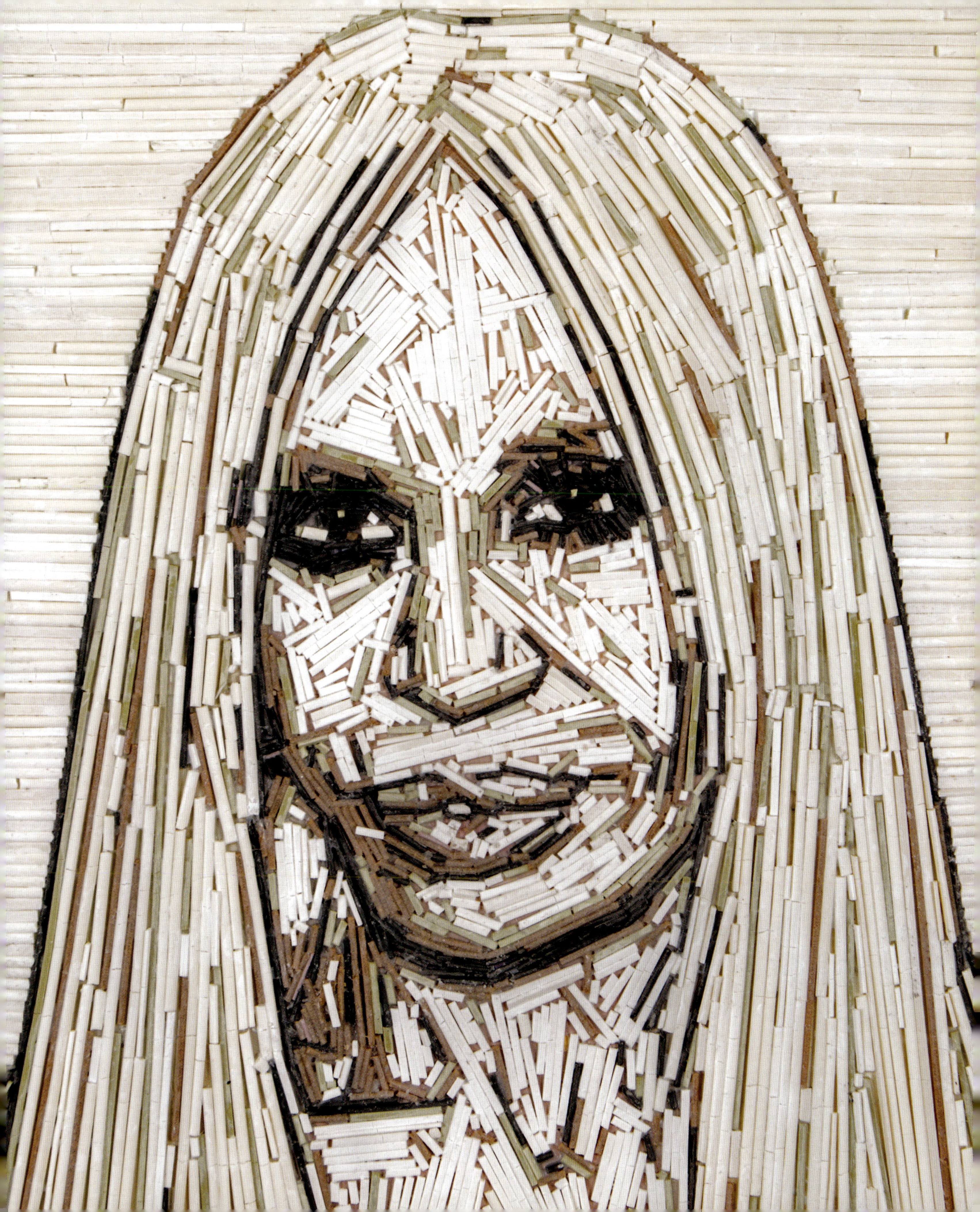

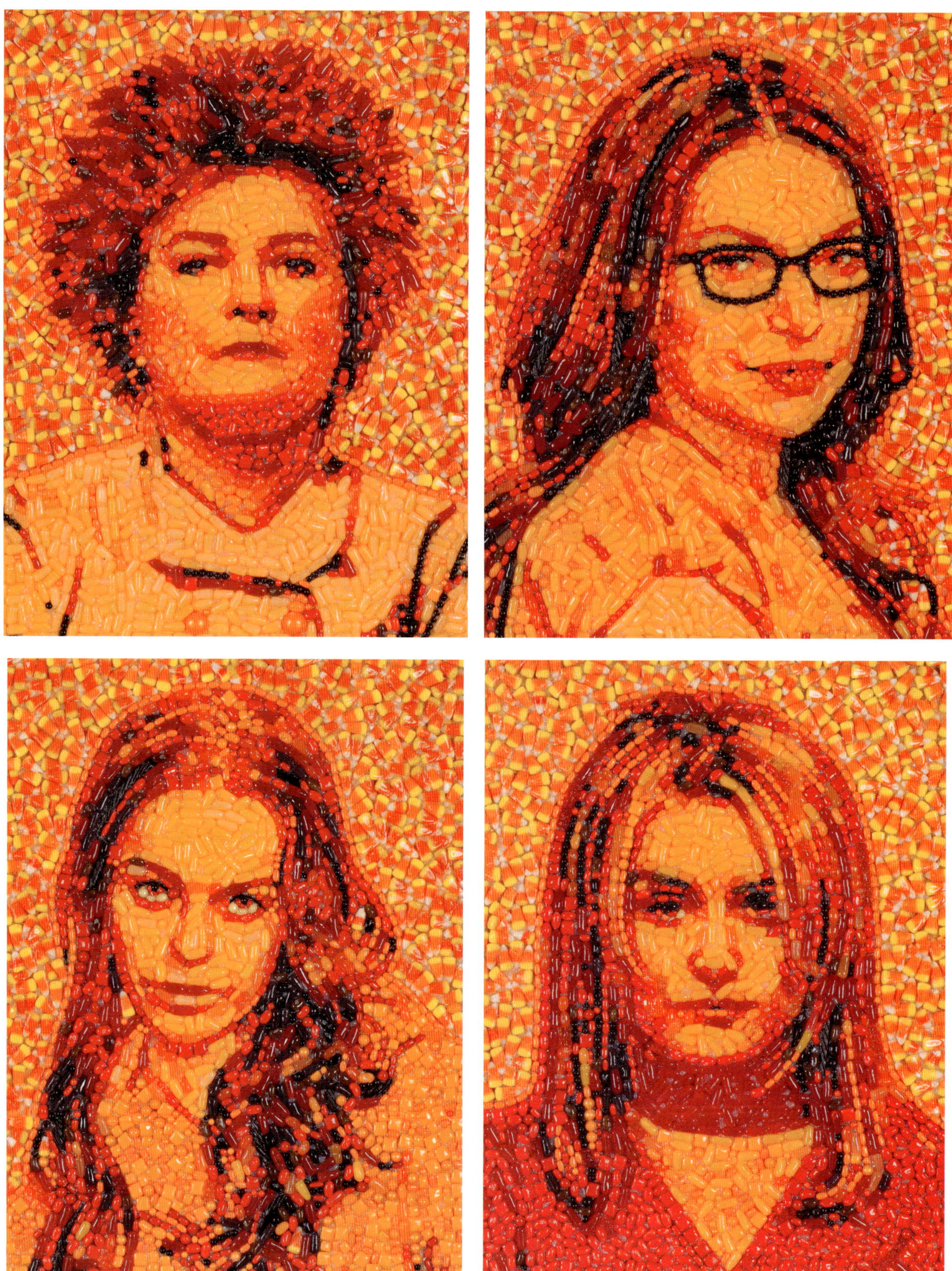

Orange Is the New Black series

TOP LEFT: RED • Orange and black candy, 2014

TOP RIGHT: ALEX • Orange and black candy, 2014

BOTTOM LEFT: PENNSATUCKY • Orange and black candy, 2014

BOTTOM RIGHT: PIPER • Orange and black candy, 2014

OPPOSITE: CRAZY EYES • Orange and black candy, 2014

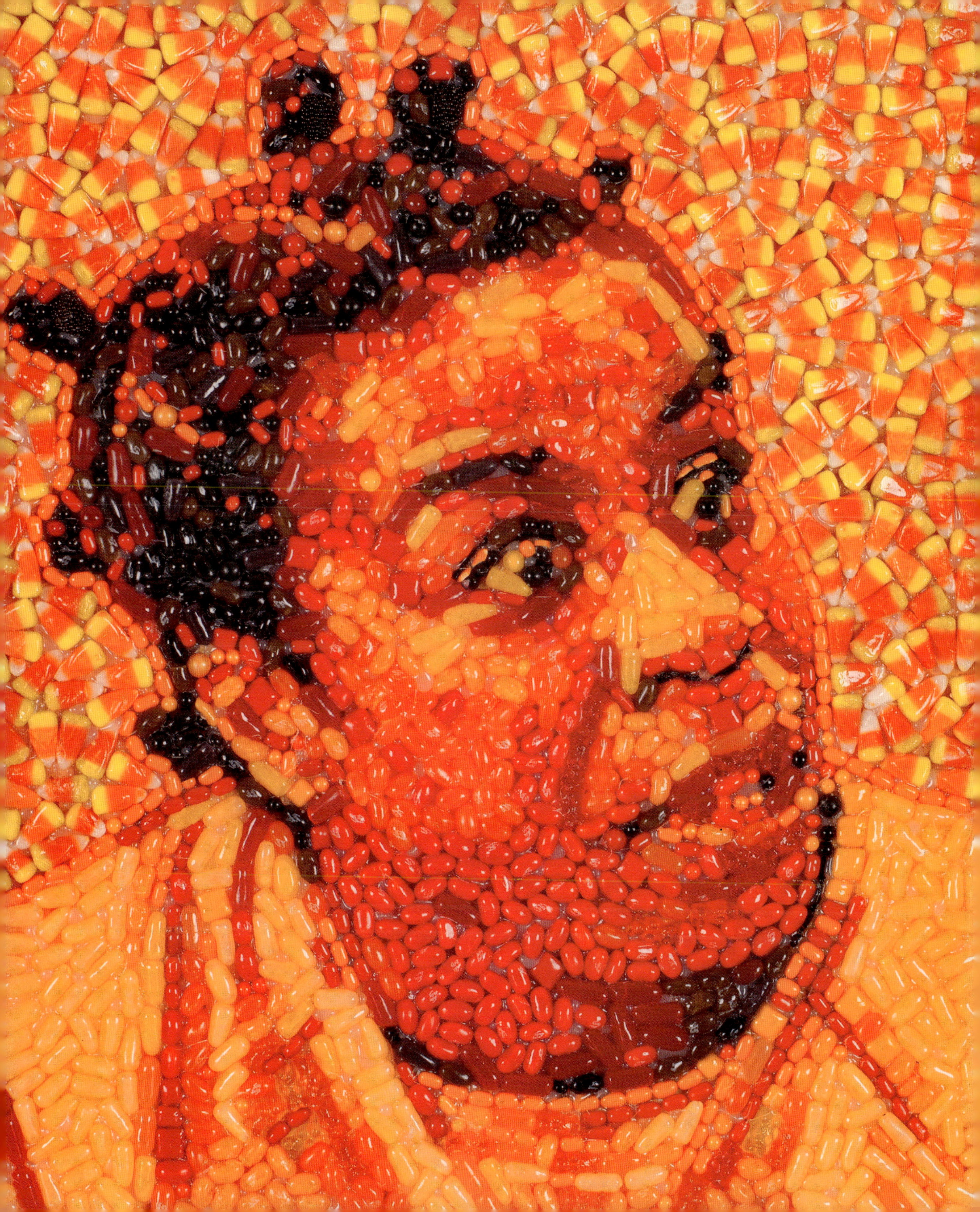

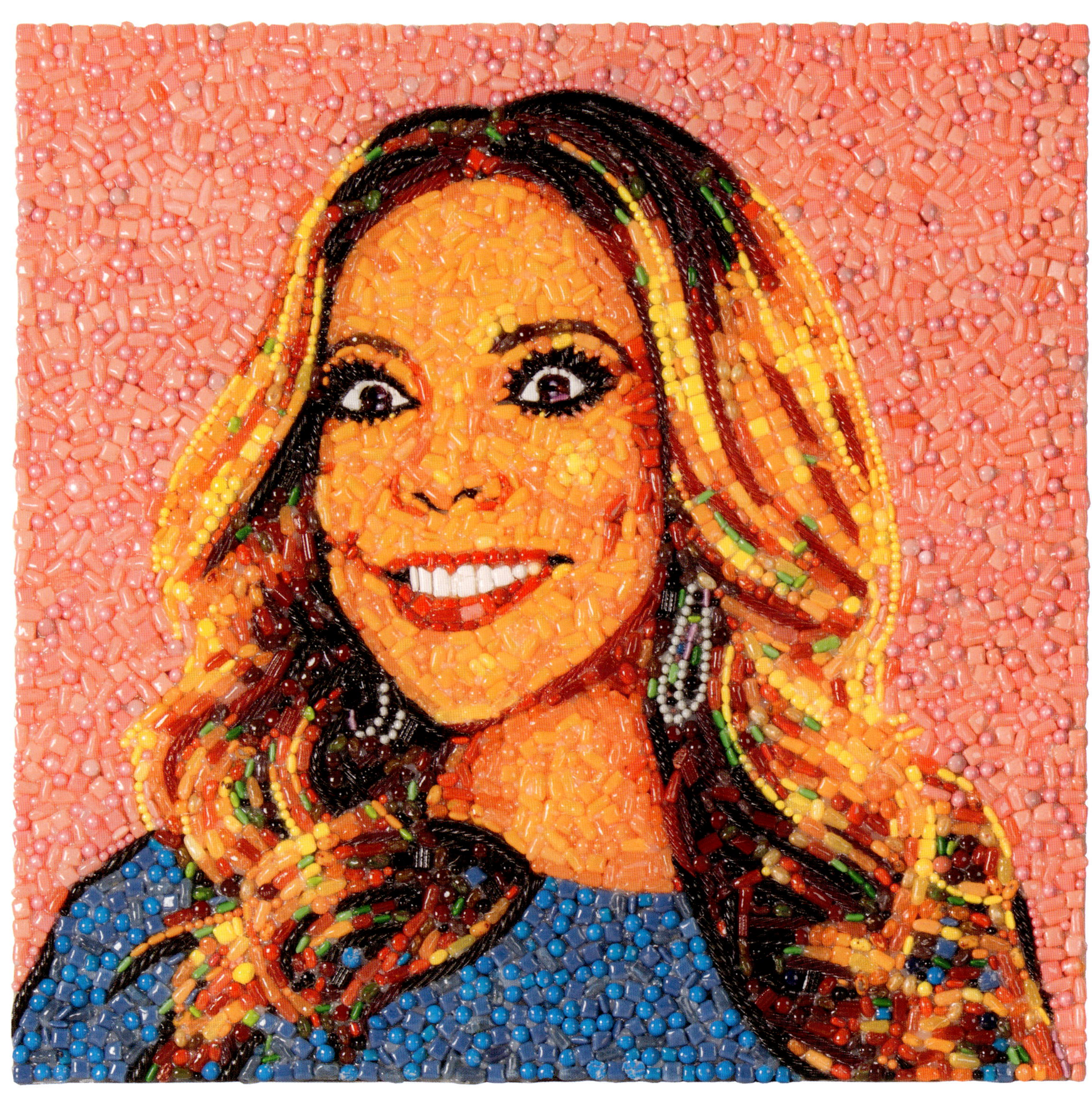

WENDY WILLIAMS • Various candies, 2017

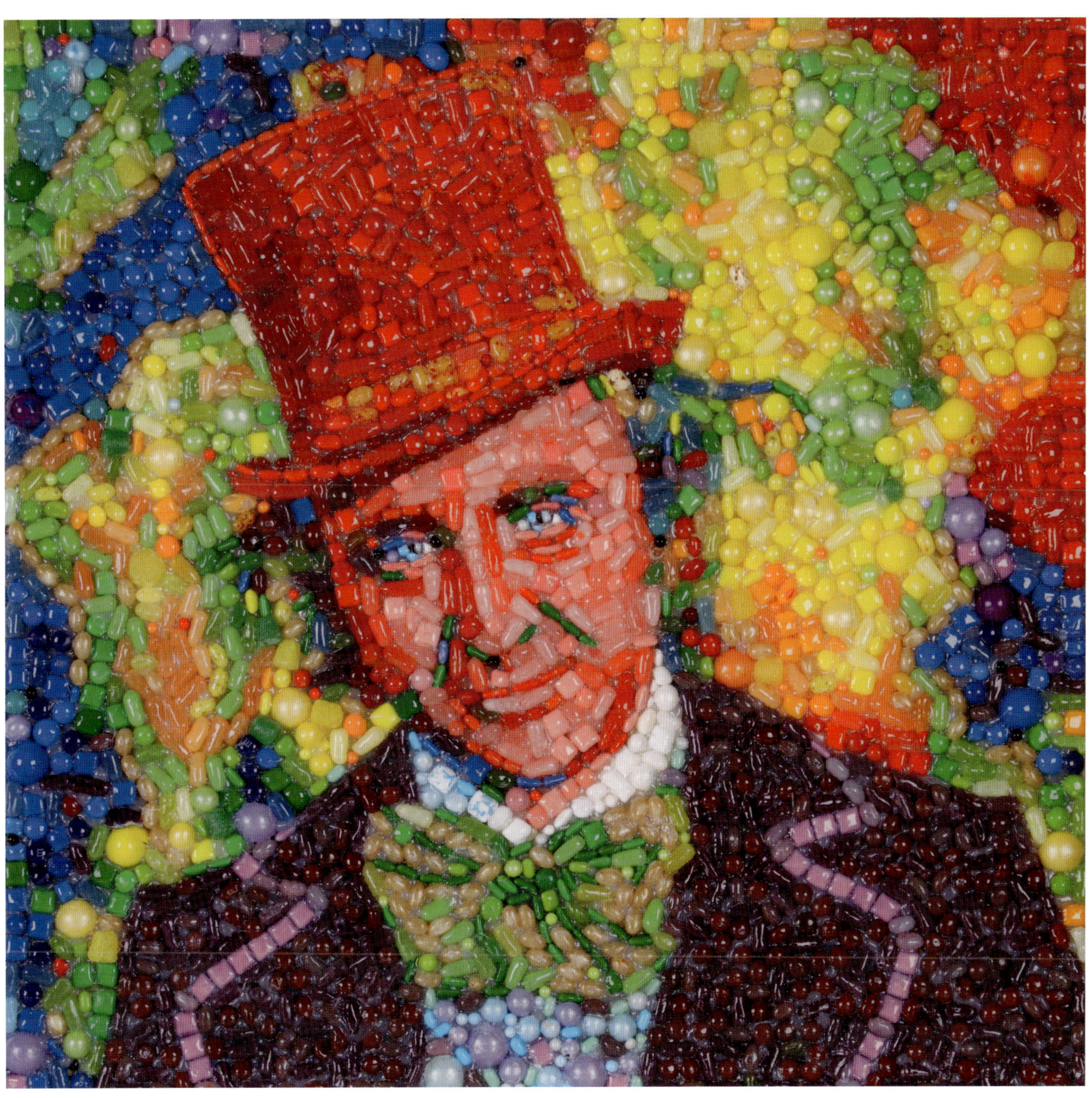

WILLY WONKA • Various candies, 2017

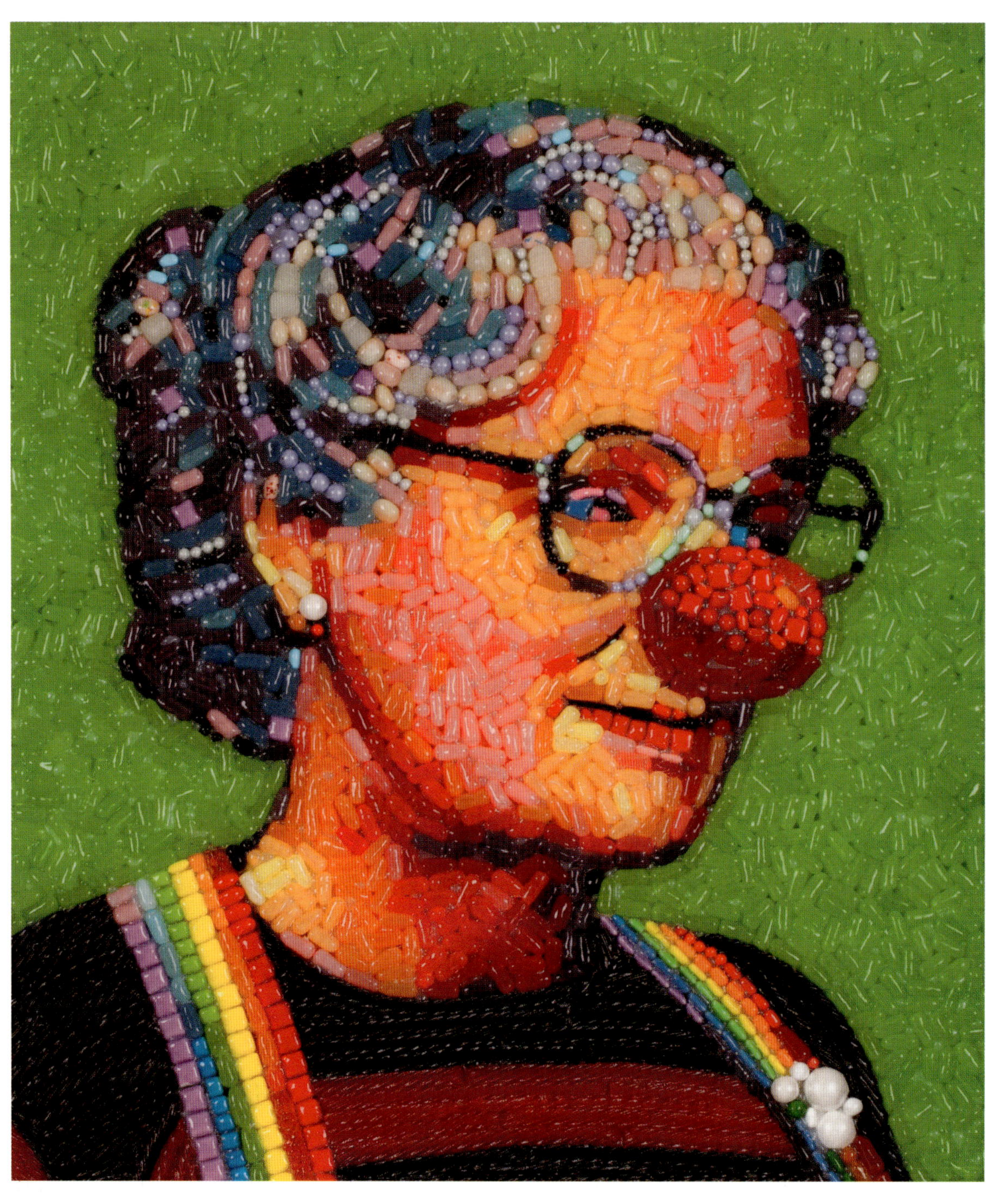

ROBIN WILLIAMS • Various candies, 2014
I made this as a tribute to Robin after he died, combining elements from his various roles: suspenders from *Mork & Mindy*, hair from *Mrs. Doubtfire*, nose from *Patch Adams*, green background from *Flubber*.

OPPOSITE: JERRY SEINFELD • Various breakfast cereals, 2000
The characters' names are spelled out in the alphabet cereal.

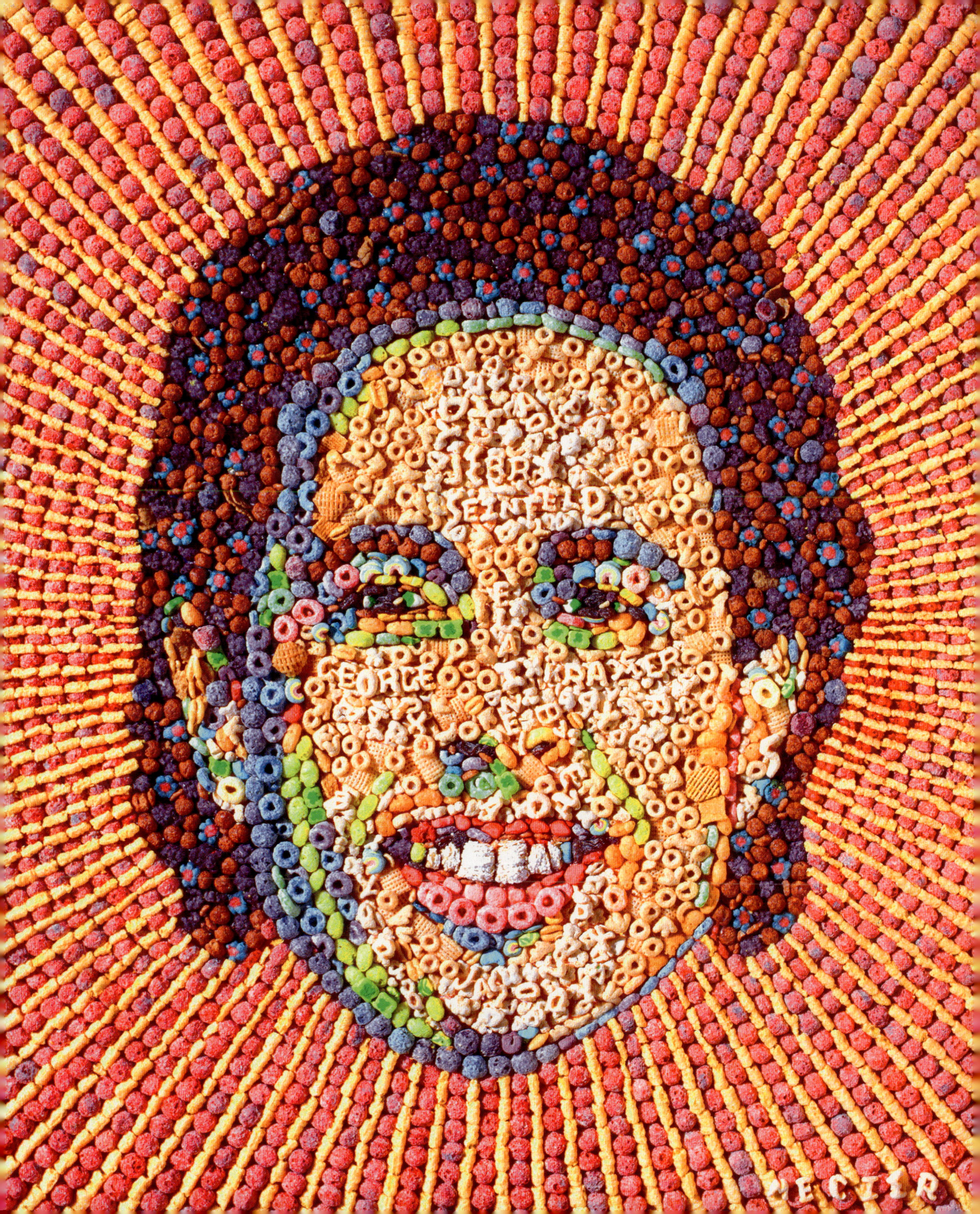
SEINFELD
GEORGE
KRAMER
MECIER

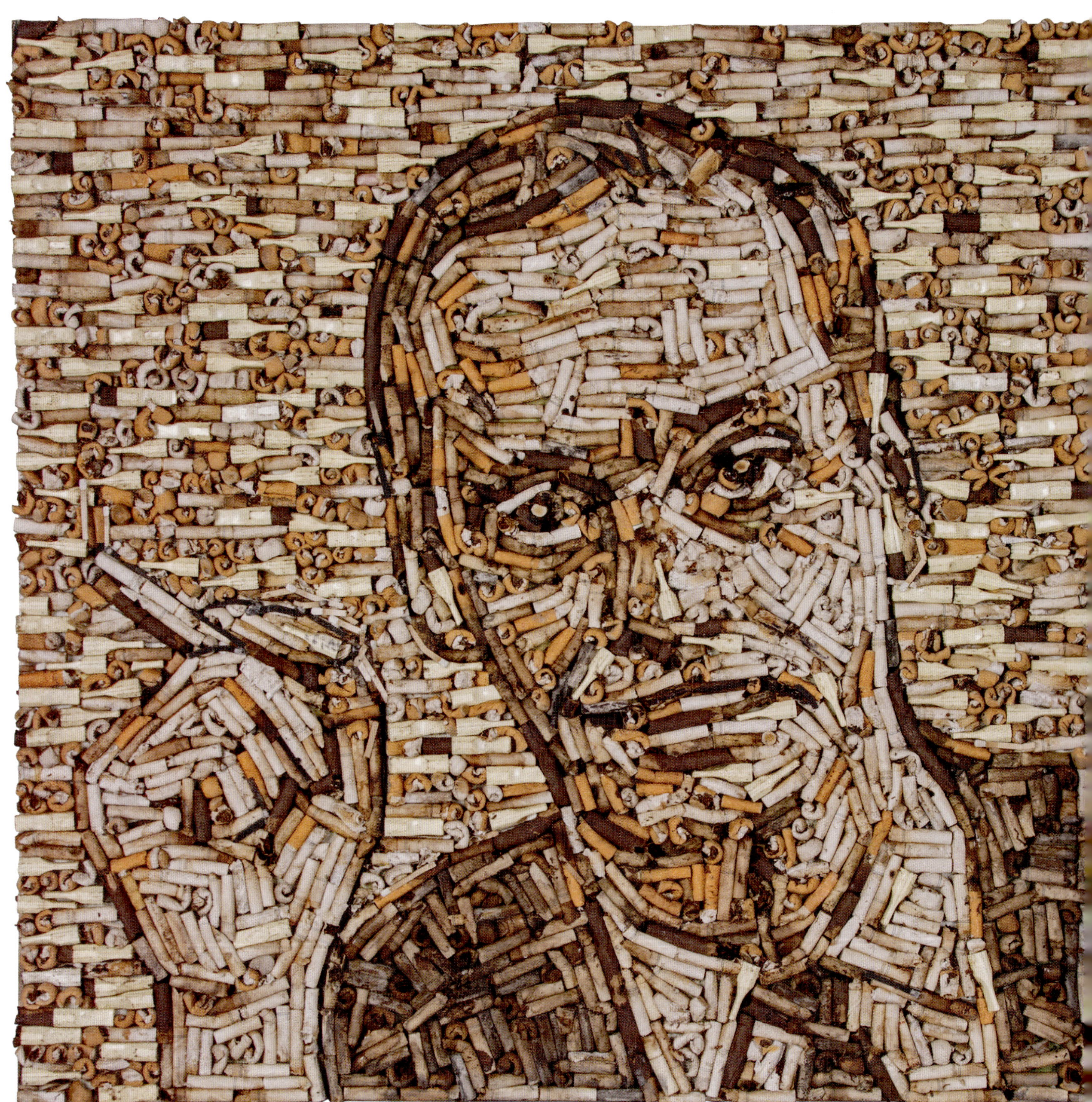

Other Stuff

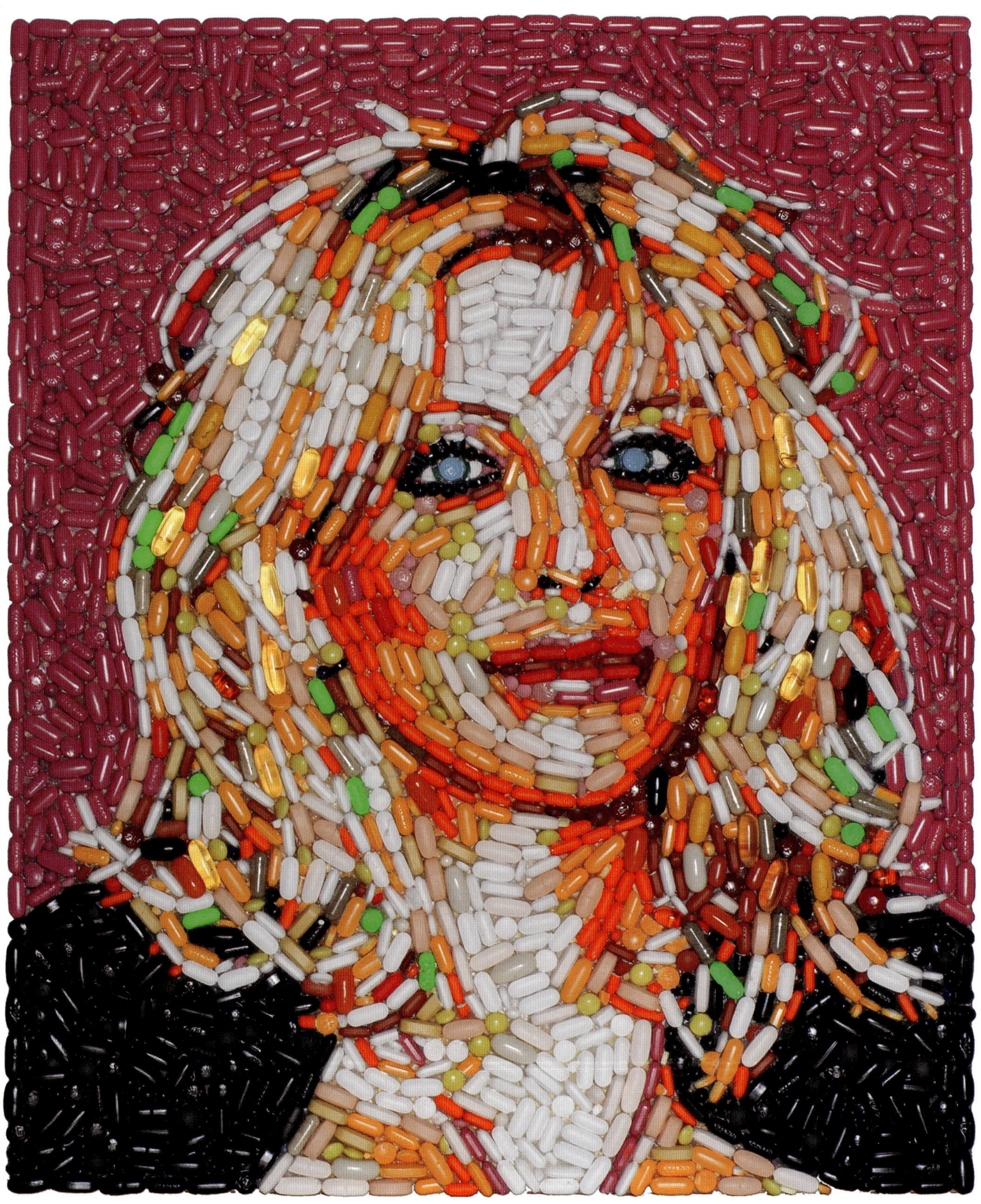

PREVIOUS SPREAD: JOHN WATERS • Cigarette butts, 2017

RIGHT: COURTNEY LOVE • Various pills, 2009

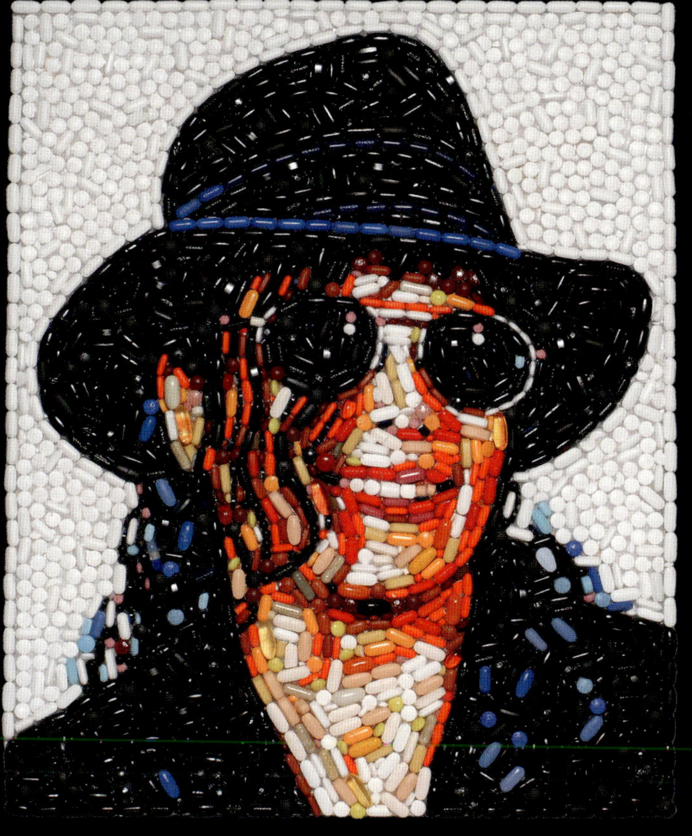

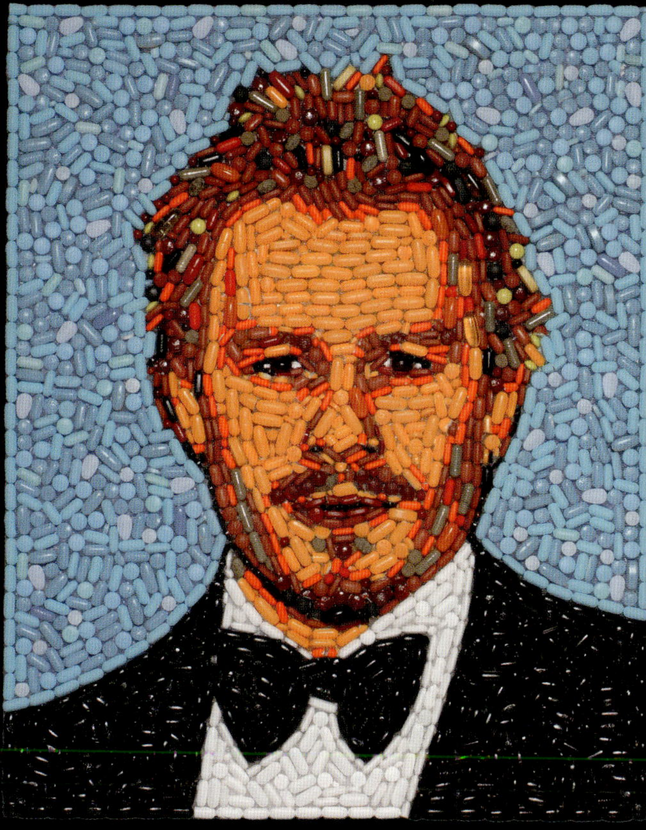

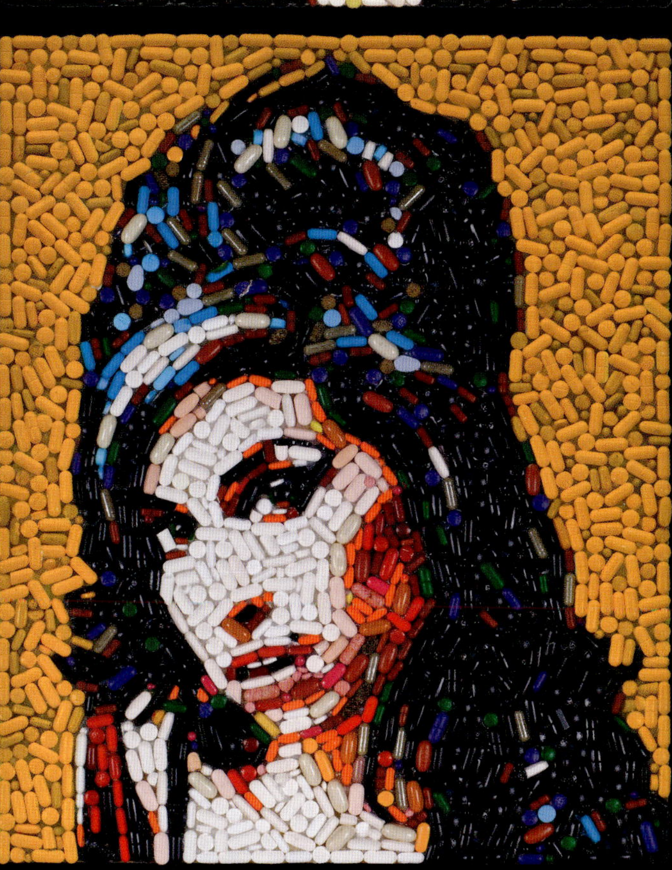

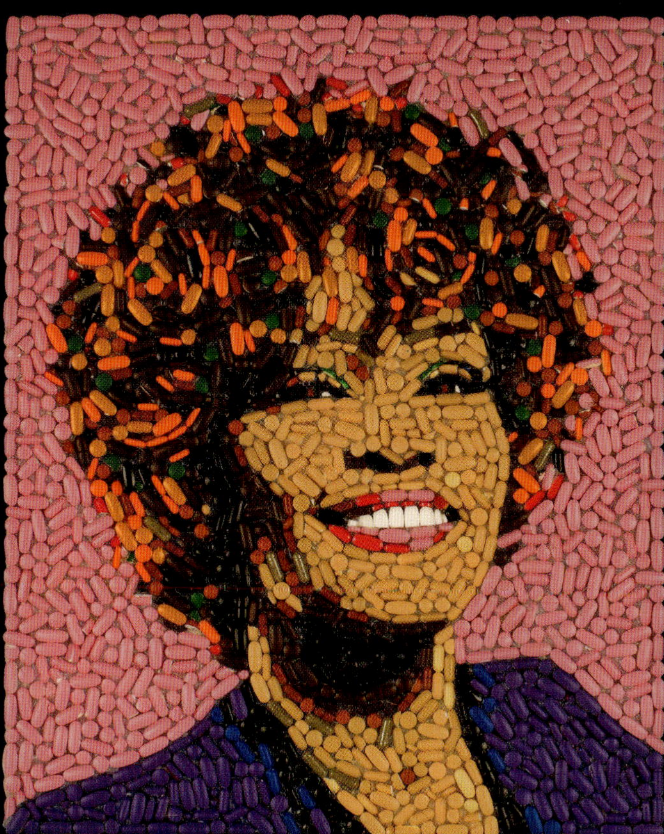

TOP LEFT: MICHAEL JACKSON • Various pills, 2009
Made as a tribute after he died.

BOTTOM LEFT: AMY WINEHOUSE • Various pills, 2011
Made as a tribute after she died.

TOP RIGHT: HEATH LEDGER • Various pills, 2009
Made as a tribute after he died. A decade after doing the Freud portrait, I continued this series for the UK edition of *Glamour* for an article about drugs in Hollywood.

BOTTOM RIGHT: WHITNEY HOUSTON • Various pills, 2012
Made as a tribute after she died.

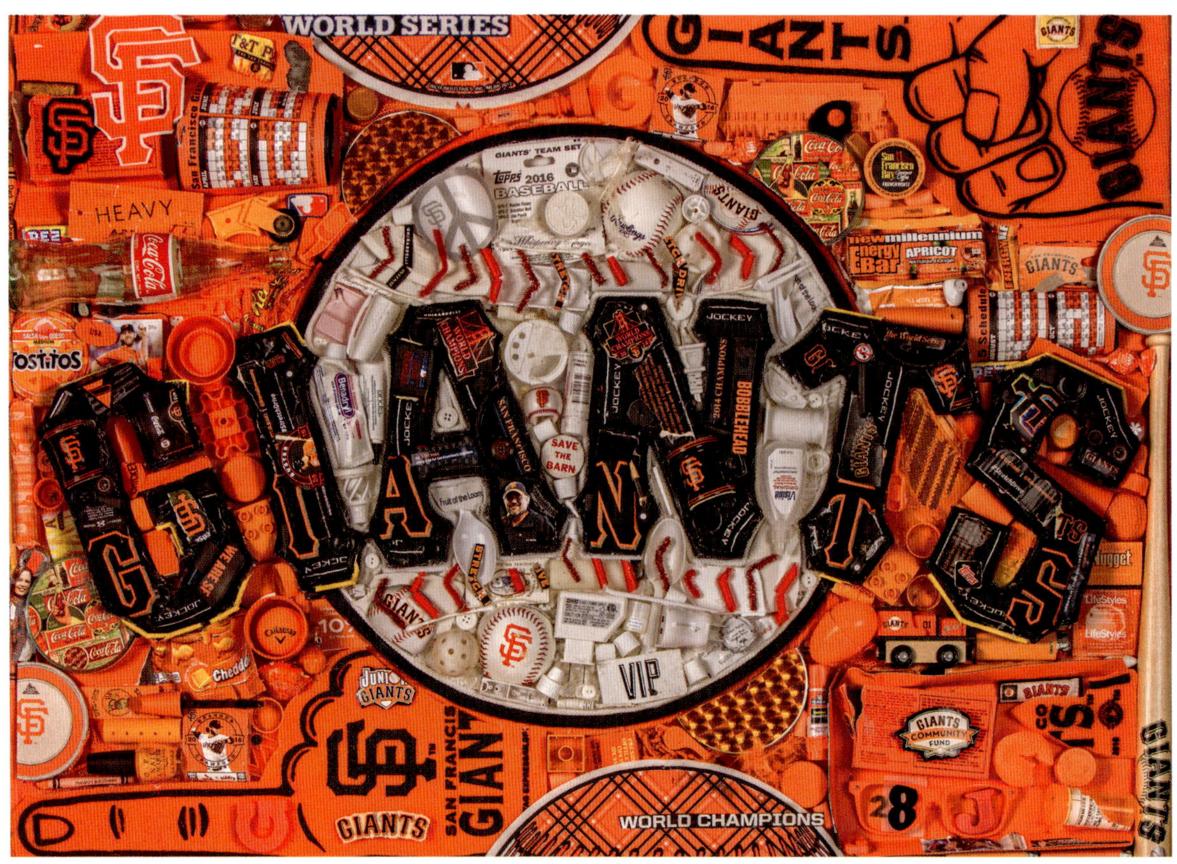

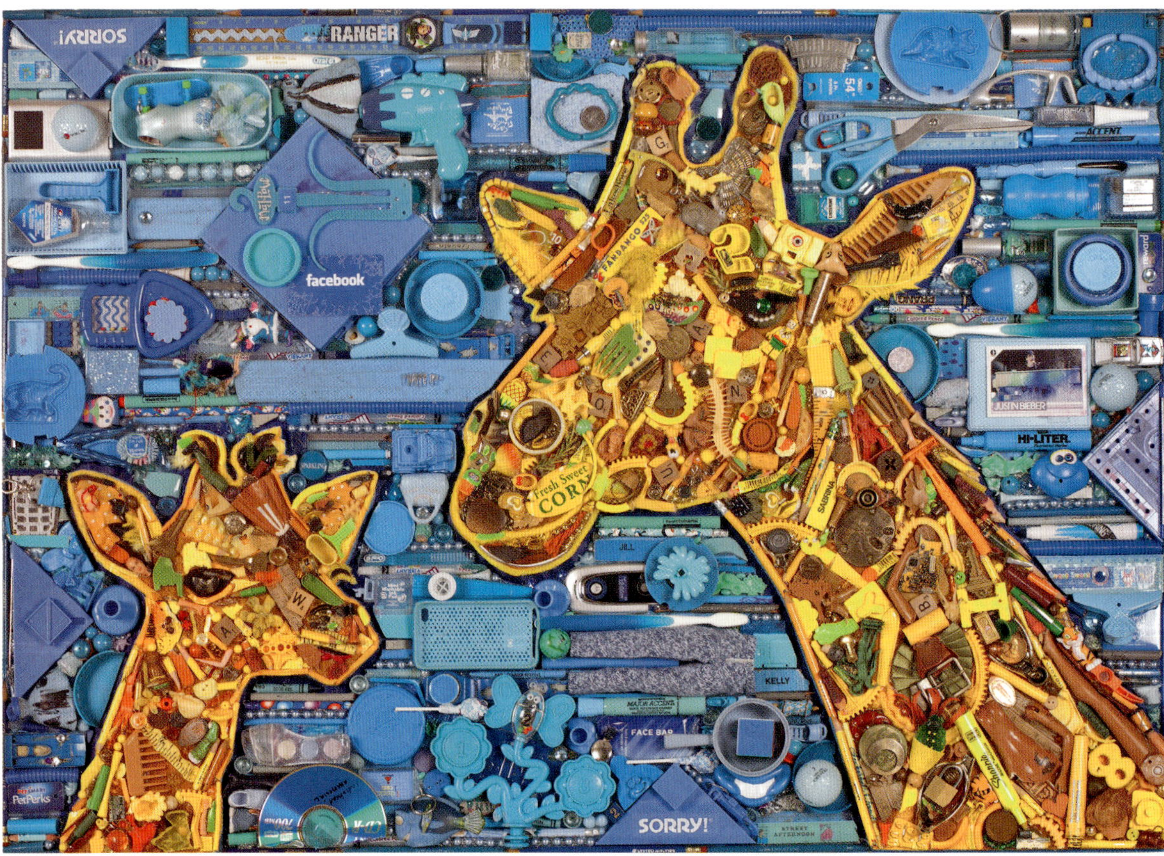

TOP: GIANTS • Various team merchandise, 2016
I made this for my favorite sister Shannon, who is a superfan.

BOTTOM: GIRAFFES • Children's toys, 2013
Commissioned by The Kaiser Permanente Oakland Medical Center for the children's waiting room.

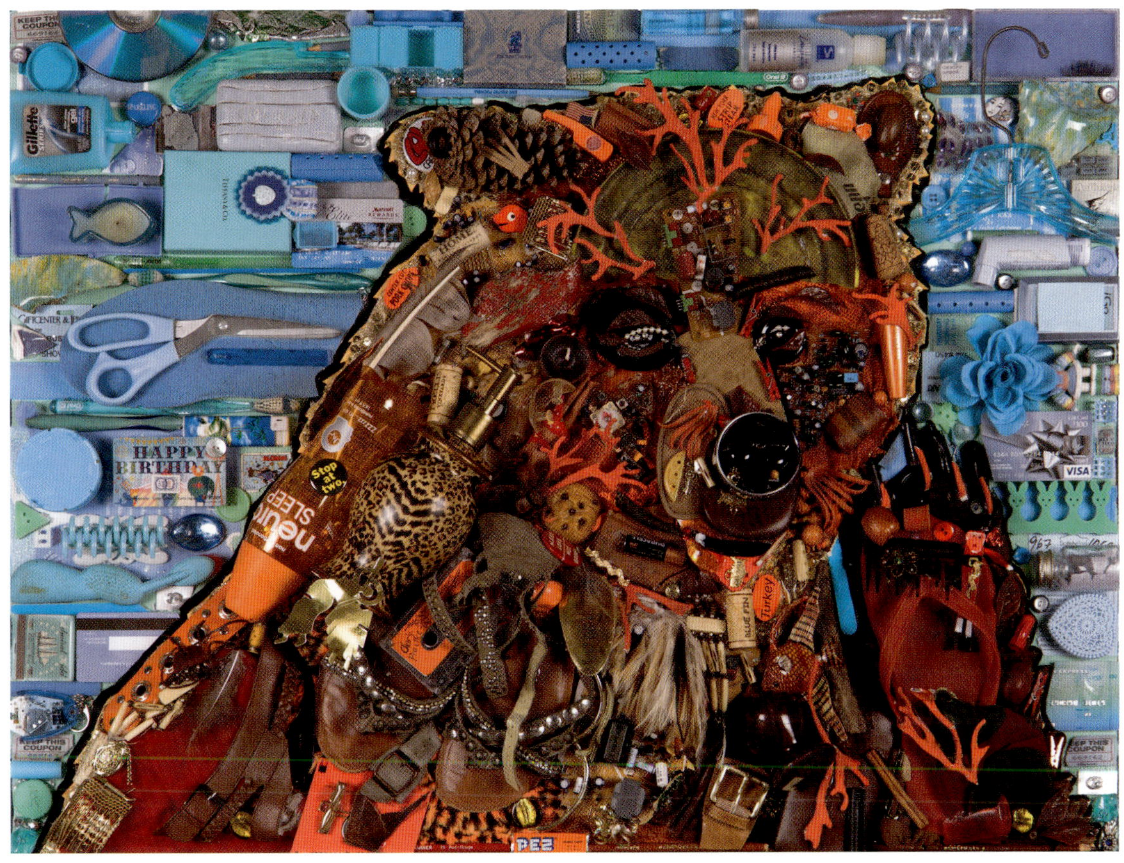

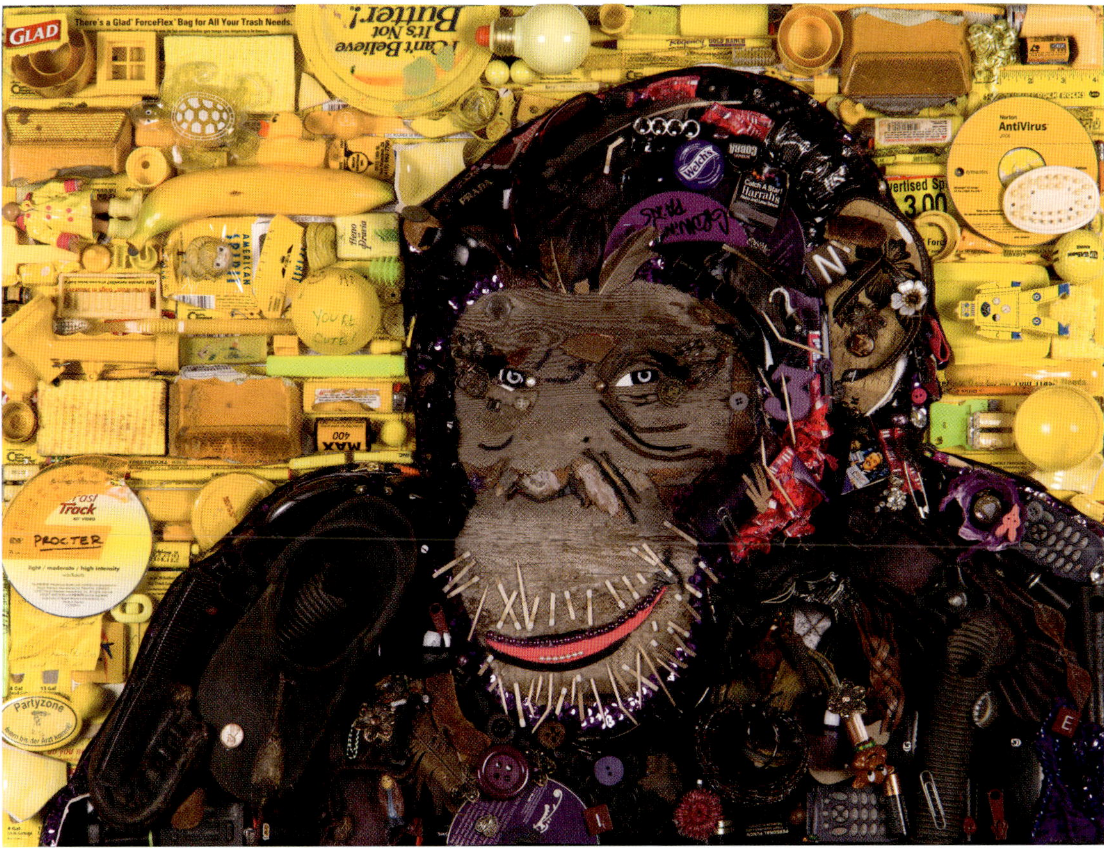

TOP: BEAR • Various plastic items, 2012

The Glad trash bag company hired me to do animal portraits out of recycling and celebrity donations to auction off for charity.

BOTTOM: APE • Various plastic items, 2012

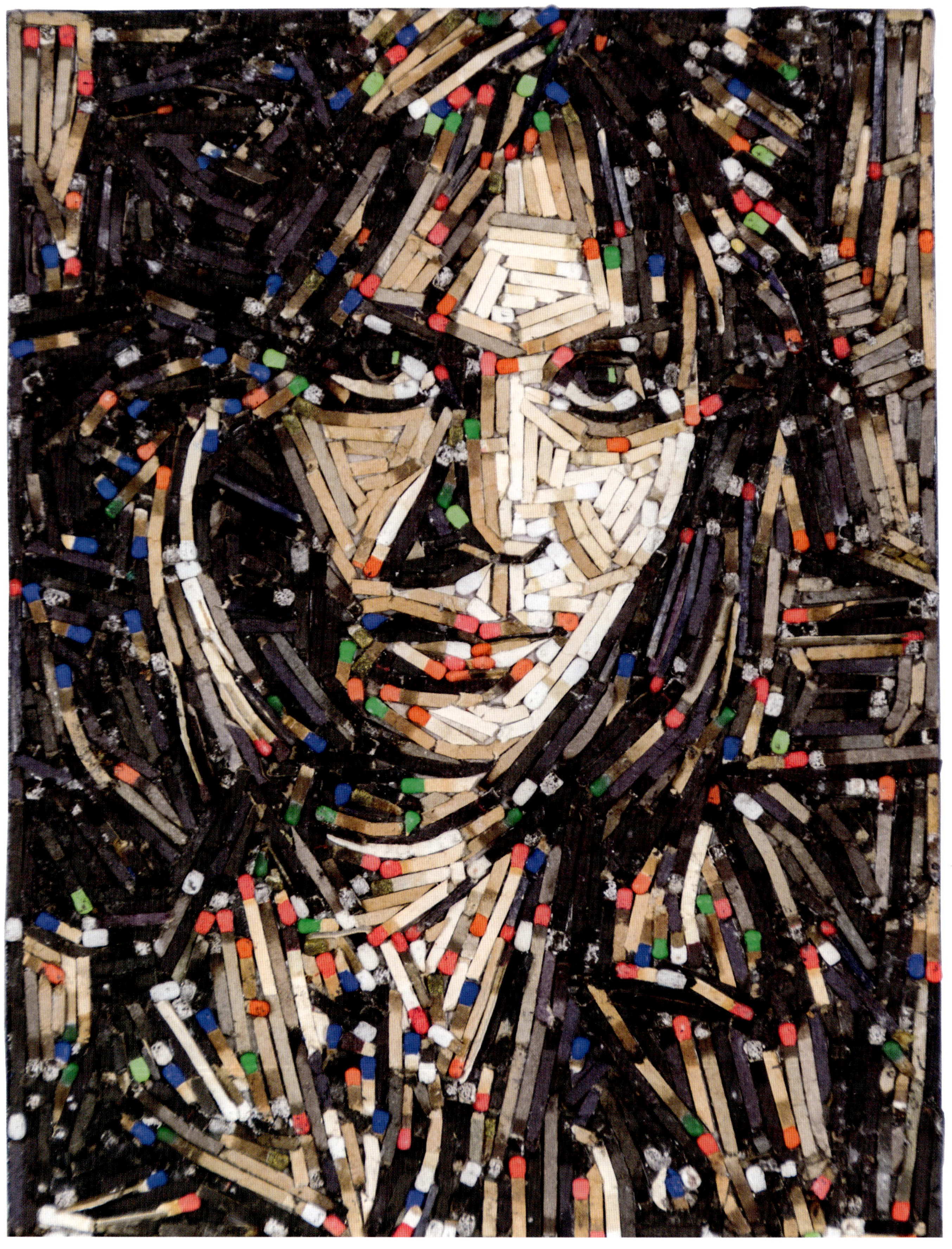

JOAN JETT • Matches, 2018

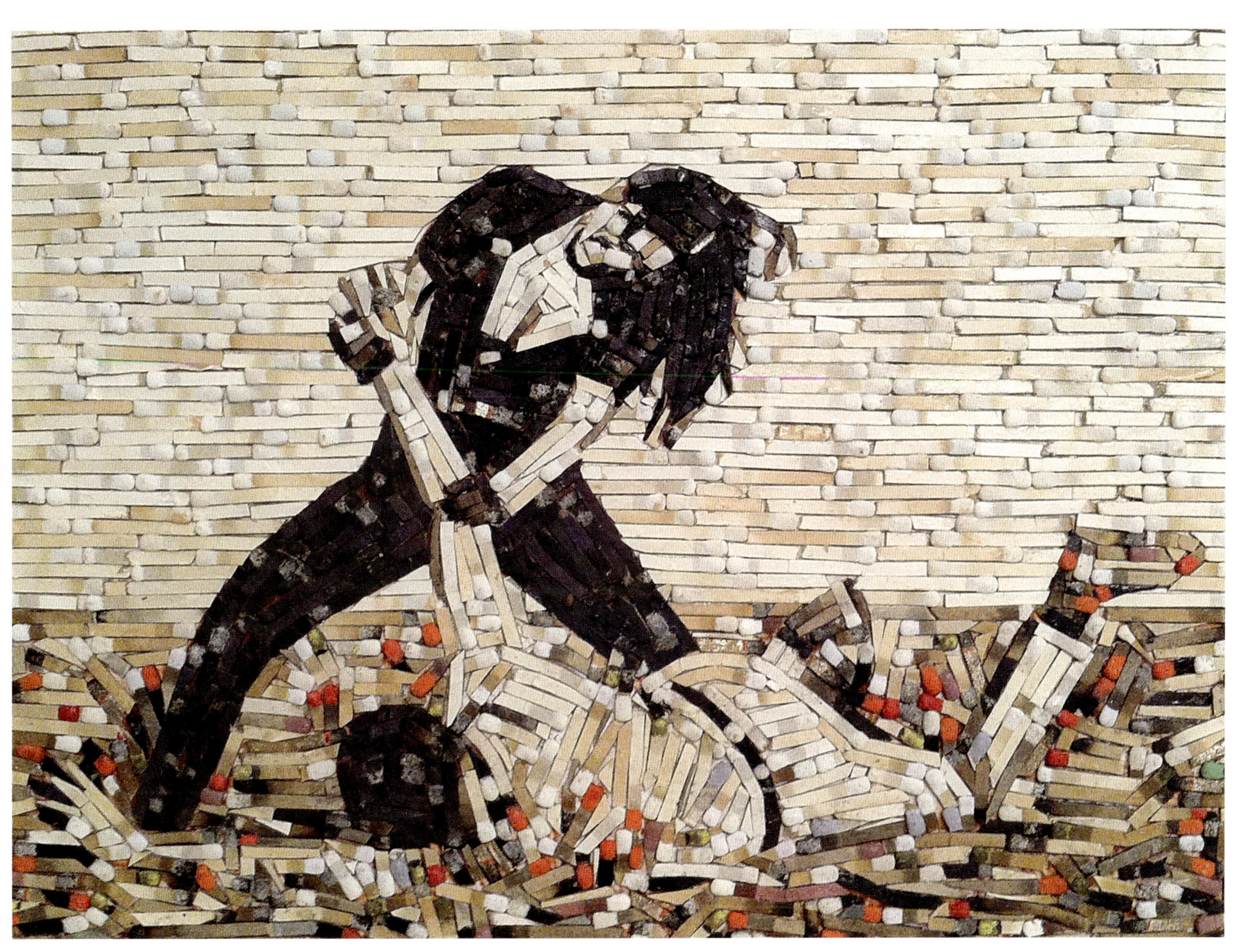

FASTER, PUSSYCAT! KILL! KILL! • Matches, 2014

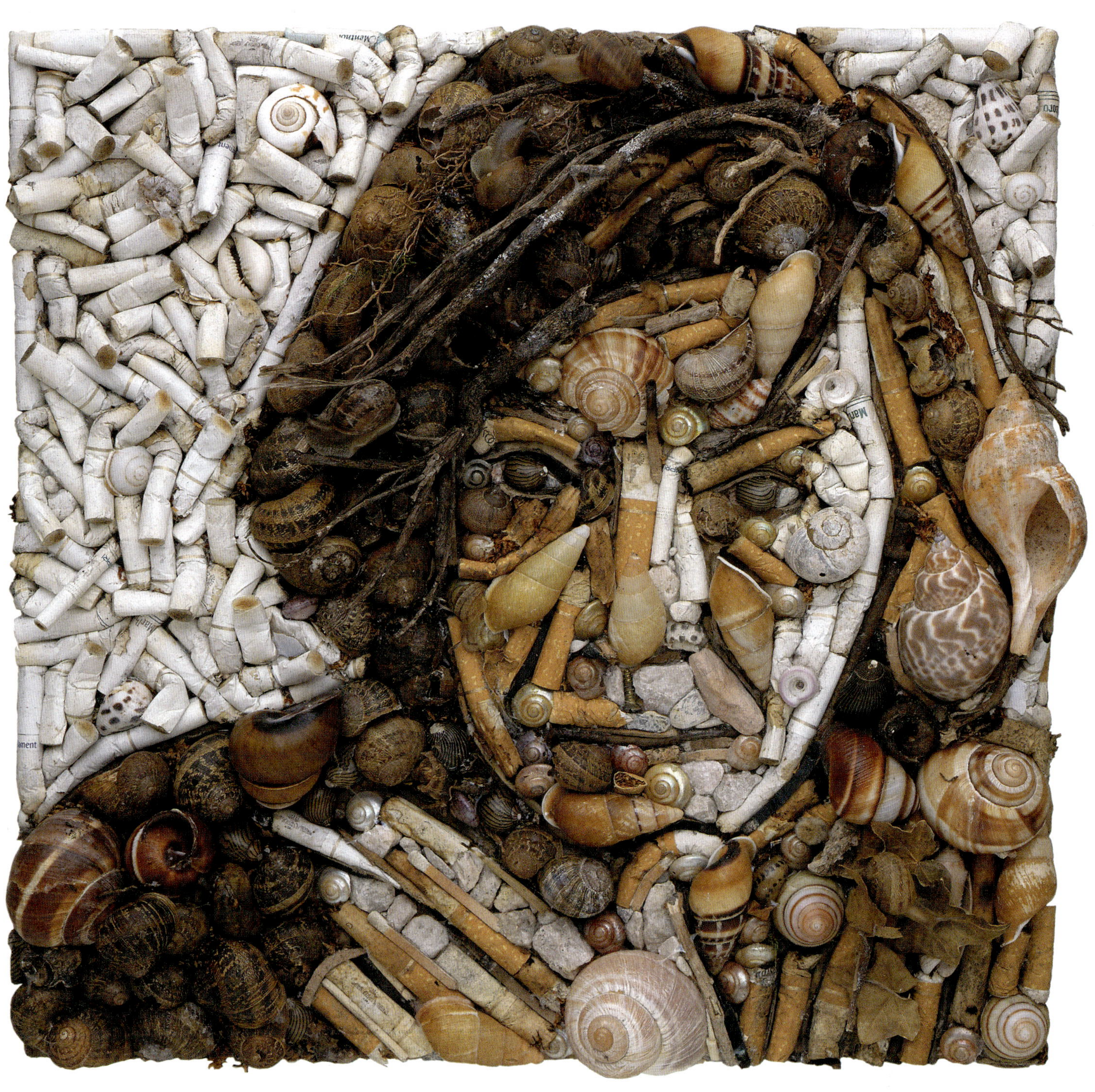

PATRICIA HIGHSMITH • Snails, roots, cigarette butts, 2006
Commissioned by the band Matmos, who released a song called "Snails and Lasers for Patricia Highsmith."
She apparently smoked a lot and had a thing for snails.

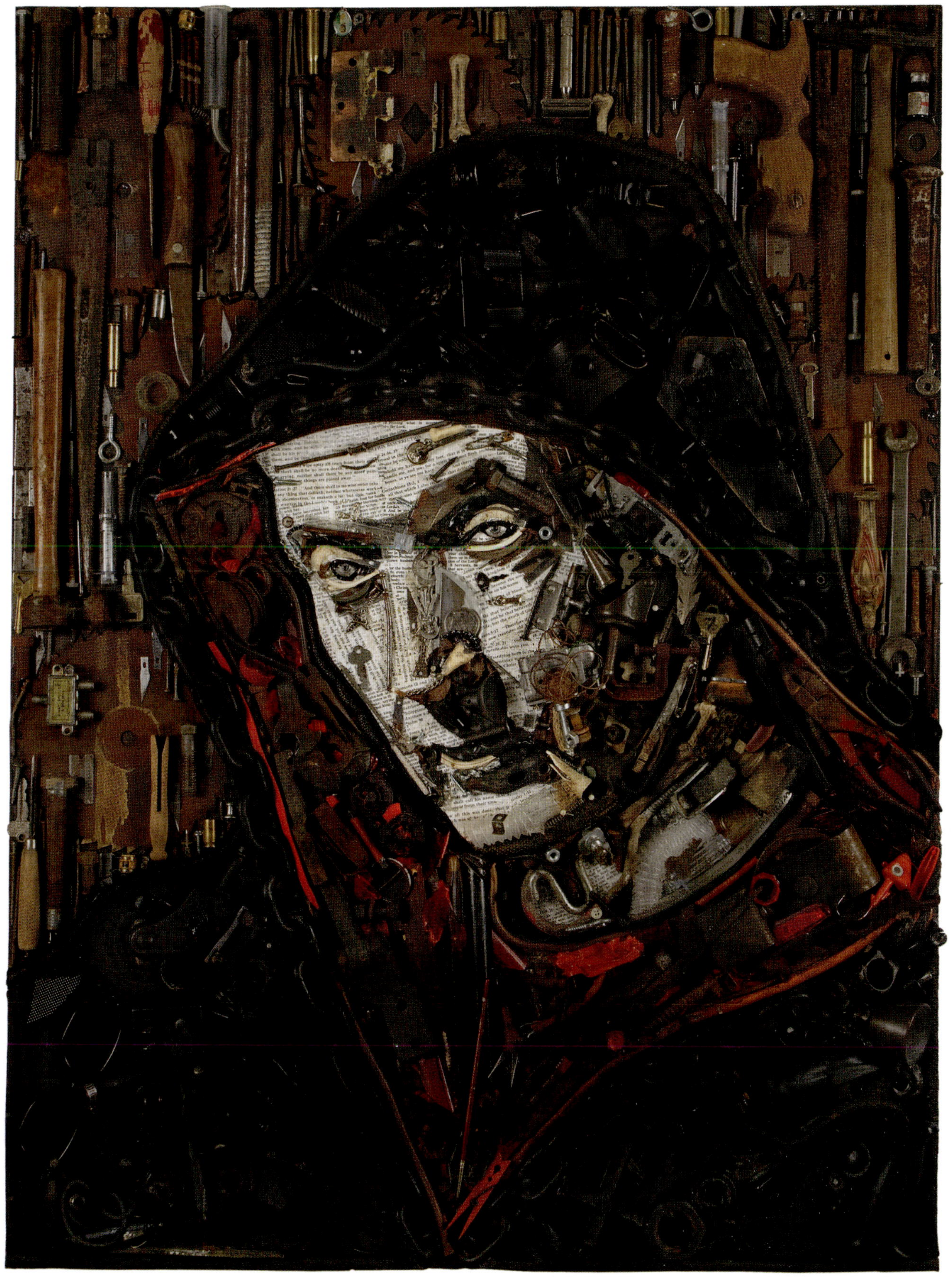

SAW • Rusty tools, nails, saws, 2010
Commissioned as a commemorative print by Lionsgate for
the release of the movie *Saw 3D: The Final Chapter*. Collection of Lionsgate.

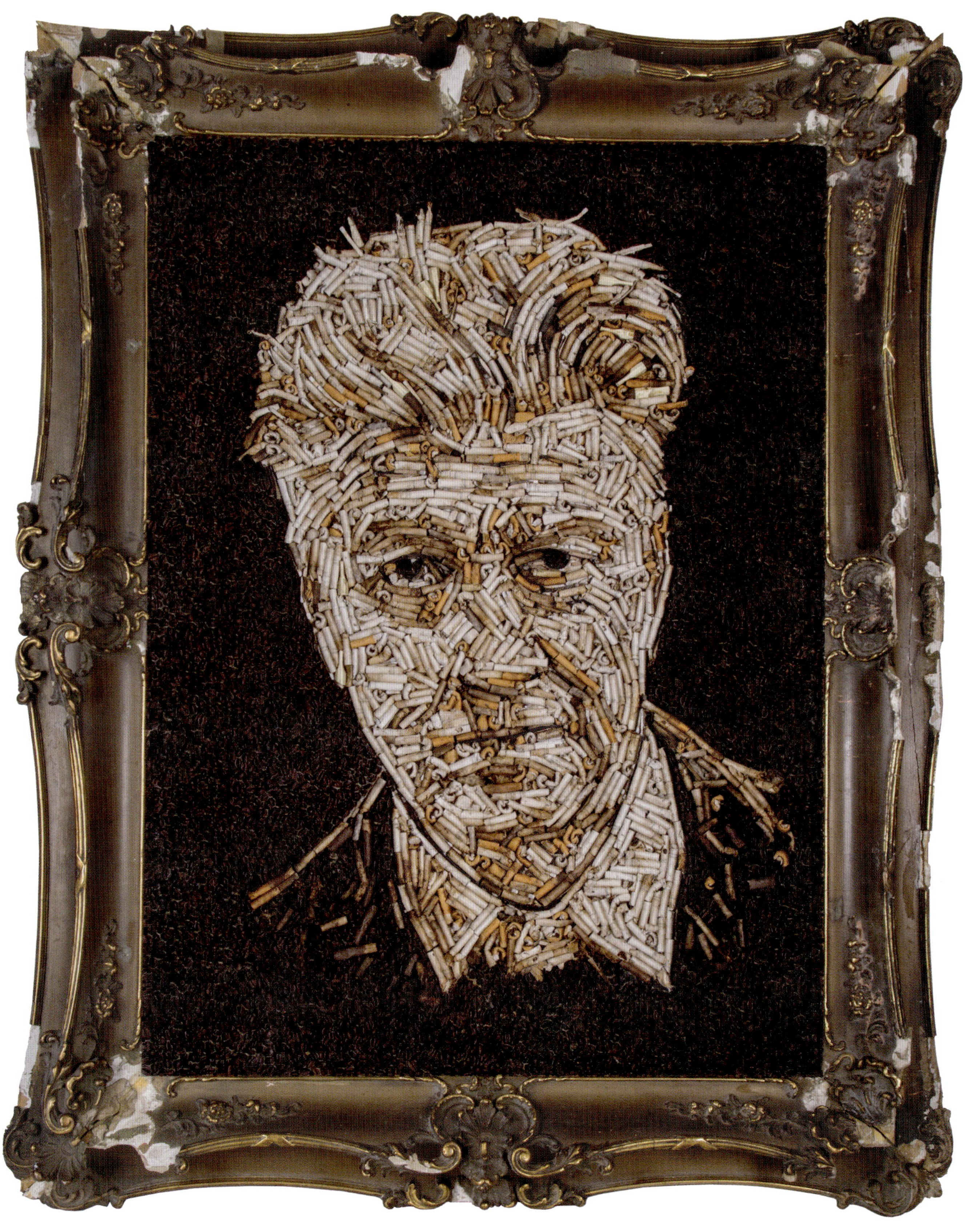

DAVID LYNCH • Coffee beans, cigarette butts, 2017

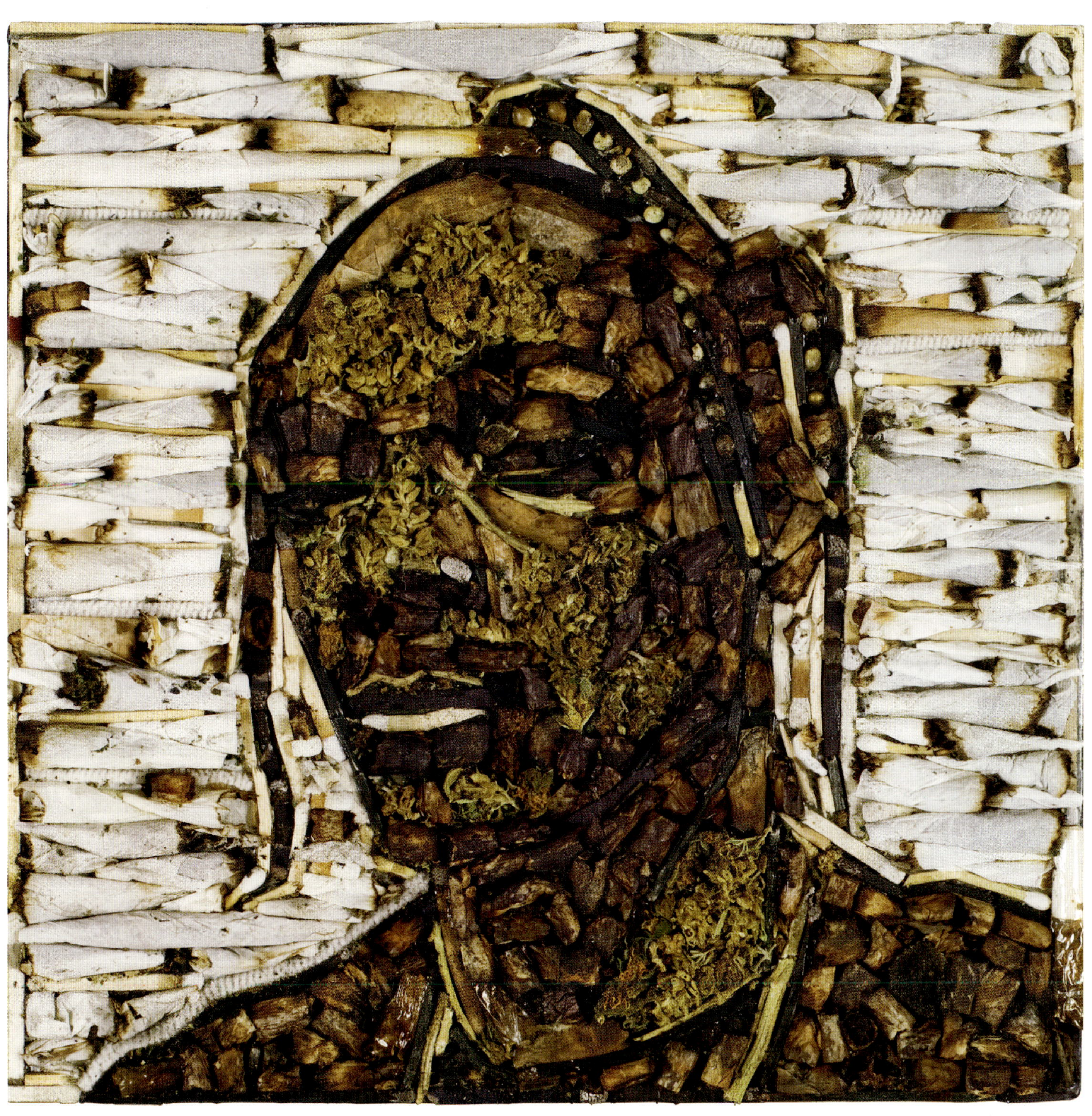

SNOOP DOGG • Cannabis bud trimmings, joints, blunt ends, pipe cleaners, matches, 2011

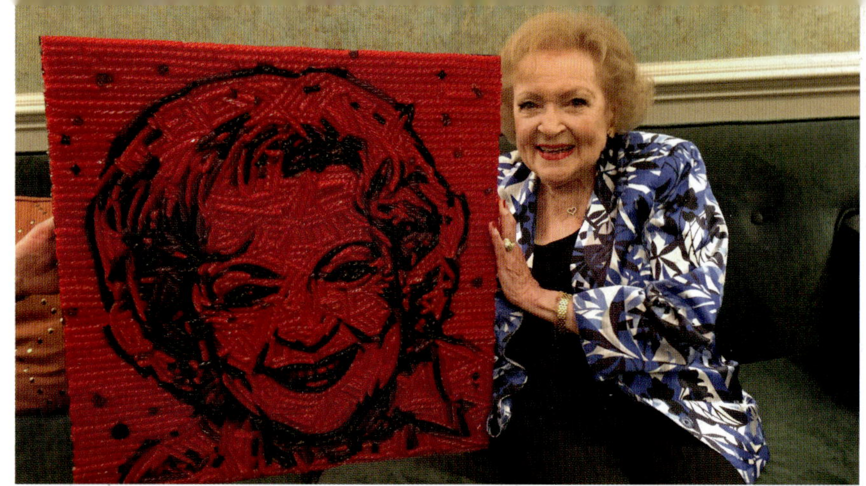

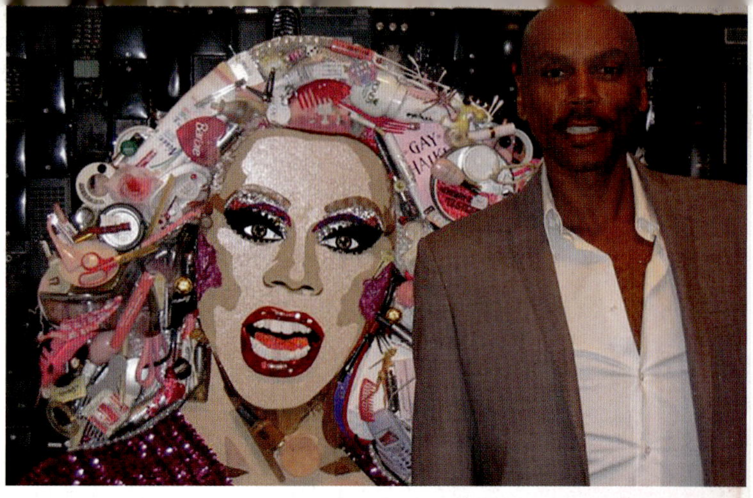

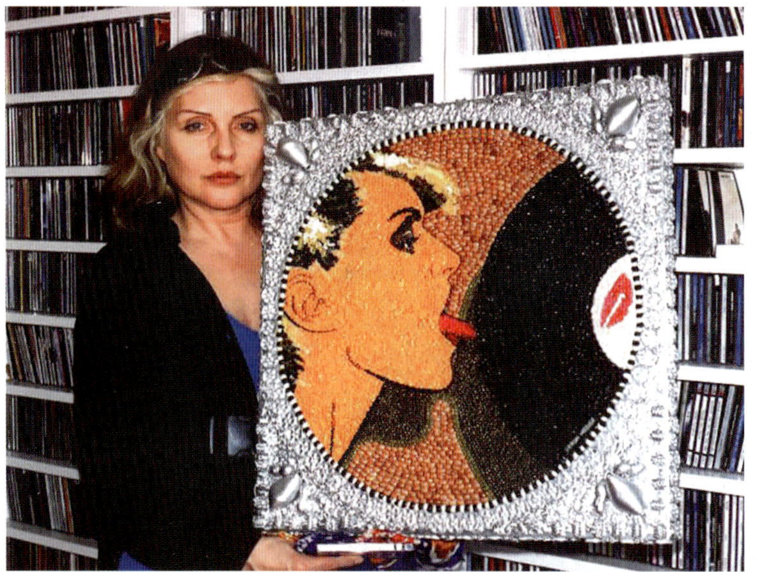

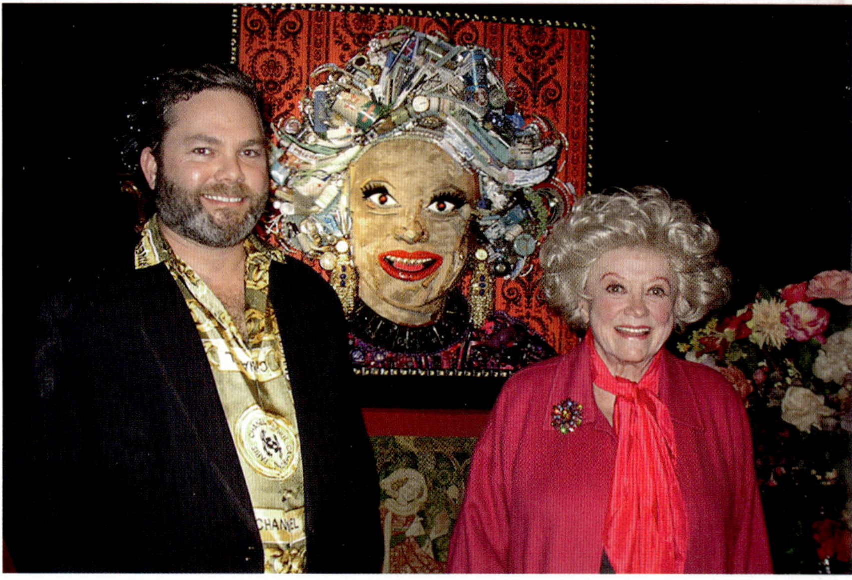
CHANEL

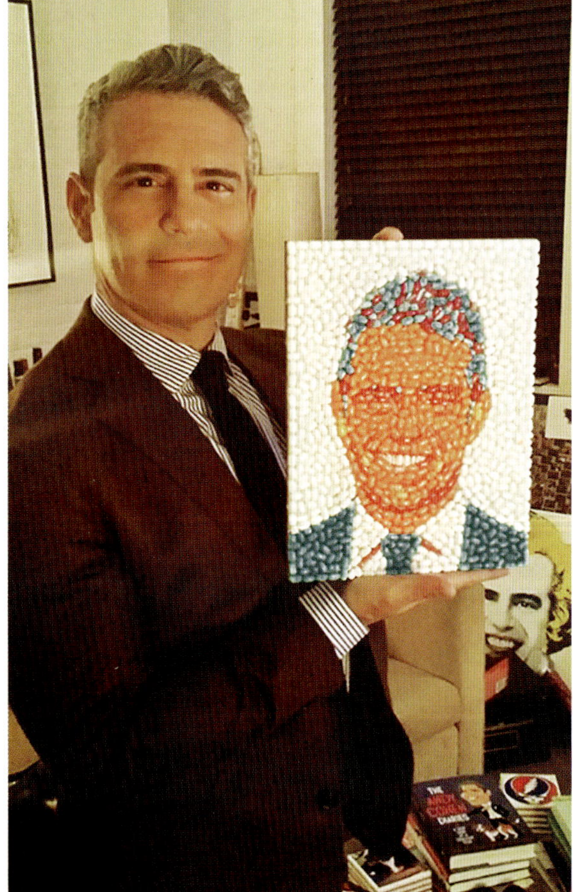

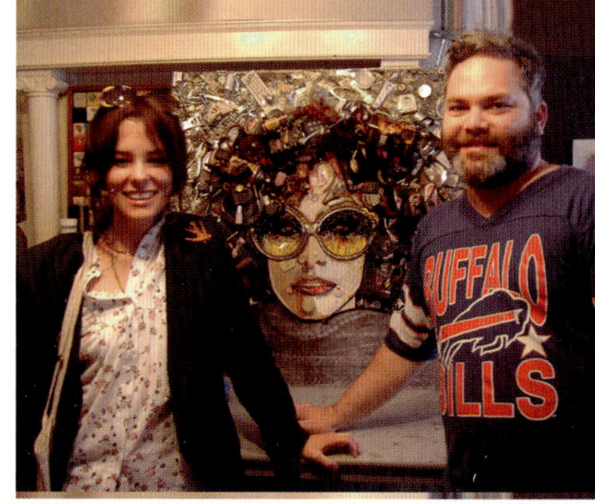
BUFFALO
BILLS

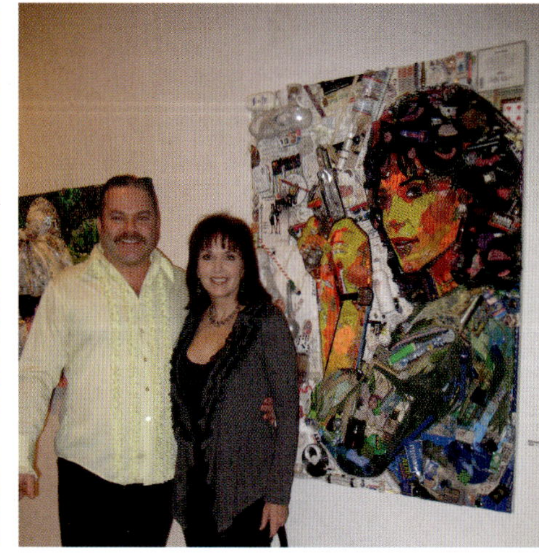

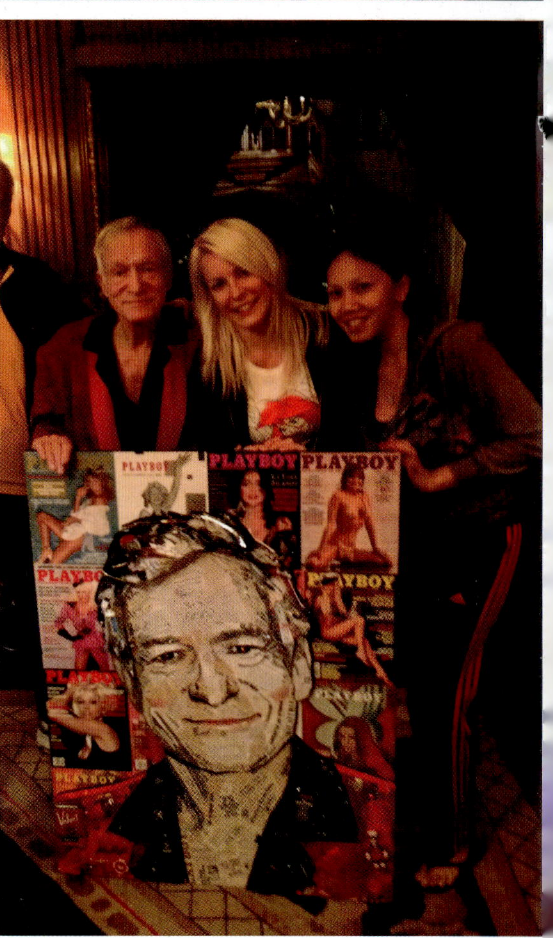
PLAYBOY
PLAYBOY
PLAYBOY

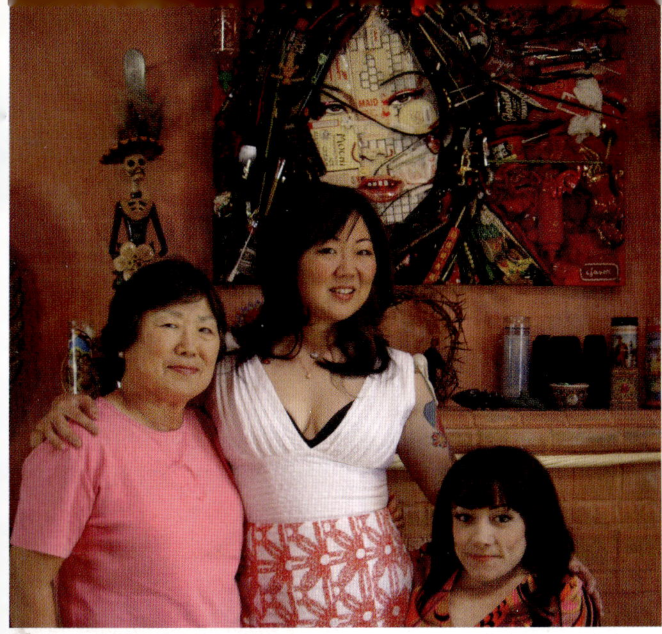
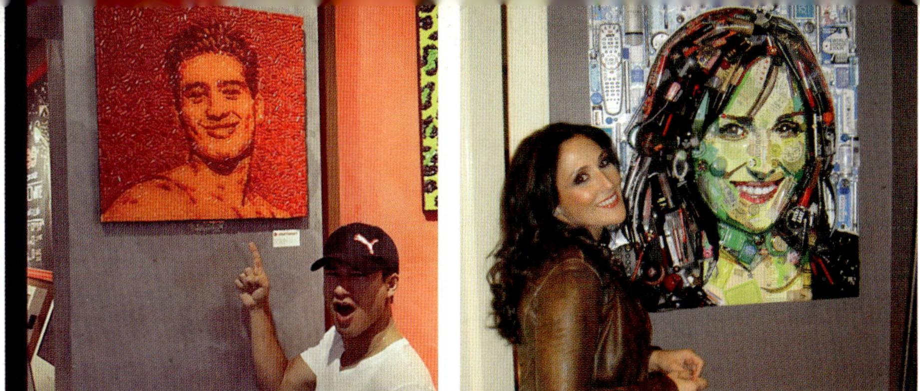
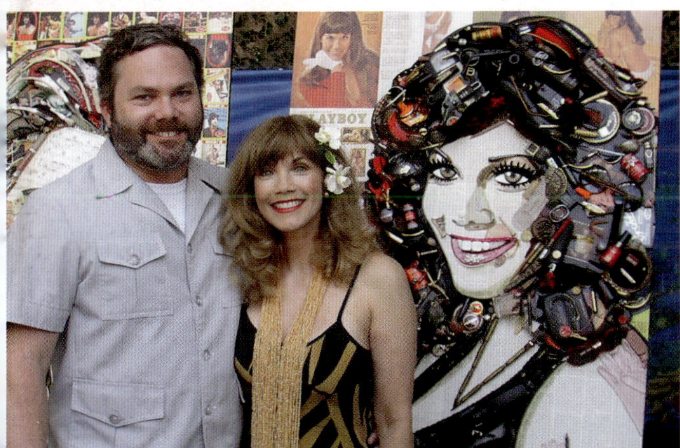
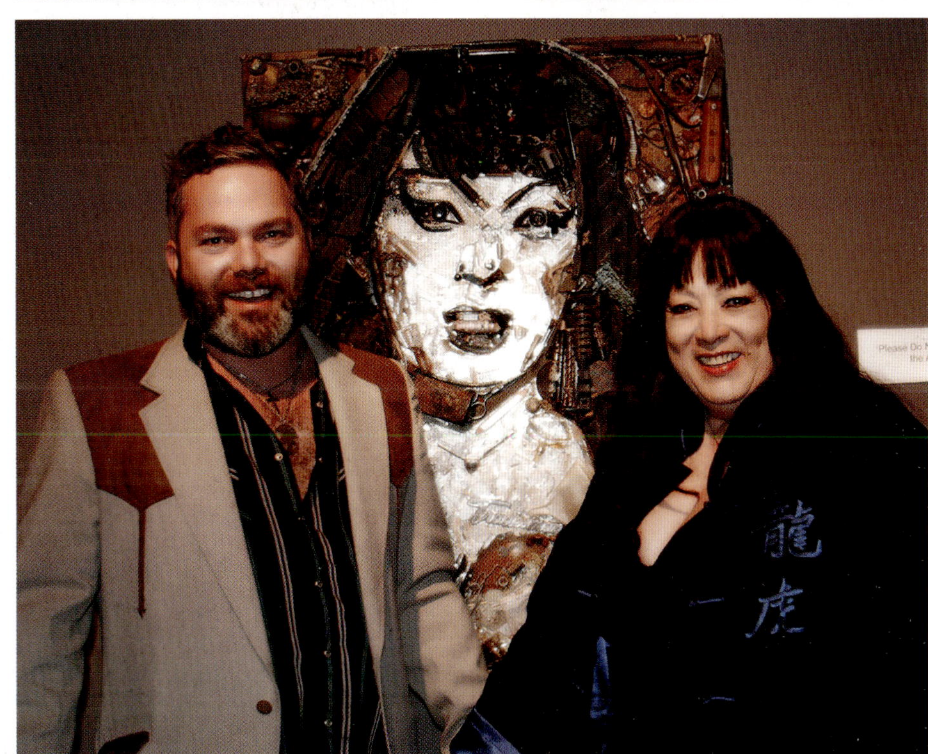
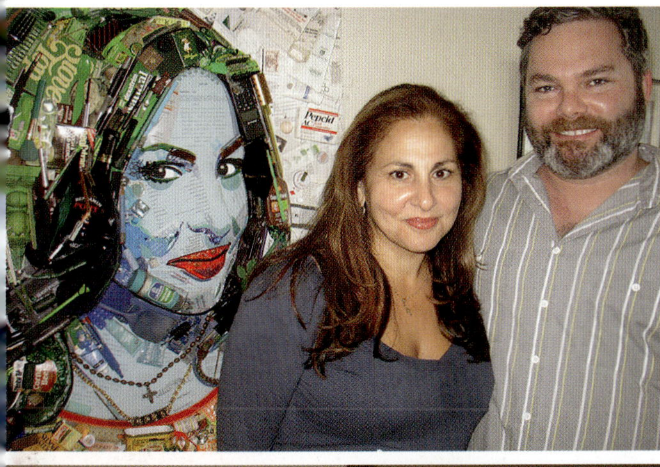
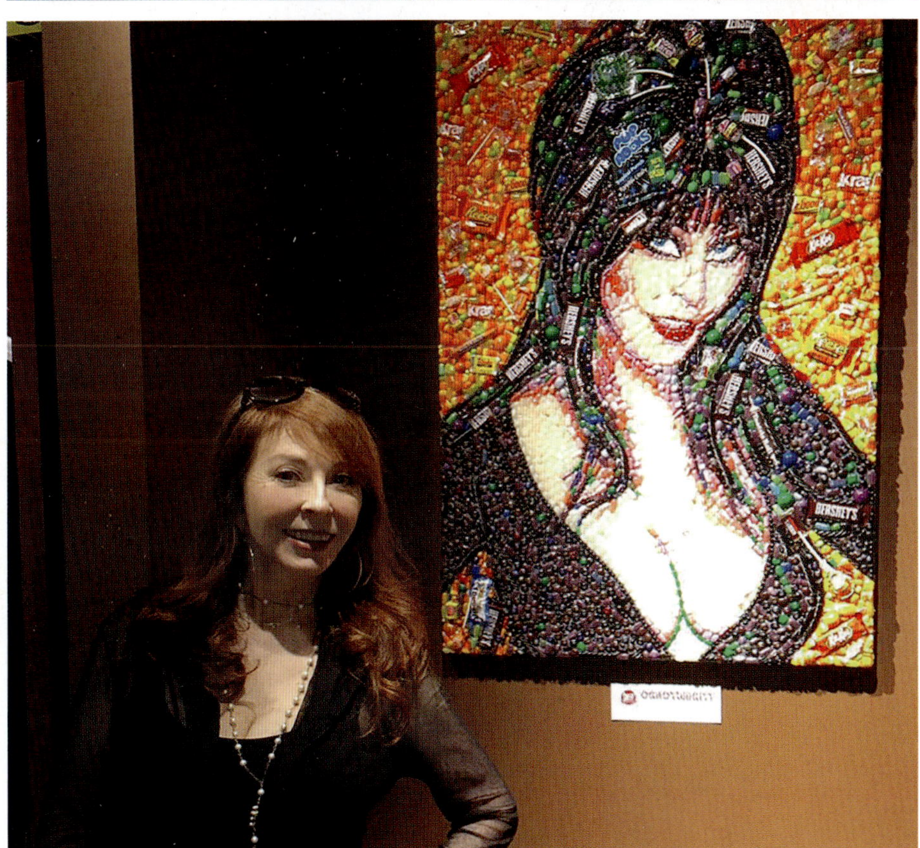
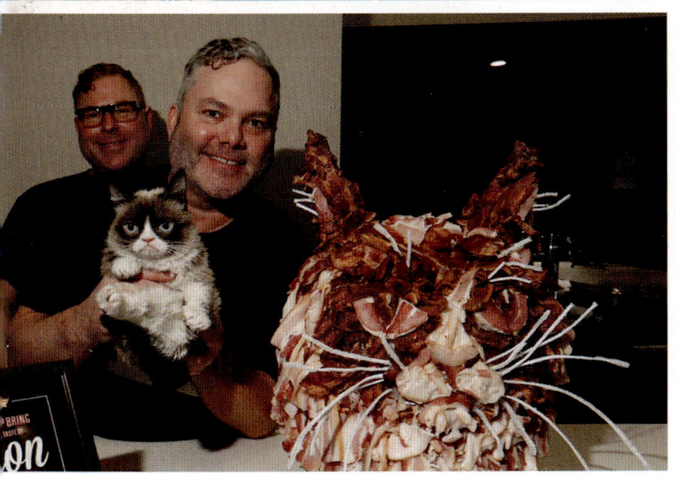

Acknowledgments

Thank you to my family, friends, and fans, and to the collectors, galleries, agents, and clients who have supported me over the years. Adam Ansell, my partner in crime, thank you for more than twenty years of perfect extreme happiness and bliss. Thanks to Jason Nakano for the gorgeous photography, to Jaina Bee and Granny's Empire of Art, and to Michael Morris and Steve Mockus for this book. To all the celebrities whom I have stalked and who mailed me their junk, thank you most of all. And to all the people who left junk on my doorstep: thank you—now please stop!

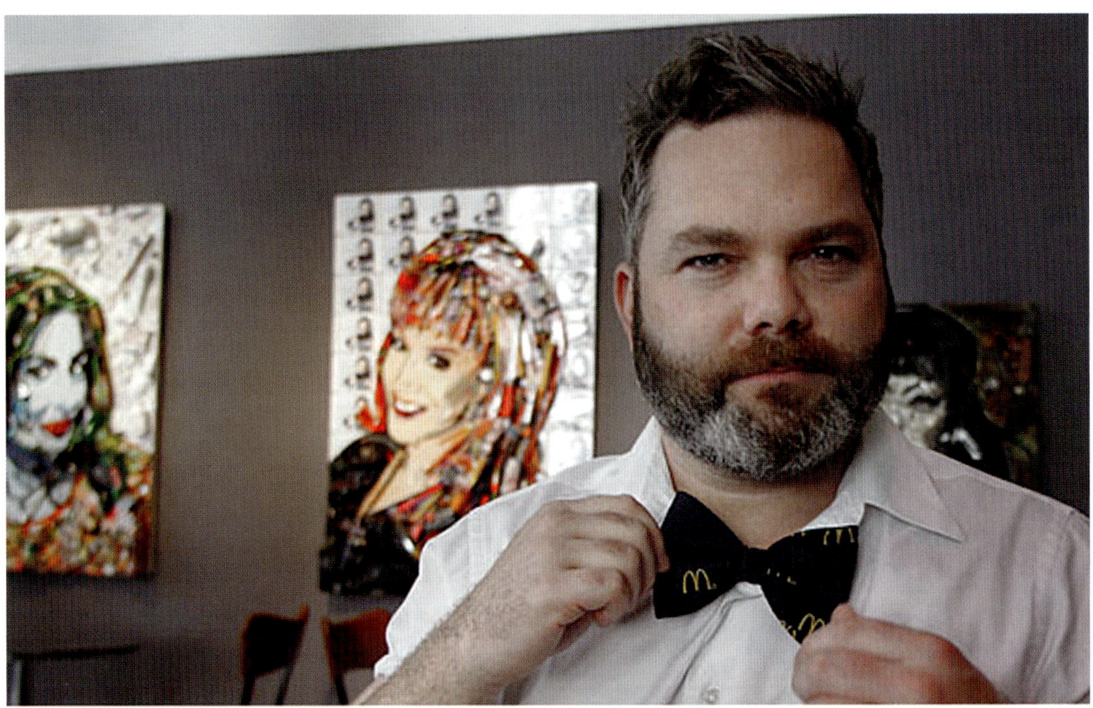

About the Author

Jason Mecier's artwork has been featured in media outlets including the *New York Times*, *Entertainment Weekly*, the *Today Show*, *Glee*, *Rachael Ray*, TMZ, Nickelodeon, Bravo, *Rolling Stone*, *People*, *Harper's*, *Seventeen*, the *Telegraph*, the *Daily Mail*, the *Advocate*, and *Soap Opera Weekly*, as well as in music videos by P!nk and Pitbull. His portraits are hanging in Ripley's Believe it or Not! museums, numerous celebrity homes, and the Playboy Mansion. He lives and works in San Francisco.